Beginning Jakarta EE Web Development

Using JSP, JSF, MySQL, and Apache Tomcat for Building Java Web Applications

Third Edition

Luciano Manelli
Giulio Zambon

Apress®

Beginning Jakarta EE Web Development: Using JSP, JSF, MySQL, and Apache Tomcat for Building Java Web Applications

Luciano Manelli
Taranto, Italy

Giulio Zambon
Harrison, ACT, Australia

ISBN-13 (pbk): 978-1-4842-5865-1
https://doi.org/10.1007/978-1-4842-5866-8

ISBN-13 (electronic): 978-1-4842-5866-8

Managing Director, Apress Media LLC: Welmoed Spahr
Acquisitions Editor: Steve Anglin
Development Editor: Matthew Moodie
Coordinating Editor: Mark Powers

Cover designed by eStudioCalamar

Cover image by Sam Erwin on Unsplash (www.unsplash.com)

Distributed to the book trade worldwide by Apress Media, LLC, 1 New York Plaza, New York, NY 10004, U.S.A. Phone 1-800-SPRINGER, fax (201) 348-4505, e-mail orders-ny@springer-sbm.com, or visit www. springeronline.com. Apress Media, LLC is a California LLC and the sole member (owner) is Springer Science + Business Media Finance Inc (SSBM Finance Inc). SSBM Finance Inc is a **Delaware** corporation.

For information on translations, please e-mail editorial@apress.com; for reprint, paperback, or audio rights, please email bookpermissions@springernature.com.

Apress titles may be purchased in bulk for academic, corporate, or promotional use. eBook versions and licenses are also available for most titles. For more information, reference our Print and eBook Bulk Sales web page at http://www.apress.com/bulk-sales.

Any source code or other supplementary material referenced by the author in this book is available to readers on GitHub via the book's product page, located at www.apress.com/9781484258651. For more detailed information, please visit http://www.apress.com/source-code.

Printed on acid-free paper

To my daughter Sara

To my son Marco

To my mum Anna

*I think that everyone has to always follow their
own dreams and fight for them*

Table of Contents

About the Authors

Luciano Manelli was born in Taranto (Italy), where he currently resides with his family. He graduated in electronic engineering at the Polytechnic of Bari at 24 years of age, and then he served as an Officer in the Navy. In 2012, he earned a PhD in computer science from the IT department, University of Bari Aldo Moro. His PhD focused on grid computing and formal methods, and he published the results in international publications. He is a professionally certified engineer and an innovation manager and, in 2014, began working for the Port Network Authority of the Ionian Sea—Port of Taranto, after working for 13 years for InfoCamere ScpA as a software developer. He has worked mainly in the design, analysis, and development of large software systems, research and development, testing, and production with roles of increasing responsibility in several areas over the years. Luciano has developed a great capability to make decisions in a technical and business context and is mainly interested in project management and business process management. In his current position, he deals with port community systems and digital innovation.

Additionally, he has written several IT books and is a contract professor at the Polytechnic of Bari and at the University of Bari Aldo Moro. You can find out more at his LinkedIn page: `it.linkedin.com/in/lucianomanelli`.

Giulio Zambon's first love was physics, but he decided to dedicate himself to software development more than 30 years ago: back when computers were still made of transistors and core memories, programs were punched on cards, and Fortran only had arithmetic IFs. Over the years, he learned a dozen computer languages and worked with all sorts of operating systems. His specific interests were in telecom and real-time systems, and he managed several projects to their successful completion. In 2001, Giulio founded his own company offering computer telephony integration (CTI) services, and he used JSP and Tomcat exclusively to develop the web side of the service platform. Back in Australia after many years in Europe, he now dedicates himself to writing software to generate and solve numeric puzzles.

About the Technical Reviewer

Luqman Saeed is a Java EE developer with Pedantic Devs. He has been doing software development for close to a decade. He started with PHP and now does Java EE full time. His goal on Udemy is to help you get productive with the powerful, modern, intuitive, and easy-to-use Java EE APIs. He will serve you the best of vanilla, pure, and awesome Java EE courses to help you master the skills needed to solve whatever development challenge you have at hand.

Introduction

In this book, you will learn to build step-by-step complete Java-based web applications focused on JSP and JSF in the Jakarta EE environment based on enterprise specifications developed by the Eclipse Foundation. The Jakarta EE open project is based on Java EE specifications (with no changes in its features) used in many enterprise applications, and its goal is the development of business applications working with packages of different vendors. The book focuses on JSF framework that simplifies the development of user interfaces allowing integration to server-side data and logic with several components, as a natural evolution of JSP which is essentially an HTML page with Java server capabilities.

So, this book can serve as a starting point for anyone who is beginning the study of web applications in Java for the first time, but it can be also interesting for developers who want to know JSF from the basics. In fact, Servlet, JSP, JSF, XML, JavaBean, and access to database are accurately analyzed and implemented with a clear project evolution: from the configuration of the world's most popular open source components OpenJDK, Tomcat, MySQL, and Eclipse to the development and the execution on a browser of several examples and complete projects.

The chapters are focused on different topics: the first chapter analyzes installation and configuration of the main components on different operating systems; six chapters are about JSP, application architectures, JSP actions, XML, and databases; two chapters are devoted to JSF; and the last chapter completes the study of the main project based on an online bookshop.

Source code for this book can be accessed via the **Download Source Code** button located at www.apress.com/9781484258651.

To follow this dissertation, it is only necessary to have minimum skills in algorithms and Java programming.

I hope that you enjoy the reading.

—Luciano Manelli

CHAPTER 1

Introducing JSP and Tomcat

Web applications (together with apps) can be considered the cornerstone of the modern technology both in private and government organizations. In fact, by interacting with a remote server, it is possible to find the needed information or to purchase something online and, in general, to use many services for your job or your personal life.

Every time you type something into a web form, an application "out there" interprets your request and prepares a web page to respond. To understand web applications, you first need to have a clear idea of what happens when you ask your browser to view a web page, either by typing a URL (Uniform Resource Locator) into the address field of your browser or by clicking a hyperlink. Figure 1-1 shows you how it works.

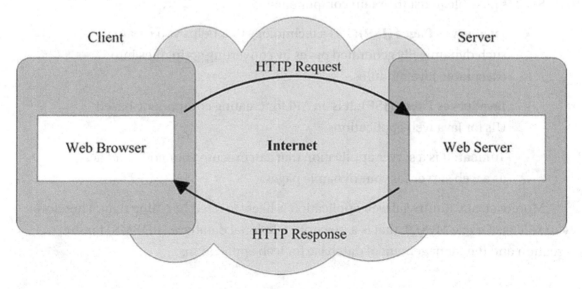

Figure 1-1. *Viewing a plain HTML page*

© Luciano Manelli and Giulio Zambon 2020
L. Manelli and G. Zambon, *Beginning Jakarta EE Web Development*,
https://doi.org/10.1007/978-1-4842-5866-8_1

The following steps show what happens when you request your browser to view a static web page:

1. When you type an address such as `www.website.com/path/whatever.html` into the address field, your browser first resolves `www.website.com` (i.e., the name of the web server) into the corresponding Internet Protocol (IP) address, usually by asking the Domain Name Server provided by your Internet service provider (ISP). Then your browser sends an HTTP (HyperText Transfer Protocol) request to the newly found IP address to receive the content of the file identified by `/path/whatever.html`.

2. In reply, the web server sends an HTTP response containing a plain-text HTML (HyperText Markup Language) page. Images and other non-textual components, such as sound and video clips, only appear in the page as hyperlinks to those resources stored either on the same server or another server on the Internet.

3. Your browser receives the response, interprets the HTML code contained in the page, requests the non-textual components from the server, and displays the lot.

So, it is possible to list the main components:

- **JavaServer Pages (JSP)**: It is a technology that helps you create such dynamically generated pages by converting script files into executable Java modules.

- **JavaServer Faces (JSF)**: It is an API for creating component-based UIs for Java web applications.

- **Tomcat**: It is a server application that can execute your code and act as a web server for your dynamic pages.

Moreover, any nontrivial web application is likely to need handling data. Therefore, you will use Oracle **MySQL** that is a powerful relational database (RDBMS) for the creation and the management of database for web applications.

Everything you need to develop JSP/JSF web applications is available for free download from the Internet; but to install all the necessary packages and tools and obtain an integrated development environment (IDE), you need to proceed with care. There is nothing more annoying than having to deal with incorrectly installed software. When something doesn't work, the problem will always be difficult to find.

In this chapter, I'll introduce you to Java servlets and JSP, and I'll show you how they work together within Tomcat to generate dynamic web pages.

You'll have to install more packages as you progress. In total, you will need at least 300MB of disk space for Java and Tomcat alone, at least 300MB of disk space for database, and twice as much space to install the Eclipse development environment useful for developing software.

To run all the examples contained in this book, you do not need large computational resources. I used a PC Intel i7 with 4 GB of memory and running Windows 7 (I also used a PC Intel i3 with 4 GB of memory and running Windows 10). I will focus on Windows operating system (OS), even if I will develop a cursory mention of package installation on macOS and Linux (Ubuntu distribution). At the time of this writing, the latest versions of all the packages you will need to install are

- **Java**: 14

- **Tomcat web server**: 9.0.34

- **Eclipse development environment**: Java IDE 2020-03

- **MySQL database**: MySQL Community Server 8.0.20

The installation of these components is explained in this chapter. In the next chapters, I also explained you how to download and configure other components: from the MySQL Java DataBase Connector (JDBC) to the Apache JavaServer Faces libraries.

Note that for security reasons, I wouldn't recommend installing something unless absolutely necessary and with no alternative, so it is easier and safer to just download a compressed version and run the relevant scripts for the respective OS. Of course, after this book is published, there will most likely be newer releases of all the aforementioned packages. Nevertheless, you should be able to adapt my instructions to install the latest versions without any problem.

Installing Java

Nothing runs without Java: on one hand, it is the runtime environment (JRE), which lets you execute Java, and on the other, it is the Java Development Kit (JDK), which lets you compile Java sources into executable classes. There are two main distributions: the Oracle JDK and the OpenJDK. I chose the second one under the open source GPL, because the Oracle JDK License has changed for releases starting from April 2019, permitting only certain uses at no cost. For more information about Oracle JDK License Update, you can go to the URL `www.oracle.com/java/technologies/javase-jdk14-downloads.html`.

Now, let's download the latest OpenJDK release. Here's what you need to do for Windows OS:

1. Go to the URL `https://jdk.java.net/14/` in Firefox browser as you can see in Figure 1-2.

2. Click the link of the zip file of Windows/x64 under Builds paragraph and the download of the archive file will start. We don't need any installer file.

3. Extract the archive file in your PC. I chose C:\.

Figure 1-2. *OpenJDK home page Firefox browser*

At this point, you should have the folder `C:\jdk-14,` that I changed in `C:\` `OpenJDK-14`, or the equivalent folders for the version you have downloaded. The Java home folder has the "bin" subfolder that will help you to develop and execute programs in Java language (with tools and utilities) and that supports the execution of programs written in the Java programming language (with an implementation of the Java Runtime Environment, class libraries, and other files). Note that since Java 11, Oracle and the OpenJDK team decided to distribute a single thing, the JDK, and to stop to duplicate some of the things the JDK in the JRE folder.

In order to be able to compile Java from the command line, you need to add the JDK path to the PATH environment variable. From the Windows `Start` menu, select `Settings` ➤ `Control Panel` ➤ `System`. When the `System Properties` dialog opens, click the "`Advanced system settings`" link that you find on the left-hand side and then on the Advanced tab. Finally, to reach the dialog that lets you modify the PATH variable, click the "`Environment Variables`" button. You will see the double dialog window shown in Figure 1-3.

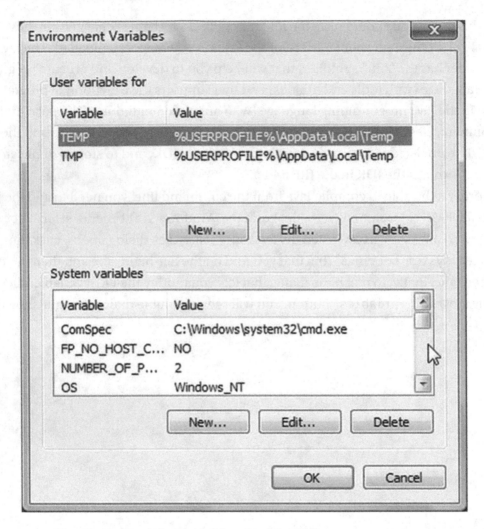

Figure 1-3. *The Environment Variables double dialog*

You might see a PATH variable on the top dialog, but what you need to do is scroll the bottom dialog by clicking the sidebar of "System variable" section until you see a variable named **Path**. Double-click it (or highlight it and click the "`Edit...`" button) and insert the text "`C:\OpenJDK-14\bin;`" in the field "Variable value" (you can also set the JAVA_HOME with the value of C:\OpenJDK-14 and then set in the Path the value %JAVA_HOME%\bin).

The semicolon at the end of the text is essential because it separates the new path from the existing ones. Do not insert additional spaces before or after.

Click the "OK" button to save the changes. Then click this button another couple of times until the system dialog closes.

What About Linux and macOS?

Linux is a complete operating system composed of free and open source software intended for personal computers. Last versions make it easy to use for non-developers, and its interface is like the Windows desktop. macOS is the operating system for Macintosh personal computers. It is a property of Apple, and it is based on a solid and secure Unix-like foundation.

Now, let's download the latest OpenJDK release for Linux OS. The simplest way is to go to the Terminal window in the Applications folder:

1. First, you need to update and upgrade the installed software of your OS.

2. Download and install the last version of the openjdk with the command `sudo apt install openjdk-14-jdk`. After inserting the password, the download will start. We don't need any installer file.

3. Now, the JDK is installed in the folder `/usr/lib/jvm/java-14-openjdk-amd64/`. If you think that can be more than one JDK installed, you can test it with the command `sudo update-alternatives --config java`.

4. At last, you can add the installed JDK to the environment variables of the `environment` file in the `/etc/` folder appending the path at the end of it (you can open and modify it using the `sudo nano /etc/environment` command and then add the following value: `JAVA_HOME=/usr/lib/jvm/java-14-openjdk-amd64/bin/`).

Now, let's download the latest OpenJDK release for macOS. Here's what you need to do:

1. Go to the URL `https://jdk.java.net/14/`. You can use Apple's browser, that is, Safari, as shown in Figure 1-4.

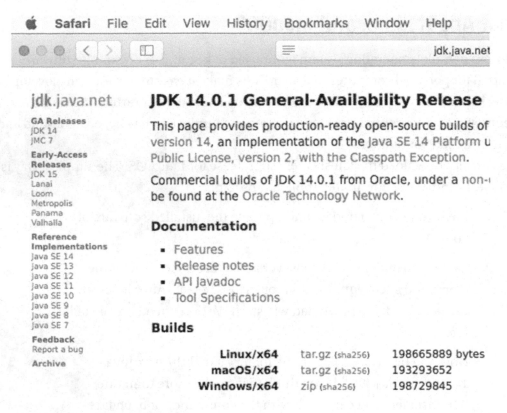

Figure 1-4. *OpenJDK home page Safari browser*

2. Click the link of the tar.gz file of macOS/x64 under Builds
    paragraph and the download of the archive file will start. We don't
    need any installer file.

3. Open the Terminal app in the Utilities folder, go to the Download
    location, and extract the downloaded file (you can use the
    command `tar -xf openjdk-14.0.1_osx-x64_bin.tar.gz`).

4. Now move the JDK to its default location (you can use the
    command `sudo mv jdk-14.0.1.jdk /Library/Java/`
    `JavaVirtualMachines/`).

5. At last, you can add the installed JDK to the environment variables
    of the bash file (setting the following value: `JAVA_HOME=$(/usr/`
    `libexec/java_home))`.

Note   Terminal (or command prompt for Windows) is a command-line interface that allows you to control your OS using a command prompt. The command sudo for a Unix-like operating systems allows to run programs or create directories by Terminal with the security privileges of a superuser (your account needs to be root or admin because administrator rights are required), and when executing it, you will be asked to enter your password.

Java Test

To test the Java installation, you can open a command-line window. The commands in the following paragraph are the same for Windows and for the other two OS. I decided to do it in Windows environment. Click the Start button and select Programs ➤ Accessories ➤ Command Prompt, or digit the command "cmd" in the search field of the Windows OS. Now type **javac** command.

If you see a screen like Figure 1-5, Java is installed.

```
C:\Users\lucky>javac
Usage: javac <options> <source files>
where possible options include:
  @<filename>                 Read options and filenames from file
  -Akey[=value]               Options to pass to annotation processors
  --add-modules <module>(,<module>)*
        Root modules to resolve in addition to the initial modules, or all modules
        on the module path if <module> is ALL-MODULE-PATH.
  --boot-class-path <path>, -bootclasspath <path>
        Override location of bootstrap class files
  --class-path <path>, -classpath <path>, -cp <path>
        Specify where to find user class files and annotation processors
  -d <directory>              Specify where to place generated class files
  -deprecation
        Output source locations where deprecated APIs are used
  --enable-preview
        Enable preview language features. To be used in conjunction with either -source or --release.
  -encoding <encoding>        Specify character encoding used by source files
  -endorseddirs <dirs>        Override location of endorsed standards path
  -extdirs <dirs>             Override location of installed extensions
  -g                          Generate all debugging info
  -g:{lines,vars,source}      Generate only some debugging info
  -g:none                     Generate no debugging info
```

Figure 1-5. *Testing Java*

If you want to test and confirm the installed Java version, go to command prompt and type **java -version** command. If you see a screen like Figure 1-6, the correct Java version is installed.

```
C:\Users\lucky>java -version
openjdk version "14" 2020-03-17
OpenJDK Runtime Environment (build 14+36-1461)
OpenJDK 64-Bit Server VM (build 14+36-1461, mixed mode, sharing)
```

Figure 1-6. *Testing Java version*

Moreover, to test the Java installation, you can also use the little application shown in Listing 1-1. In this example, you can use a smart editor as Notepad++ or a different text editor.

To create the source code for your first Java program, you have to

- Declare a class with name "Hello".

- Declare the main method "public static void main(String args[])".

- Type the command "System.out.println("Hello World")" for displaying the text Hello World on the command prompt window.

Listing 1-1. Hello.java

```
class Hello {
   public static void main(String args[]){
     System.out.println("Hello World");
   }
}
```

Now, save the file as **Hello.java** in your working folder. Open again the command window and, after changing to your work directory, type "javac Hello.java" to compile the application. It should return the prompt without saying anything. It also means that you have correctly updated the Path system variable. If you want to know more about what the javac compiler is doing, type –verbose between javac and the name of the file. You will see a file named Hello.class in your work directory. Now, to run the application, type "java Hello" on Command Prompt as shown in Figure 1-7.

```
C:\Users\lucky\OneDrive\Desktop>javac Hello.java

C:\Users\lucky\OneDrive\Desktop>java Hello
Hello World
```

Figure 1-7. *Testing a Java class*

Note that all the code described in this book is available for download from the Apress website. In this case, you can simply type the code; in others, you don't need to retype it, even if I think that it is important that you improve your programming skills developing in the Eclipse environment. You can find the examples in folders with the same names as the corresponding chapters.

Installing Tomcat

This is the Java web server of Apache's Tomcat service, which is the servlet container that allows you to run JSP and in which Java code can run (Tomcat 9 is the latest version). It is easier and safer to just download a zipped version and run the relevant scripts for the respective OS.

Tomcat listens to three communication ports of your PC (8005, 8009, and 8080). Before you install Tomcat, you should check whether some already installed applications are listening to one or more of those ports. To do so, use the command netstat that displays detailed information about your computer's network communications.

In Windows OS, you can open a terminal window and type the command `netstat /a`. It will display a list of active connections in tabular form. The second column of the table will look like this:

```
Local Address
0.0.0.0:135
0.0.0.0:445
0.0.0.0:3306
```

The port numbers are the numbers after the colon. If you see one or more of the ports Tomcat uses, after installing Tomcat, you will have to change the ports it listens to.

Here's how to install Tomcat 9 correctly:

1. Go to the URL `https://tomcat.apache.org/download-90.cgi`. Immediately below the second heading ("`Quick Navigation`"), you will see four links: `KEYS`, `9.0.34`, `Browse`, and `Archives`.

2. By clicking `9.0.34`, you will be taken toward the bottom of the same page to a heading with the same version number. Below the version heading, you will see the subheading "`Core`". Below that,

you will see the link for the zip download, arranged as follows: zip (pgp, sha512) apache-tomcat-9.0.34.zip. Click `zip link` to download the file apache-tomcat-9.0.34.zip (11.5MB).

3. Unzip the downloaded file in C:/. At this point, you should have the folder `C:\apache-tomcat-9.0.34`. I prefer to maintain the default folder name in this case because I can use different server versions without confusion. In fact, a very business situation includes different environments (such as development, test, and delivery), so remember to maintain consistency between the server versions to prevent bugs or different behaviors.

4. Now, you can configure the server creating in the folder C:\apache-tomcat-9.0.34\bin the file setenv.bat with the following code:

```
set "JRE_HOME=C:\OpenJDK-14"
set "JAVA_HOME=C:\OpenJDK-14"
exit /b 0
```

Now the server is ready to start up. Go to C:\apache-tomcat-9.0.34\bin and double-click startup.bat file or open a command window, go to bin folder, and type startup.bat as in Figure 1-8.

```
C:\apache-tomcat-9.0.34\bin>startup.bat
Using CATALINA_BASE:   "C:\apache-tomcat-9.0.34"
Using CATALINA_HOME:   "C:\apache-tomcat-9.0.34"
Using CATALINA_TMPDIR: "C:\apache-tomcat-9.0.34\temp"
Using JRE_HOME:        "C:\OpenJDK-14"
Using CLASSPATH:       "C:\apache-tomcat-9.0.34\bin\bootstrap.jar;C:\apache-tomcat-9.0.34\bin\tomcat-juli.jar"
```

Figure 1-8. *Starting up Tomcat server*

A second window is generated: if there are no problems, it will end with the code line that indicates the startup time, as shown in Figure 1-9. In this window, it will be also written the log of our applications.

```
rectory [C:\apache-tomcat-9.0.34\webapps\manager]
06-May-2020 17:24:41.484 INFO [main] org.apache.catalina.startup.HostConfig.deployDirectory Deployment of web applicatio
n directory [C:\apache-tomcat-9.0.34\webapps\manager] has finished in [38] ms
06-May-2020 17:24:41.485 INFO [main] org.apache.catalina.startup.HostConfig.deployDirectory Deploying web application di
rectory [C:\apache-tomcat-9.0.34\webapps\ROOT]
06-May-2020 17:24:41.538 INFO [main] org.apache.catalina.startup.HostConfig.deployDirectory Deployment of web applicatio
n directory [C:\apache-tomcat-9.0.34\webapps\ROOT] has finished in [52] ms
06-May-2020 17:24:41.545 INFO [main] org.apache.coyote.AbstractProtocol.start Starting ProtocolHandler ["http-nio-8080"]

06-May-2020 17:24:41.557 INFO [main] org.apache.catalina.startup.Catalina.start Server startup in [978] milliseconds
```

Figure 1-9. *Starting up Tomcat window*

To see that Tomcat is working properly, open a browser and type localhost:8080. You should see the page shown in Figure 1-10 (Firefox in the example).

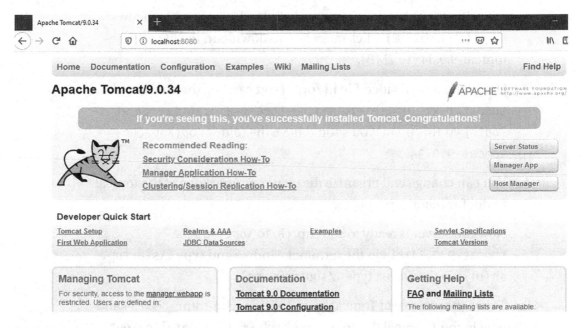

Figure 1-10. *The localhost home page*

A URL like `http://localhost:8080/` that you saw in the previous figure specifies that on the host side, the port number for HTTP is 8080 instead of 80, which is the standard port for HTTP. This is because Tomcat expects and routes HTTP traffic through port 8080. This is appropriate if you intend to use Tomcat to handle requests for JSP pages and place it behind a server (typically, the Apache web server) that handles static HTTP/HTTPS. But if you intend to use Tomcat to handle HTTP/HTTPS as well, you should change its default ports 8080 and 8443 to 80 and 443, respectively.

What About Linux and macOS?

Here's how to install Tomcat 9 correctly in Linux:

1. Go to the URL `https://tomcat.apache.org/download-90.cgi`. Immediately below the second heading ("Quick Navigation"), you will see four links: KEYS, 9.0.34, Browse, and Archives.

2. By clicking `9.0.34`, you will be taken toward the bottom of the same page to a heading with the same version number. Below the version heading, you will see the subheading "`Core`". Below that, you will see the link for the tar.gz download, arranged as follows: tar.gz (pgp, sha512). Click tar.gz link to download the file apache-tomcat-9.0.34 (10.7MB).

3. Unzip the downloaded file in /opt/ (you can use the command `sudo tar xf /Downloads/apache-tomcat-9.0.35.tar.gz -C /opt/`). At this point, you should have the folder `/opt/apache-tomcat-9.0.34`.

4. You can change and organize the owner permissions of the tomcat folder for security purposes.

5. Now the server is ready to start up. Go to `\opt\apache-tomcat-9.0.34\bin` in the terminal window and type `.\startup.sh` (to stop the server, type `./shutdown.sh`).

6. To see the console of Tomcat, go to \opt\apache-tomcat-9.0.34 and type in the Terminal the command `tail -f logs/catalina.out`.

7. At last, you can open a browser and type localhost:8080.

Here's how to install Tomcat 9 correctly in macOS:

1. Go to the URL `https://tomcat.apache.org/download-90.cgi`. Immediately below the second heading ("Quick Navigation"), you will see four links: KEYS, 9.0.34, Browse, and Archives.

2. By clicking `9.0.34`, you will be taken toward the bottom of the same page to a heading with the same version number. Below the version heading, you will see the subheading "`Core`". Below that,

you will see the link for the tar.gz download, arranged as follows: tar.gz (pgp, sha512). Click tar.gz link to download the file apache-tomcat-9.0.34 (10.7MB).

3. Unzip the downloaded file in `/usr/local` (you can use in the Downloads folder the command `sudo tar xf apache-tomcat-9.0.35.tar.gz -C /usr/local/`). At this point, you should have the folder `/usr/local/apache-tomcat-9.0.34`.

4. You can change and organize the owner permissions of the tomcat folder for security purposes.

5. Now the server is ready to start up. Go to `/usr/local/apache-tomcat-9.0.34/bin` in the terminal window and type `./startup.sh` (to stop the server, type `./shutdown.sh`). The JRE_HOME is set in a correct way because it points to the folder `\usr\` defined in the previous paragraph or to the defined JAVA_HOME folder.

6. To see the console of Tomcat, go to `/usr/local/apache-tomcat-9.0.34` and type in the Terminal the command `tail -f logs/catalina.out`.

7. At last, you can open a browser and type localhost:8080.

With Java and Tomcat in place, we can finally begin playing with JSP!

Introduction to HTML

You can find on the Internet several websites that describe HTML, Cascading Style Sheets (CSS), and JavaScript in detail. Therefore, instead of attempting to cover everything there is to know about them, I will introduce a few key concepts for anyone who is beginning the study of web development for the first time.

HyperText Markup Language (HTML) is the standard "tag" markup language used for creating html pages (with extension .htm or .html). Therefore, it is the base for JSP pages. HTML documents are organized as a hierarchy of elements that normally consist of content enclosed between a pair of start and end tags.

The schema is

```
<TAG attributes>contents</TAG>
```

15

You can nest HTML elements inside each other, and in fact, without nesting, no HTML page would be possible. The tag can be organized in the following way (with indentation):

```
<TAG1 attributes >
        <TAG2 attributes >
              content 2
        </TAG2>
</TAG1>
```

For example, the tags <html> and </html> delimit the whole HTML document. However, some elements are empty, in which case you can usually replace the end tag with a slash immediately before the closing bracket of the start tag, as in <img src="mypict.gif"/>.

You can insert comments in the following way:

```
<!-- comments -->
```

Each tag can have some attributes with some values:

```
<tag1 attribute1= "value1" attribute2= "value2">
```

The html document presents two sections:

```
<head>...</head>
<body>...</body>
```

It is possible defining

- Bold characters: <b>

- Underline characters: <u>

- Italic characters: <i>

- Newline:

- Paragraph: <p>

- Heading: from <h1> to <h6>

The title tag defines a title for the HTML document.

The style tag defines style information for the HTML document: it can be inline for a section of the page or general (in this case, it is defined in the head tag of the html page).

Listing 1-2 shows the simplest possible HTML page. Copy the code in a text document and then save the file as basic.html. Double-click the file and the html page will be open in the predefined browser.

Listing 1-2. basic.html

```html
<html>
        <head><title>Page title</title></head>
                <style type="text/css">
                    body {background-color:gray; font-size=10pt;}
                </style>
        <body>
                <b>Bold characters</b>
                <u>Underline characters</u>
                <i>Italic characters</i>
                A newline<br>
                <p>A paragraph</p>
                <h1>A heading</h1>
        </body>
</html>
```

Figure 1-11 shows the outcome of Listing 1-2.

Figure 1-11. *A basic HTML page*

Essentially, an HTML document consists of text, images, audio and video clips, active components such as scripts and executables, and hyperlinks. A browser then interprets and renders the components in sequence, mostly without inserting any empty space or newline between them.

At last, it is possible defining tables:

- <table>...</table>: It opens/closes a table.

- <tr>...</tr> ("table row"): It creates a row.

- <td>...</td> ("table data"): It creates a cell.

A table consists of rows and columns, with cells containing text, images, and other components. In almost every chapter of this book, you'll find examples of tables. Tables are an easy way to present components in an organized fashion.

Listing 1-3. table.html

```
<table border="1">
   <tr>
       <td> content 1</td>
       <td> content 2</td>
   </tr>
   <tr>
       <td> content 3</td>
       <td> content 4</td>
   </tr>
 </table>
```

Listing 1-3 shows the code that generates the simple table of Figure 1-12.

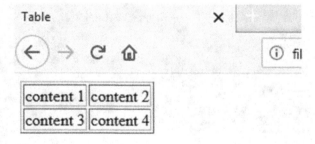

Figure 1-12. *An HTML-generated table*

To turn your web pages into an interactive experience, you have to give users the ability to make choices and type or upload information (i.e., when you create a new email, you type data in an online form!). To achieve this, you use the form element, which accepts data from the user and sends it to the server.

This book is full of examples of input forms. But a summary of all possible input elements as shown in Figure 1-13 might be useful as a reference. The browser was Firefox.

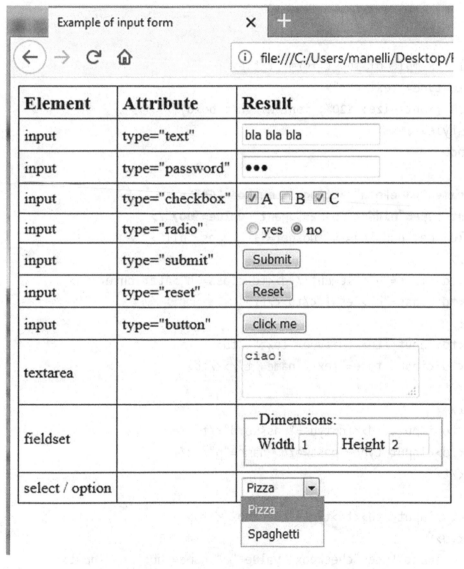

Figure 1-13. *An HTML form with examples of all input elements*

The various types of the input element let the user enter a string of text or a password, check one or more check boxes, choose one of several radio buttons, submit a form, or reset a form's fields. The textarea element lets the user enter several lines of text, while the fieldset element lets you group several input fields under one or more headings. To present multiple choices, you use the select element, which contains one option element for each alternative. Listing 1-4 shows the source code of Figure 1-13.

Listing 1-4. form.html

```html
<html>
<head>
  <title>Example of input form</title>
  <style type="text/css">
    td.h {font-size: 120%; font-weight: bold}
    </style>
  </head>
<body>
<form name="nameForm" action="" method="GET">
  <input type="hidden" name="agent" value="007"/>
  <table  cellpadding="5" border="1" rules="all">
    <tr>
      <td class="h">Element</td><td class="h">Attribute</td>
      <td class="h">Result</td></tr>
    <tr>
      <td>input</td><td>type="text"</td>
      <td><input type="text" name="t"/></td>
      </tr>
    <tr>
      <td>input</td><td>type="password"</td>
      <td><input type="password" name="p"/></td>
      </tr>
    <tr>
      <td>input</td><td>type="checkbox"</td>
      <td>
        <input type="checkbox" value="a" name="abc">A</input>
        <input type="checkbox" value="b" name="abc">B</input>
```

```
    <input type="checkbox" value="c" name="abc">C</input>
    </td>
  </tr>
<tr>
  <td>input</td><td>type="radio"</td>
  <td>
    <input type="radio" name="yn" value="y">yes</input>
    <input type="radio" name="yn" value="n">no</input>
    </td>
  </tr>
<tr>
  <td>input</td><td>type="submit"</td>
  <td><input type="submit"/></td>
  </tr>
<tr>
  <td>input</td><td>type="reset"</td>
  <td><input type="reset"/></td>
  </tr>
<tr>
  <td>input</td><td>type="button"</td>
  <td><input type="button" value="click me" name="b"/></td>
  </tr>
<tr>
  <td>textarea</td><td></td>
  <td><textarea name="ta">Default text</textarea></td>
  </tr>
<tr>
  <td>fieldset</td><td></td>
  <td><fieldset>
    <legend>Dimensions:</legend>
    Width <input type="text" size="3" name="w"/>
    Height <input type="text" size="3" name="h"/>
    </fieldset></td>
  </tr>
<tr>
```

```
    <td>select / option</td><td></td>
    <td><select name="food">
      <option value="pizza" selected >Pizza</option>
      <option value="spaghetti">Spaghetti</option>
      </select></td>
    </tr>
  </table>
 </form>
</body>
</html>
```

I've highlighted two lines. The first line, which contains the form element, shows that the action attribute is set to the empty string. The action attribute defines the URL of the page that must handle the request form. An empty string means that the same page displaying the form will also handle it. The second highlighted line shows how you can use the input element to set parameters without the user being aware of it (unless he or she peeks at the source, that is).

If you fill in the form as shown in Figure 1-13 and click the Submit button (or hit the Enter key), you'll see in the address field of your browser that the following string appears at the end of the URL (I've inserted newlines for readability):

```
?agent=007
&t=bla+bla+bla
&p=abc
&abc=a
&abc=c
&yn=n
&ta=ciao!
&w=1
&h=2
&food=pizza
```

The browser has translated each input element into a string parameter-name=parameter-value. Notice that each space in the text fields has been replaced by a plus sign, including the spaces within the password. Also notice that the parameter abc appears twice, because I checked two of the three available check boxes. To avoid seeing all the parameters in the browser, use in the form element the attribute method="POST".

Moreover, the POST method is more secure because data are stored in the request body of the HTTP and it has no restrictions on data length.

For more information, you can simply go to www.w3schools.com/ that is one of the more important and complete sites for web development site.

What Is JSP?

JSP is a technology that lets you add dynamic content to web pages. In absence of JSP, to update the appearance or the content of plain static HTML pages, you always have to do it by hand. Even if all you want to do is change a date or a picture, you must edit the HTML file and type in your modifications. Nobody is going to do it for you, whereas with JSP, you can make the content dependent on many factors, including the time of the day, the information provided by the user, the user's history of interaction with your website, and even the user's browser type. This capability is essential to provide online services in which you can tailor each response to the viewer who made the request, depending on the viewer's preferences and requirements. A crucial aspect of providing meaningful online services is for the system to be able to *remember* data associated with the service and its users. That's why databases play an essential role in dynamic web pages. But let's take it one step at a time.

Viewing a JSP Page

With JSP, the web page doesn't actually exist on the server. As you can see in Figure 1-14, the server creates it fresh when responding to each request.

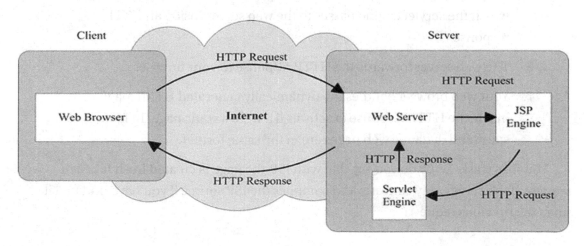

Figure 1-14. *Viewing a JSP page*

The following steps explain how the web server creates the web page:

1. As with a normal page, your browser sends an HTTP request to the web server. This doesn't change with JSP, although the URL probably ends in `.jsp` instead of `.html` or `.htm`.

2. The web server is not a normal server, but rather a Java server, with the extensions necessary to identify and handle Java servlets. The web server recognizes that the HTTP request is for a JSP page and forwards it to a JSP engine.

3. The JSP engine loads the JSP page from disk and converts it into a Java servlet. From this point on, this servlet is indistinguishable from any other servlet developed directly in Java rather than JSP, although the automatically generated Java code of a JSP servlet is not always easy to read, and you should never modify it by hand.

4. The JSP engine compiles the servlet into an executable class and forwards the original request to another part of the web server called the *servlet engine*. Note that the JSP engine only converts the JSP page to Java and recompiles the servlet if it finds that the JSP page has changed since the last request. This makes the process more efficient than with other scripting languages (such as PHP) and therefore faster.

5. The servlet engine loads the servlet class and executes it. During execution, the servlet produces an output in HTML format, which the servlet engine passes to the web server inside an HTTP response.

6. The web server forwards the HTTP response to your browser.

7. Your web browser handles the dynamically generated HTML page inside the HTTP response exactly as if it were a static page. In fact, static and dynamic web pages are in the same format.

You might ask, "Why do you say that with JSP, the page is created fresh for each request, if the server only converts and compiles the JSP source if you have updated it since the previous request?"

What reaches your browser is the output generated by the servlet (i.e., by the converted and compiled JSP page), not the JSP page itself. The same servlet produces different outputs depending on the parameters of the HTTP request and other factors. For example, suppose you're browsing the products offered by an online shop. When you click the image of a product, your browser generates an HTTP request with the product code as a parameter. As a result, the servlet generates an HTML page with the description of that product. The server doesn't need to recompile the servlet for each product code.

The servlet queries a database containing the details of all the products, obtains the description of the product you're interested in, and formats an HTML page with that data. This is what dynamic HTML is all about!

Plain HTML is not capable of interrogating a database, but Java is, and JSP gives you the means of including snippets of Java inside an HTML page.

Hello World!

A small example of JSP will give you a more practical idea of how JSP works. Let's start once more from HTML. Listing 1-5 shows you a plain HTML page to display "Hello World!" in your browser's window.

Listing 1-5. hello.html

```html
<html>
        <head>
                <title>Hello World static HTML</title>
        </head>
        <body>
                Hello World!
        </body>
</html>
```

Create the folder %CATALINA_HOME%\webapps\ROOT\tests\ and store in it `hello.html`. Then type the following URL in your browser to see the web page:

`http://localhost:8080/tests/hello.html`

Normally, to ask your browser to check that the syntax of the page conforms to the XHTML standard of the World Wide Web Consortium (W3C), you would have to start the page with the following lines:

```
<?xml version="1.0" encoding="UTF-8"?>
<!DOCTYPE html PUBLIC "-//W3C//DTD XHTML 1.0 Strict//EN"
  "http://www.w3.org/TR/xhtml1/DTD/xhtml1-strict.dtd">
```

You'd also have to replace

```
<html>
```

with

```
<html xmlns="http://www.w3.org/1999/xhtml">
```

However, for this simple example, I prefer to keep the code to what's essential. Figure 1-15 shows you how this page will appear in your browser.

Figure 1-15. *"Hello World!" in plain HTML*

If you direct your browser to show the page source, not surprisingly, you'll see exactly what's shown in Listing 1-5. To obtain the same result with a JSP page, you only need to insert a JSP directive before the first line, as shown in Listing 1-6, and change the file extension from `.html` to `.jsp`.

Listing 1-6. "Hello World!" in a Boring JSP Page

```
<%@page language="java" contentType="text/html"%>
<html>
        <head>
                <title>Hello World dynamic HTML</title>
        </head>
        <body>
```

```
            Hello World!
      </body>
</html>
```

As with `hello.html`, you can view, as shown in Figure 1-16, `hello.jsp` by placing it in Tomcat's `ROOT\tests` folder and then type the following URL in your browser to see the web page:

```
http://localhost:8080/tests/hello.jsp
```

Hello World!

Figure 1-16. *"Hello World!" in JSP*

Obviously, there isn't much point in using JSP for such a simple page. It only pays to use JSP if you include dynamic content. Check out Listing 1-7 for something more juicy.

Listing 1-7. hello.jsp

```
<%@page language="java" contentType="text/html"%>
<html>
      <head>
            <title>Hello World dynamic HTML</title>
      </head>
      <body>
            Hello World!
            <%
            String userAgent = request.getHeader("user-agent");
            out.println("<br/>user-agent " + userAgent);
            %>
      </body>
</html>
```

The code within the <% ... %> pair is a scriptlet written in Java. When Tomcat's JSP engine interprets this module, it creates a Java servlet like that shown in Listing 1-8 (with some indentation and empty lines removed).

Listing 1-8. Java Code from the "Hello World!" JSP Page

```
out.write("\r\n");
out.write("<html>\r\n");
out.write("<head><title>Hello World dynamic
 HTML </title></head>\r\n");
out.write("<body>\r\n");
String userAgent = request.getHeader("user-agent");
out.println("<br/>User-agent: " + userAgent);
out.write("\r\n");
out.write("Hello World!\r\n");
out.write("</body>\r\n");
out.write("</html>\r\n");
```

As I said before, this servlet executes every time a browser sends a request to the server. However, before the code shown in Listing 1-8 executes, the server binds the variable out to a character stream associated with the content of the HTML response. As a result, everything written to out ends up in the HTML page that you'll see in your browser. As you can see, Tomcat copies the scriptlet in your JSP file into the servlet and sends everything outside the scriptlet directly to the output. This should clarify how HTML and Java work together in a JSP page.

As the variable out is defined in each servlet, you can use it within any JSP module to insert something into the response (more on variables in Chapter 2).

Another such "global" JSP variable is request (of type HttpServletRequest). The request contains the IP address from which the request was originated, that is, of the remote computer with the browser (remember that this code runs on the server). The request also contains information about the browser. When some browsers send a request, they provide somewhat misleading information, and the format is complex.

The line that prints the userAgent informations, in the code in Listing 1-7, tells you the used browser and whether the browser is running on a Windows system or a Mac.

Figure 1-17 shows the generated page as it appears in a browser.

Hello World!
User-agent: Mozilla/5.0 (Windows NT 6.1; Win64; x64; rv:72.0) Gecko/20100101 Firefox/72.0

Figure 1-17. *hello.jsp with Firefox*

Installing MySQL

In this section, I will explain how to install MySQL. I prefer manual installation because it offers some benefits and more control: you can back up or move databases in seconds and you can install and reinstall MySQL anywhere (also on USB drive). It will be also useful the installation of the MySQL Workbench, which is a user-friendly tool for the management of the database.

To install MySQL, do the following steps:

1. Go to `https://dev.mysql.com/downloads/mysql/`, the MySQL Community Server page, as shown in Figure 1-18 and agree the privacy policy.

2. Ensure that the selected platform is "Microsoft Windows" and click the download of the without installer version "Windows (x86, 64-bit), ZIP Archive" under "Other Downloads" section.

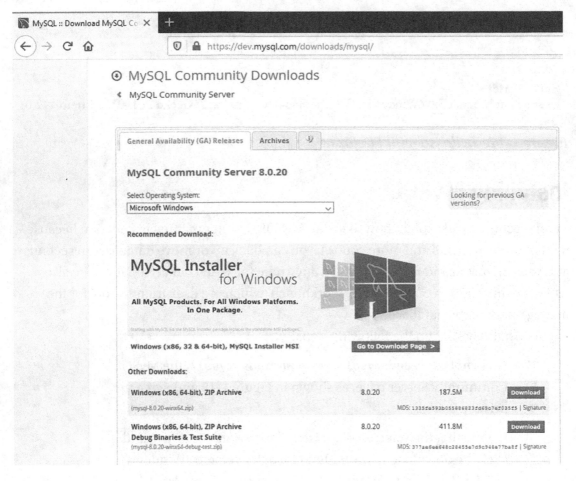

Figure 1-18. *MySQL download page*

3.   Before you can download the package, you will have to log in as a
     user or register to be one, or, if you want, you can skip this step.

4.   Finally, you can download the without installer version (mysql-
     8.0.20-winx64.zip): it has a dimension of 187.5M. This package
     contains MySQL database server.

5.   Extract the zip file into C folder: drive and rename the folder from
     "mysql-8.0.20-winx64" to "mysql".

6.   Now, create the "data" folder. I chose in the same folder mysql,
     even if I recommend always placing the data folder on another
     drive. This prevents loss of data and makes easy reinstallation.

7. Now, you must initialize the data directory manually before
    MySQL can be started. Open a command window and type under
    the bin folder

    ```
    C:\mysql\bin>mysqld --console --initialize
    ```

    The `--console` option enables writing the diagnostic output to
    console (if you omit this option, the server writes output to the
    error log in the data folder).

You will get the following result on the console shown in Listing 1-9.

Listing 1-9. Log of Database Initialization

```
2020-05-11T22:35:02.223801Z 0 [System] [MY-013169] [Server] C:\mysql\bin\
mysqld.exe (mysqld 8.0.20) initializing of server in progress as process
7472
2020-05-11T22:35:02.243301Z 1 [System] [MY-013576] [InnoDB] InnoDB
initialization has started.
2020-05-11T22:35:17.626425Z 1 [System] [MY-013577] [InnoDB] InnoDB
initialization has ended.
2020-05-11T22:35:47.786871Z 6 [Note] [MY-010454] [Server] A temporary
password is generated for root@localhost: >7<s#XV!lsKz
```

The string I have highlighted in bold is the generated password for root user (which
is the default administrative account in the MySQL grant system) displayed in the stream
during the initialization. Now, you are ready to work with your database. Open two
console windows: in the first, start the database with the command

```
C:\mysql\bin>mysqld.exe -console
```

Listing 1-10 shows the starting up of the server. The command --console lets you see
the startup logs being printed.

Listing 1-10. Log of Database Starting Up

```
C:\mysql\bin>mysqld.exe --console
2020-05-12T09:00:22.716177Z 0 [System] [MY-010116] [Server] C:\mysql\bin\
mysqld.exe (mysqld 8.0.20) starting as process 4188
2020-05-12T09:00:22.767345Z 1 [System] [MY-013576] [InnoDB] InnoDB
initialization has started.
2020-05-12T09:00:25.311052Z 1 [System] [MY-013577] [InnoDB] InnoDB
initialization has ended.
2020-05-12T09:00:27.089744Z 0 [System] [MY-011323] [Server] X Plugin ready
for connections. Bind-address: '::' port: 33060
2020-05-12T09:00:27.880666Z 0 [Warning] [MY-010068] [Server] CA certificate
ca.pem is self signed.
2020-05-12T09:00:28.129496Z 0 [System] [MY-010931] [Server] C:\mysql\bin\
mysqld.exe: ready for connections. Version: '8.0.20'  socket: ''  port:
3306  MySQL Community Server - GPL.
```

In the second, connect to the database with user and password and start the mysql console with the command

```
C:\mysql\bin>mysql -u root -p
```

After typing the password when prompted (Enter password: ***********), you will see the welcome message on the console, as shown in Listing 1-11.

Listing 1-11. Log of Database Connection

```
C:\mysql\bin>mysql -u root -p
Enter password: ***********
Welcome to the MySQL monitor.  Commands end with ; or \g.
Your MySQL connection id is 8
Server version: 8.0.20
Copyright (c) 2000, 2020, Oracle and/or its affiliates. All rights
reserved.
Oracle is a registered trademark of Oracle Corporation and/or its
affiliates. Other names may be trademarks of their respective
owners.
```

```
Type 'help;' or '\h' for help. Type '\c' to clear the current input
statement.
mysql>
```

Now the *command-line interface (CLI)* is activated; you can note the change of the prompt command I have highlighted.

At last, I recommend changing the password with the command

```
mysql> ALTER USER 'root'@'localhost' IDENTIFIED BY 'root';
```

The string I have highlighted in bold is the new password I used.

Then, run the command

```
mysql> FLUSH PRIVILEGES;
```

It tells the server to reload the grant tables: this operation puts your new changes into effect.

Finally, if you want to stop the database, enter exit in the prompt to stop the command-line client and then type

```
C:\mysql\bin>mysqladmin.exe -u root -p shutdown
Enter password: ****
```

The command *mysqladmin* invokes the administrative utility to connect to MySQL server as root user and tell it to shut down.

The console writes the following message as shown in Listing 1-12.

Listing 1-12. Log of Server Shut Down

```
2020-05-12T16:03:03.527360Z 20 [System] [MY-013172] [Server] Received
SHUTDOWN from user root. Shutting down mysqld (Version: 8.0.20).
2020-05-12T16:03:03.531865Z 0 [System] [MY-013105] [Server] C:\mysql\bin\
mysqld.exe: Normal shutdown.
2020-05-12T16:03:05.704839Z 0 [System] [MY-010910] [Server] C:\mysql\bin\
mysqld.exe: Shutdown complete (mysqld 8.0.20)  MySQL Community Server - GPL.
```

Now you can install Workbench. Do the following steps for Windows:

1. Go to `https://dev.mysql.com/downloads/workbench/`, the MySQL Community Server page, as shown in Figure 1-19.

2. Ensure that the selected platform is "Microsoft Windows" and click the download installer version "Windows (x86, 64-bit), MSI Installer" under "Other Downloads" section.

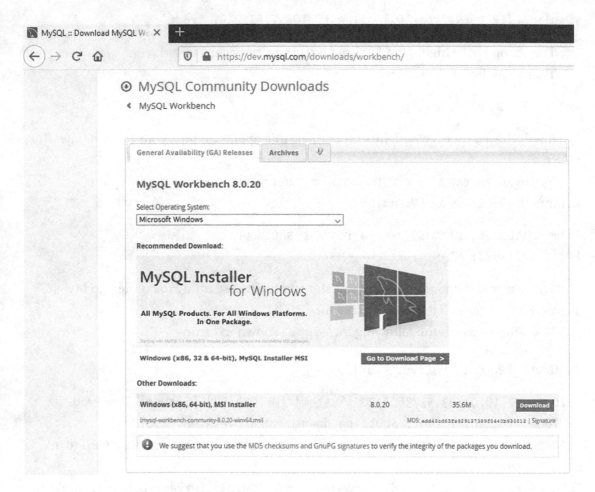

Figure 1-19. MySQL Workbench download page

3. Before you can download the package, you will have to log in as a user or register to be one, or, if you want, you can skip this step.

4. Finally, you can download the installer version (mysql-workbench-community-8.0.20-winx64.msi): it has a dimension of 35.6M.

5. Be aware that Workbench requires "Microsoft .NET Framework 4.5.2" and the "Visual C++ 2015-2019 Redistributable Package". However, if some packages are not installed, the installer will guide you to download and install the latest binary compatible version with your operating system.

6. When you execute the mysql-workbench-community-8.0.20-winx64.msi installer, the wizard starts as shown in Figure 1-20.

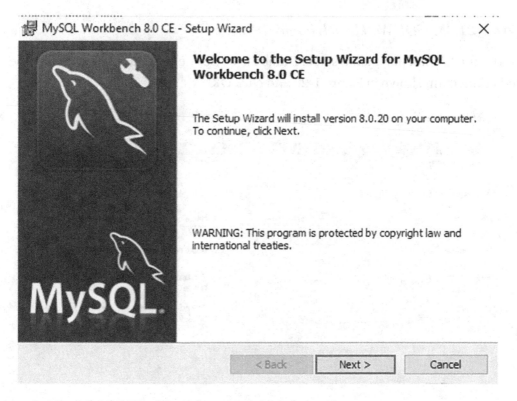

Figure 1-20. *MySQL Workbench setup wizard*

After finishing the installation, we can start the Workbench, as shown in Figure 1-21.

Figure 1-21. *MySQL Workbench home*

From the Workbench menu, select Database ➤ Connect to Database…. Select the stored connection shown in Figure 1-22 and click OK!

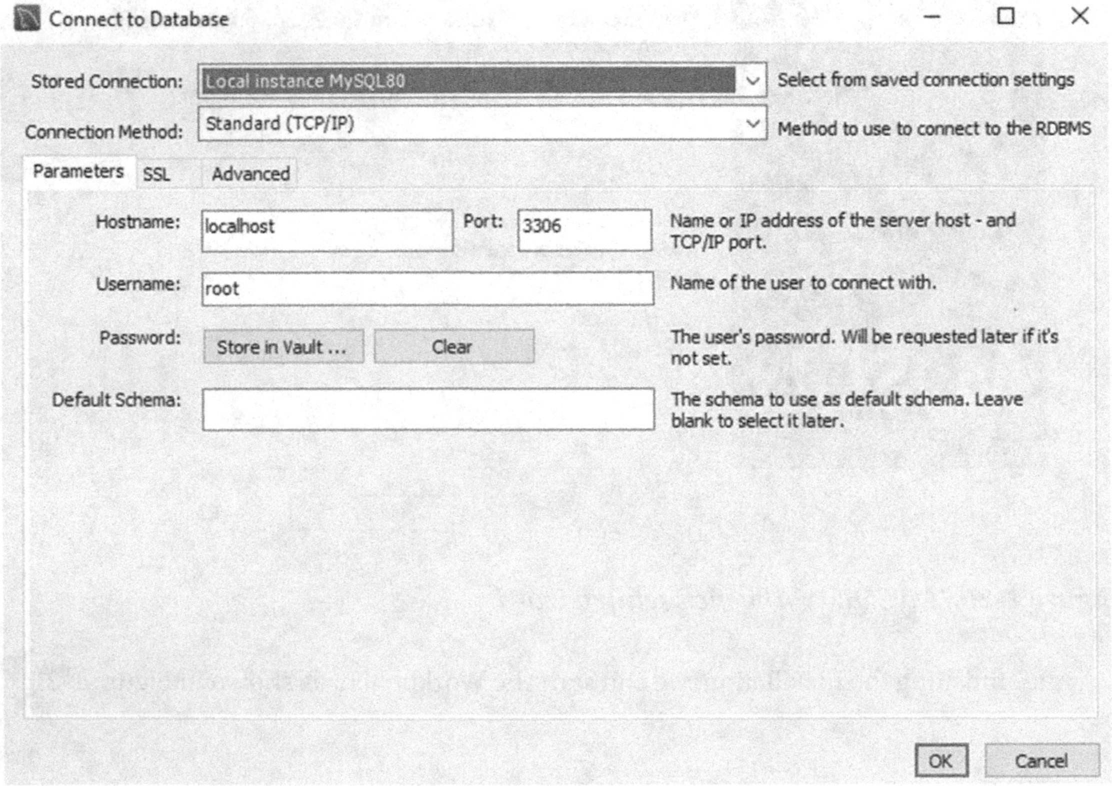

Figure 1-22. *MySQL Workbench—Connect to Database*

Figure 1-23 shows the authentication panel. Now, set to "root" the password and confirm!

Figure 1-23. *MySQL Workbench—database authentication*

Now, it is also possible to work with Workbench.

What About Linux and macOS?

Here's how to install MySQL correctly in Linux. The simplest way is to go to the Terminal window in the Applications folder:

1. Download and install the last version of the MySQL with the command `sudo apt install mysql-server`. After inserting the password, the download will start. We don't need any installer file.

2. Change and organize the owner permissions of the mysql folder for security purposes.

Now, the steps are the same that for Windows OS. You must initialize the data directory manually, before MySQL can be started, typing in the Terminal under the bin folder the command `mysqld -console --initialize`. Then start the MySQL console (use the command `sudo mysql`) and change password. You can start and stop the server by typing the following commands:

```
sudo /etc/init.d/mysql start
sudo /etc/init.d/mysql stop
```

You can also download the Workbench file mysql-workbench-community_8.0.20-1ubuntu20.04_amd64.deb (that is similar to an installer package for Linux systems) from MySQL site. Then you can run the file (you can use the command `sudo dpkg -i mysql-workbench-community_8.0.20-1ubuntu20.04_amd64.deb`). Now you can work with Workbench. It is installed on your system in the Applications folder.

Here's how to install MySQL correctly in macOS. To install MySQL, do the following steps:

1. Go to `https://dev.mysql.com/downloads/mysql/`, the MySQL Community Server page in Safari browser.

2. Ensure that the selected platform is "macOS" and click the download of the without installer version "macOS 10.15 (x86, 64-bit), Compressed TAR Archive" under "Other Downloads" section.

3. Open a Terminal window and unpack it at the typically installation location (/usr/local/mysql).

4. Change and organize the owner permissions of the mysql folder for security purposes.

Now, the steps are the same that for Windows OS. You must initialize the data directory manually, before MySQL can be started, typing in the Terminal under the bin folder the command `mysqld -console --initialize`. You can start and stop the server by typing the following commands:

```
sudo /usr/local/mysql/support-files/mysql.server start
sudo /usr/local/mysql/support-files/mysql.server stop
```

You can also download the Workbench file mysql-workbench-community-8.0.20-macos-x86_64.dmg from MySQL Workbench site, after selecting the macOS operating system. Double-click the downloaded file and, in the installation window, drag the icon of MySQL Workbench onto the icon of Applications as suggested. Now you can launch the application: the first time you would get the warning "Workbench is an application downloaded from the internet. Are you sure you want to open it?", just click "open". Now you can work with Workbench.

Installing Eclipse

Although it's possible to build web applications by compiling Java modules from the command line, it's more efficient to use an integrated development environment (IDE). This way, you can concentrate on the more creative part of developing software, rather than fix inconsistency and fiddle with folder hierarchies.

An IDE integrates all the applications that you need to develop software—from a source editor and a compiler to tools to automate the application building process and a debugger—into a single application. When developing in Java or in another object-oriented language, an IDE also includes tools to visualize class and object structure as well as inheritance and containment. Another advantage of using an IDE is that it propagates changes you make to individual modules. For example, if you rename a class, the IDE can automatically update its occurrences throughout your project files.

As the applications you develop become more complex, it makes more and more sense to use an IDE. That's why, before continuing to our next project, I will tell you how to install and configure Eclipse.

Eclipse is an extremely powerful and extensible IDE, well suited for web application development. The Eclipse Foundation makes a new release four times a year (in March, June, September, and December), due to continuous integration and delivery in the software industry (the so-called rolling release). To develop the examples contained in this book, I used Eclipse IDE 2020-03, March 2020.

Once you've installed Eclipse to develop web applications, you can use it for any other software development task, for example, developing and debugging applications written in Java, C++, and even Fortran, which is still widely used in the scientific community.

Furthermore, whatever task related to software development you need to perform, it's likely that somebody has already developed an Eclipse plug-in for it. The website `http://marketplace.eclipse.org/` lists about 2000 plug-ins organized in dozens of categories. In fact, Eclipse itself consists of a core platform that executes plug-ins, plus a series of plug-ins that implement most of its functionality. Therefore, the standard packages available for download from the Eclipse website already include dozens of plug-ins.

In this section, I'll only explain how to install the standard Eclipse configuration for Java EE development, which is what you need as you go through the rest of this book.

First of all, you need to download the package. To do so, go to `www.eclipse.org/downloads/packages/` and click the Windows 64-bit link of Eclipse IDE for Java EE Developers, as shown in Figure 1-24.

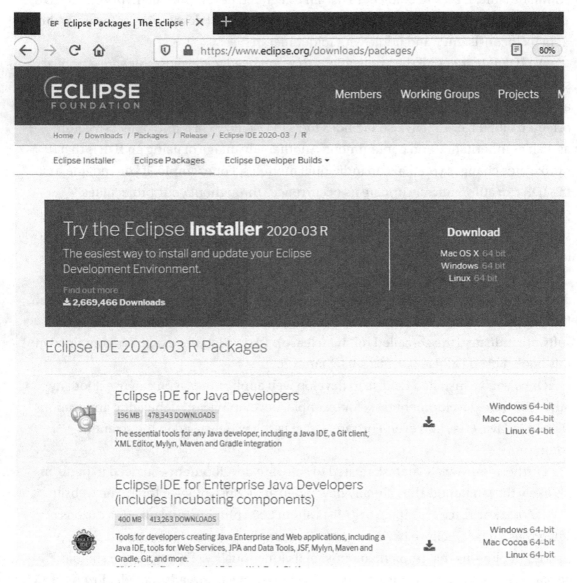

Figure 1-24. *Downloading Eclipse*

The website will suggest a mirror site for the download. The installation of Eclipse is very easy: expand the downloaded eclipse-jee-2020-03-R-win32-x86_64.zip and download the Eclipse IDE for Enterprise Java Developers.

File and move the `eclipse` folder to a convenient place. For no particular reason, I chose to move it to `C:\`. Old habits are difficult to change. You might like to move the Eclipse folder to `C:\Program Files\`.

To execute Eclipse, double-click `eclipse.exe`, which you find immediately inside the eclipse folder.

When it starts, Eclipse asks you to select a workspace. The workspace is the folder where Eclipse stores your development projects. Therefore, it makes sense to place it on a drive or in a directory that you back up regularly. Before clicking the `OK` button, check the box marked "`Use this as the default and do not ask again`". It will make your life easier. I chose C:\Users\manelli\, which is my user's home directory. The first time it executes, Eclipse displays a Welcome screen. To enter the screen where you do development, click the Workbench icon, as shown in Figure 1-25.

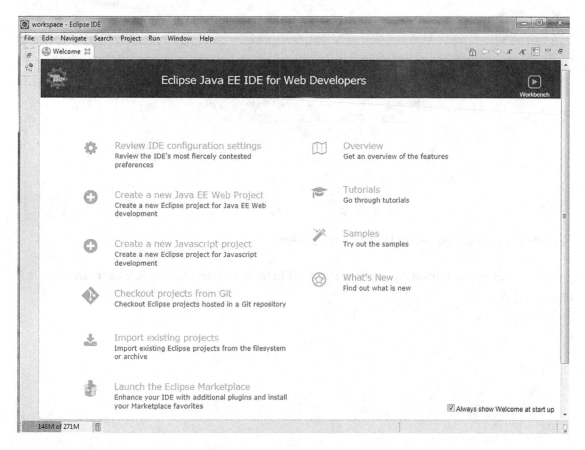

Figure 1-25. *Eclipse—the Welcome screen*

41

Once you see the Workbench screen, select the `Servers` tab and click the `new server wizard` link, as shown in Figure 1-26.

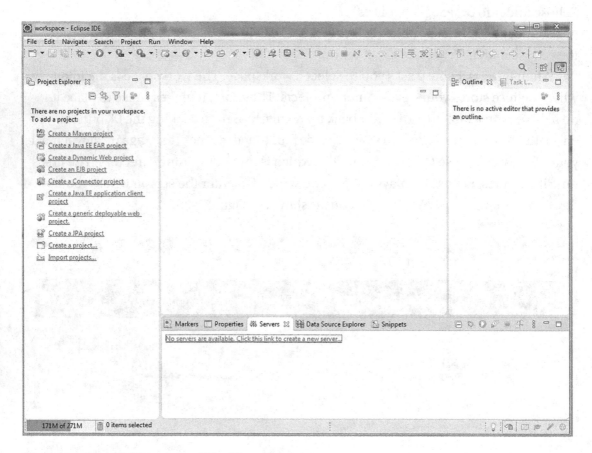

Figure 1-26. *Eclipse—the Workbench screen*

The screen that comes up is where you tell Eclipse to use Tomcat 9, as shown in Figure 1-27.

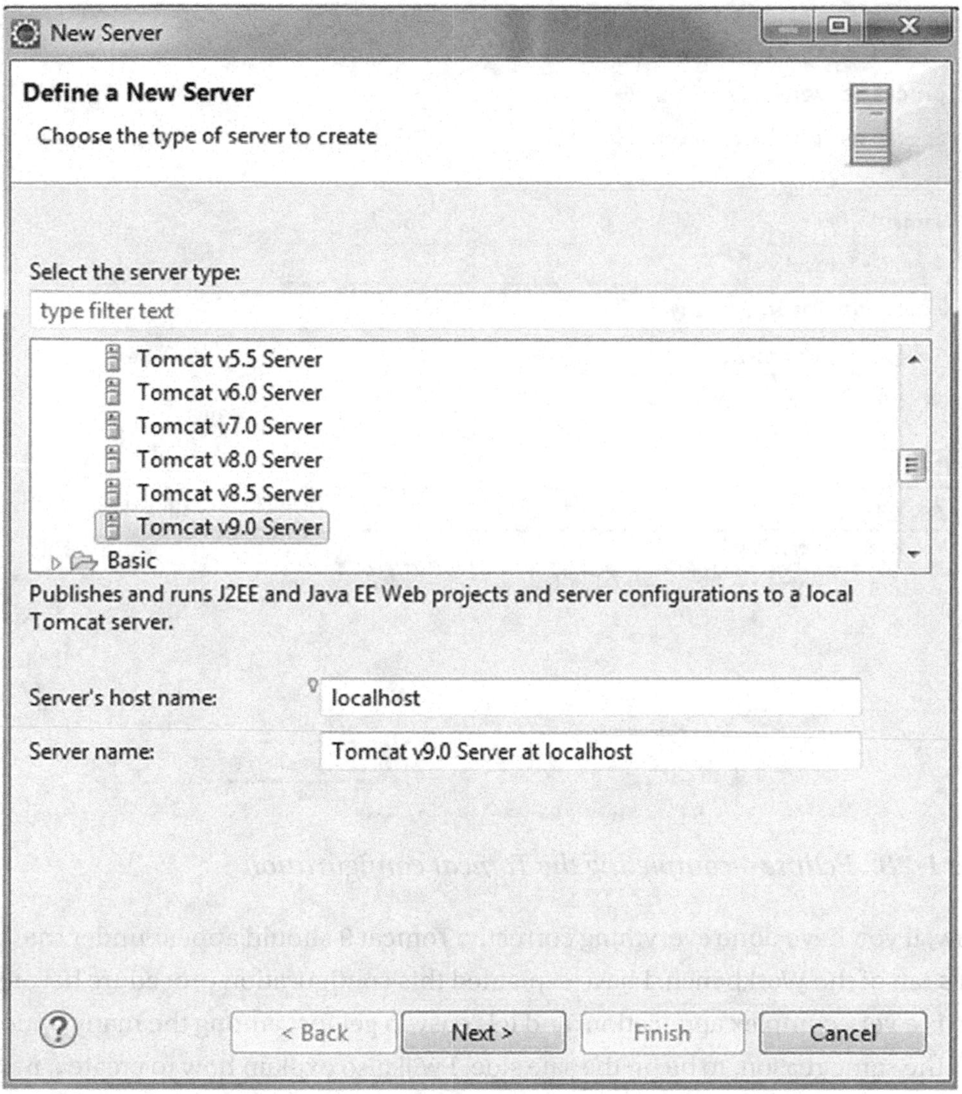

Figure 1-27. *Eclipse—choosing Tomcat 9 as localhost*

Next (and last), you need to tell Eclipse where to find Tomcat 9 and what version of JDK to use, as shown in Figure 1-28.

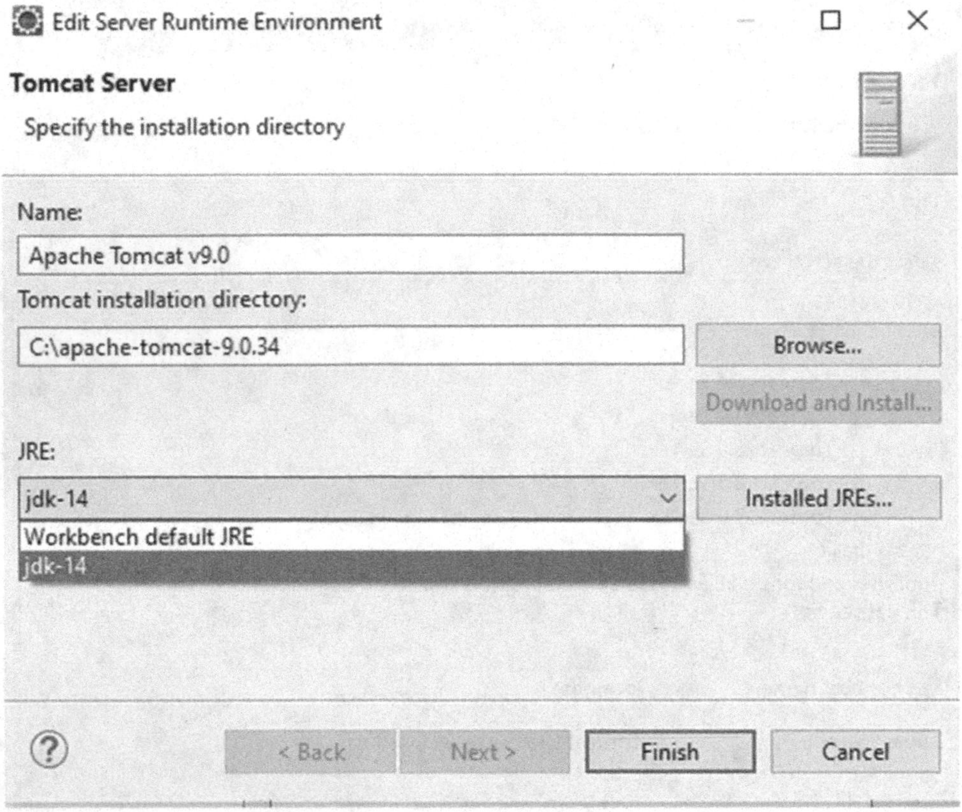

Figure 1-28. Eclipse—completing the Tomcat configuration

Now, if you have done everything correctly, Tomcat 9 should appear under the Servers tab of the Workbench. I have explained this configuration procedure because Eclipse is a very complex application, and it is easy to get lost among the many options.

For the same reason, to be on the safe side, I will also explain how to create a new web project. Later, you will learn how to import into Eclipse the example projects included in the software package of this book.

At last, you can verify that Eclipse uses the correct JDK. Go to Help ➤ About Eclipse IDE and click "Installation Detail" button. You can see the path and the name of the installed and used JDK, as shown in Figure 1-29.

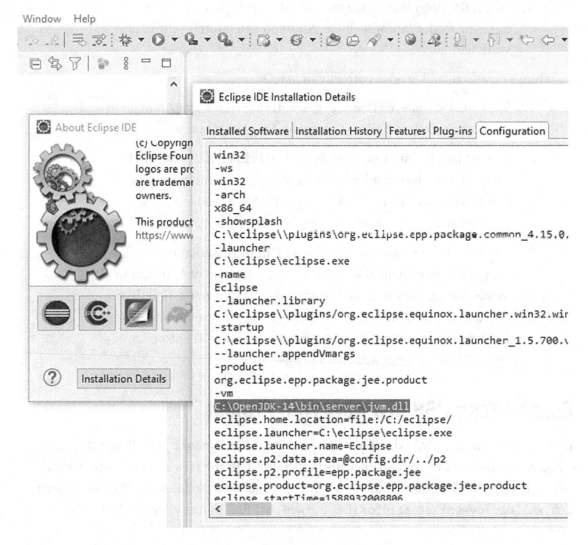

Figure 1-29. *Eclipse Configuration*

What About Linux and macOS?

Here's how to install Eclipse correctly in Linux:

1. Type the URL www.eclipse.org/downloads/packages/ and go to the section Eclipse IDE for Enterprise Java Developers.

2. By clicking the Linux 64-bit link of Eclipse IDE, you will be forwarded to the download page that suggests a mirror site for the download. Clicking that link, the download of the file eclipse-jee-2020-03-R-incubation-linux-gtk-x86_64.tar.gz starts (399M).

45

3. Unzip the downloaded file in /home/. At this point, you should have the folder /home/eclipse. Now you can launch Eclipse and work with it.

Here's how to install Eclipse correctly in macOS:

1. Type the URL `www.eclipse.org/downloads/packages/` and go to the section Eclipse IDE for Enterprise Java Developers.

2. By clicking the Mac Cocoa 64-bit link of Eclipse IDE, you will be forwarded to the download page that suggests a mirror site for the download. Clicking that link, the download of the file eclipse-jee-2020-03-R-incubation-macosx-cocoa-x86_64.dmg starts (401M).

3. Double-click the downloaded file and, in the installation window, drag the icon of Eclipse Workbench onto the icon of Applications as suggested. Now you can launch the application: the first time you would get the warning "Eclipse is an application downloaded from the internet. Are you sure you want to open it?", just click "open". Now you can work with Eclipse.

Eclipse Test: JSP in a New Web Project

In the menu bar of the Workbench, select File ➤ New ➤ Dynamic Web Project, type a project name (e.g., test), and click the Next button. In the new screen, named Java, click again the Next button. In the new screen, named Web Module, tick the box Generate web.xml deployment descriptor (i.e., the web.xml file) before clicking the Finish button.

The new project will appear in the Project Explorer pane (i.e., on the left-hand side) of the Workbench as shown in Figure 1-30.

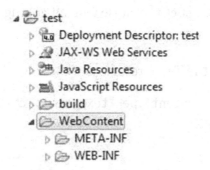

Figure 1-30. Eclipse—the test project

Now, expand it as shown in Figure 1-31, right-click the WebContent folder and select "New ➤ JSP File".

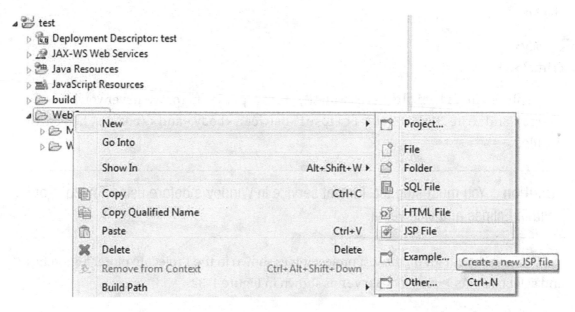

Figure 1-31. Eclipse—the test project

In the new JSP screen that appears, replace the default name NewFile.jsp with index.jsp and click the Finish button.

Eclipse shows the newly created file in the Project Explorer pane and opens it in the central pane of the Workbench for you to edit. Listing 1-13 shows its content. For me, the newly created file is located in the folder C:\Users\manelli\workspace\test\WebContent\. If, for any reason, you edit the file with some other editor, to see the latest version within Eclipse, you need to right-click it in Eclipse's Project Explorer and select

Refresh. But I suggest that you stick to Eclipse with all editing, because it is very easy to make a mistake otherwise.

Listing 1-13. index.jsp of the Test Project

```
<%@ page language="java" contentType="text/html; charset=ISO-8859-1"
pageEncoding="ISO-8859-1"%>
<!DOCTYPE html>
<html>
<head>
<meta charset=ISO-8859-1">
<title>Insert title here</title>
</head>
<body>

</body>
</html>
```

Replace "Insert title here" with "My first project" (or whatever you like, of course), and write "Hello from Eclipse!" between <body> and </body>. Then save the file.

Caution   You must stop the Tomcat service in Windows before using Tomcat from within Eclipse and vice versa.

Position the cursor on the test project folder shown in the Project Explorer, right-click, and select Run As ➤ Run on Server as shown in Figure 1-32.

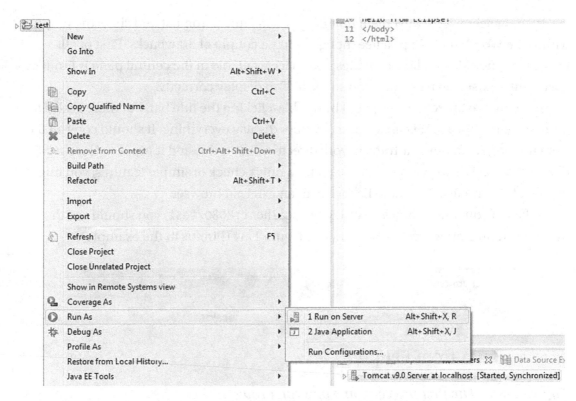

Figure 1-32. *Eclipse—the run on Tomcat of the first project*

When a screen comes up, click Finish. You will be rewarded with what is shown in Figure 1-33.

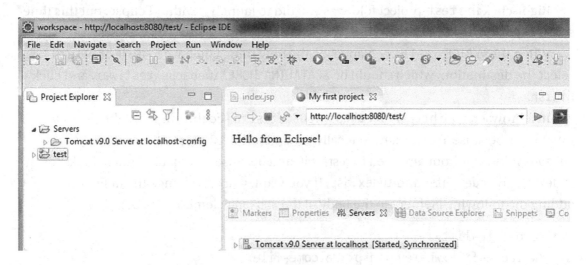

Figure 1-33. *Eclipse—the output of the first project*

It might seem very convenient that Eclipse can launch Tomcat and show the output within the Workbench. In practice though, it has a couple of drawbacks. First of all, because of the side and bottom panes, the space available in the central pane is limited. As a result, most web pages are "too squeezed" to display correctly.

You can maximize the web panel by double-clicking the title bar, but there is also a more important reason: Eclipse doesn't always display everything. It should copy all files from the project folder to a Tomcat work directory, but it doesn't! It tends to "lose" CSS files and images. This means that, except for a quick check of simple features, you might do what I do and use Tomcat in Eclipse with an external browser.

In fact, if you open a browser and type localhost:8080/test, you should see the same result on a browser page as shown in Figure 1-34 (Firefox in the example).

Figure 1-34. *The first project home page on browser*

A second choice is to use Tomcat externally. To see the output of the test project outside Eclipse, first of all, stop the "internal" Tomcat by right-clicking it under the Servers tab of the Workbench and selecting Stop. Then, start the Tomcat service in Windows.

Right-click the test-project folder as you did to launch it within Eclipse, but this time select Export ➤ WAR File.

When the WAR Export screen appears, the only thing you have to do is browse to select the destination, which should be %CATALINA_HOME%\webapps\test.war, and click Finish.

In a browser, type http://localhost:8080/test to see the output of the project. This works because Tomcat automatically expands all WAR files it discovers in its webapps folder, without any need to restart it, and because by default Tomcat looks for index.html, index.htm, and index.jsp. If you want, you can change the default by adding the following element to the body of the web-app element of web.xml:

```
<welcome-file-list>
    <welcome-file>whatever.jsp</welcome-file>
</welcome-file-list>
```

Listing the HTML-Request Parameters

With JSP you can generate dynamic web pages. That's settled. But the utility of dynamic pages goes well beyond recognizing what browser the viewer is using or displaying different information on different days. What really matters is to be able to adapt the content of a web page on the basis of who the viewer is and what the viewer wants.

Each HTML request includes a series of parameters, which are usually the results of what the viewer enters into a form before hitting the "Submit" button. Additional parameters can also be part of the URL itself. For example, pages in multilingual websites sometimes have URLs ending with "?lang=en" to tell the server that it should format the requested page in English.

Listing 1-14—that you can insert in your Eclipse Project test—shows a simple JSP page that lists all the HTML-request parameters. It is a useful little tool you can use to easily check what your HTML pages actually send to the server.

Listing 1-14. req_params.jsp

```
<%@page language="java" contentType="text/html"%>
<%@page import="java.util.*, java.io.*"%>
<%
  Map        map = request.getParameterMap();
  Object[] keys = map.keySet().toArray();
  %>
<html><head><title>Request Parameters</title></head><body>
  Map size = <%=map.size()%>
  <table border="1">
    <tr><td>Map element</td><td>Par name</td><td>Par value[s]</td></tr>
<%
    for (int k = 0; k < keys.length; k++) {
      String[] pars = request.getParameterValues((String)keys[k]);
      out.print("<tr><td>" + k + "</td><td>'" + keys[k] + "'</td><td>");
      for (int j = 0; j < pars.length; j++) {
        if (j > 0) out.print(", ");
        out.print("'" + pars[j] + "'");
        }
```

```
        out.println("</td></tr>");
        }
  %>
    </table>
</body></html>
```

The interesting bits are in the lines I have highlighted in bold. The first one tells you that the parameters are stored in an object of type `Map` and shows you how to retrieve the list of the parameter names.

The second highlighted line shows you how to insert the value of a Java variable directly into the output (i.e., into the HTML page), by enclosing it between the pair `<%=` and `%>`. This is different from using a scriptlet, in which you can use JSP to build dynamicity into a web page.

The third highlighted line shows how to request the values of each parameter you know the name of. I said "values" instead of "value" because each parameter can appear more than once within the same request. For example, if you view the URL

```
http://localhost:8080/test/req_params.jsp?a=b&c=d&a=zzz&empty=&empty=&1=22
```

you get what you see in Figure 1-35.

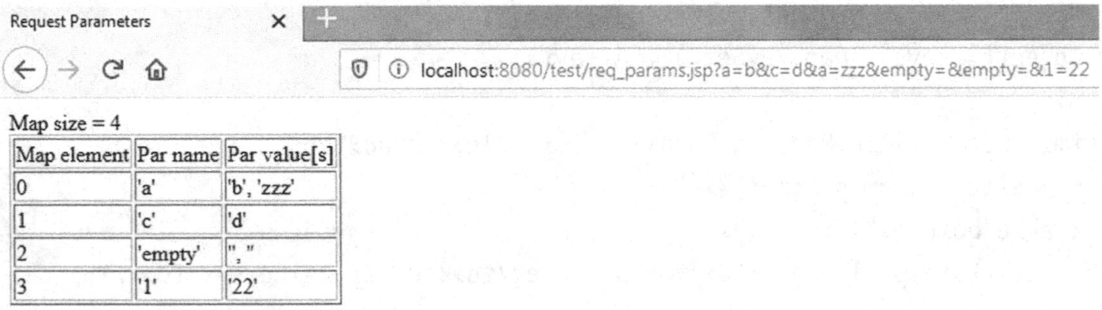

Map size = 4

Map element	Par name	Par value[s]
0	'a'	'b', 'zzz'
1	'c'	'd'
2	'empty'	'', ''
3	'1'	'22'

Figure 1-35. *Output of req_params.jsp*

Notice that the parameter aptly named `empty` appears twice in the query string, which results in two empty strings in the parameter map. Also, looking at the parameter a, you'll notice that the values are returned in the same order in which they appear in the query string.

Summary

In this chapter, you learned how to install Java and Tomcat and how to check that they work correctly. You then learned how to install the Eclipse IDE, how to configure it to use the latest versions of Java and Tomcat, and how to create JSP applications from scratch.

After explaining what happens on the server when you click a link in your browser to view a new page, I introduced servlet and JSP technologies and explained what role they play in a web server.

Then, I showed you a simple HTML page and how you can begin to add dynamic content to it with JSP.

Finally, you learned how to use JSP to display the HTTP-request parameters.

Perhaps this was not the most exciting chapter, but you now have in place a basic development and run environment, without which you wouldn't be able to proceed. And you have had your first taste of JSP.

In the next chapter, you'll learn more about JavaServer Pages and how you can best structure web applications.

CHAPTER 2

JSP Elements

A JSP page is made out of a page template, which consists of HTML code and JSP elements such as *scripting* elements, *directive* elements, and *action* elements. In the previous chapter, after explaining how to install Java, Tomcat, and Eclipse, I introduced you to JSP and explained JSP's role within web applications. In this chapter, I'll describe in detail the first two types of JSP elements. For the action elements, refer to the next chapters.

Introduction

Scripting elements consist of code delimited by particular sequences of characters. The scriptlets, which you encountered in the examples in Chapter 1 and delimited by the pair <% and %>, are one of the three possible types of scripting elements. The other two are declarations and expressions.

All scripting elements are Java fragments capable of manipulating Java objects, invoking their methods, and catching Java exceptions. They can send data to the output, and they execute when the page is requested. Tomcat defines several *implicit objects: application, config, exception, out, pageContext, request, response, and session.*

Directive elements are messages to the JSP container (i.e., Tomcat). Their purpose is to provide information on the page itself necessary for its translation. As they have no association with each individual request, directive elements do not output any text to the HTML response.

The first line of the hello.jsp example was a directive:

```
<%@page language="java" contentType="text/html"%>
```

Besides page, the other directives available in JSP pages are include and taglib.

Action elements specify activities that, like the scripting elements, need to be performed when the page is requested, because their purpose is precisely to encapsulate activities that Tomcat performs when handling an HTTP request from a client. Action elements can use, modify, and/or create objects, and they may affect the way data is sent

55

to the output. There are more than a dozen standard actions: `attribute`, `body`, `element`, `fallback`, `forward`, `getProperty`, `include`, `param`, `params`, `plugin`, `setProperty`, `text`, and `useBean`. For example, the following action element includes in a JSP page the output of another page:

```
<jsp:include page="another.jsp"/>
```

In addition to the standard action elements, JSP also provides a mechanism that lets you define custom actions, in which a prefix of your choice replaces the prefix `jsp` of the standard actions. The *tag extension mechanism* lets you create libraries of custom actions, which you can then use in all your applications. Several custom actions became so popular within the programming community that Sun Microsystems (now Oracle) decided to standardize them. The result is JSTL, the JSP Standard Tag Library.

The *Expression Language* (EL) is an additional JSP component that provides easy access to external objects (i.e., Java beans). EL was introduced in JSP 2.0 as an alternative to the scripting elements, but you can also use EL and scripting elements together.

In the next sections, I will first go through the scripting elements, because they are easier to understand and you can use them to glue together the rest. Then, I will describe the implicit objects and the directives. To help you find the correct examples in the software package for this chapter, I divided them in folders named according to the section title and the functionality tested (e.g., request object - body).

Scripting Elements and Java

Scripting elements let you embed Java code in an HTML page. Every Java executable—whether it's a free-standing program running directly within a runtime environment or a servlet executing in a container such as Tomcat—boils down to instantiating classes into objects and executing their methods. This might not be so apparent with JSP, since Tomcat wraps every JSP page into a class of type `Servlet` behind the scenes, but it still applies.

A Java method consists of a sequence of operations—executed when the method is called—with the scope to instantiate objects, allocate memory for variables, calculate expressions, perform assignments, or execute other specific instructions.

In this section, I'll summarize the syntax of Java while keeping JSP in mind.

Scriptlets

A scriptlet is a block of Java code enclosed between <% and %>. For example, this code includes two scriptlets that let you switch an HTML element on or off depending on a condition:

```
<% if (condition) { %>
<p>This is only shown if the condition is satisfied</p>
<%   } %>
```

Expressions

An expression scripting element inserts into the page the result of a Java expression enclosed in the pair <%= and %>. For example, in the following snippet of code, the expression scripting element inserts the current date into the generated HTML page:

```
<%@page import="java.util.Date"%>
Server date and time: <%=new Date()%>
```

You can use within an expression scripting element any Java expression, provided it results in a value. In practice, it means that every Java expression will do, except the execution of a method of type void. For example, `<%=(condition) ? "yes" : "no"%>` is valid, because it calculates to a string. You would obtain the same output with the scriptlet `<%if (condition) out.print("yes") else out.print("no");%>`.

Note that an expression is not a Java statement. Accordingly, it has no semicolon at the end.

Declarations

A declaration scripting element is a Java variable declaration enclosed between <%! and %>. It `results` in an instance variable shared by all requests for the same page.

Data Types and Variables

Java makes available primitive data types similar to the basic types of C/C++ (see Table 2-1).

Table 2-1. *Java Data types*

Name	Class	Description
byte	Byte	1-byte signed integer (−128 to +127)
short	Short	2-byte signed integer (−32,768 to +32,767)
int	Integer	4-byte signed integer (−2,147,483,648 to +2,147,483,647)
Long	Long	8-byte signed integer (approximately -10^{19} to $+10^{19}$)
Float	Float	32-bit signed floating point (8-bit exponent, 23-bit precision)
Double	Double	64-bit signed floating point (11-bit exponent, 52-bit precision)
Char	Character	16-bit unsigned Unicode
boolean	Boolean	Either true or false

The second column of Table 2-1 gives you the names of the so-called *wrapper classes* that Java makes available for each primitive type. These classes provide some useful static methods to manipulate numbers. For example, `Integer.parseInt(String s, int radix)` interprets a string as a number in the base set by the second argument and returns it as an `int` value (e.g., `Integer.parseInt("12", 16)` and `Integer. parseInt("10010", 2)` both return 18).

Programs in Java can be platform-independent because all platform dependencies are "hidden" inside libraries. The wrapper classes I just mentioned are in the java.lang library, together with dozens of other general classes such as String and Math. You can find the full documentation of the Java 13 platform at `https://docs.oracle.com/en/java/javase/13/docs/api/index.html`.

Here are some examples of how you can declare variables and initialize them:

```
String aString = "abcdxyz";
int k = aString.length();  // k is then set to 7
char c = aString.charAt(4);  // c is set to 'x'
static final String NAME = "John Doe";
```

The `final` keyword in the last example of declarations makes the variable unchangeable. This is how you define constants in Java. The `static` keyword indicates that a variable is to be shared by all objects within the same application that are instantiated from the class.

The use of static variables in JSP requires some further comment. In JSP, you can declare variables in three ways:

```
<% int k = 0; %>
<%! int k = 0; %>
<%! static int k = 0; %>
```

The first declaration means that a new variable is created for each incoming HTTP client request; the second one means that a new variable is created for each new instance of the servlet; and the third one means that the variable is shared among all instances of the servlet.

Tomcat converts each JSP page into a subclass of the HTTP Servlet class (`javax. servlet.http.HttpServlet`). Normally, Tomcat instantiates each one of these classes only once and then creates a Java thread for each incoming request. It then executes the same servlet object within each thread. If the application runs on a distributed environment or for high numbers of requests, Tomcat can instantiate the same servlet more than once. Therefore, only the third declaration guarantees that the variable will be shared among all requests.

Tomcat keeps the servlet code buried deep in the folder named `work`. For example, the servlet generated from `webapps\ROOT\test\a.jsp` is in `work\Catalina\ localhost\_\org\apache\jsp\test\` and is named `a_jsp.java`.

You're free to name your variables as you like, though your case-sensitive string of characters must begin with a letter, a dollar, or an underscore and not contain a space. That said, be aware that the following keywords are reserved and will cause a compilation error: `abstract`, `assert`, `boolean`, `break`, `byte`, `case`, `catch`, `char`, `class`, `const`, `continue`, `default`, `do`, `double`, `else`, `enum`, `extends`, `final`, `finally`, `float`, `for`, `goto`, `if`, `implements`, `import`, `instanceof`, `int`, `interface`, `long`, `native`, `new`, `package`, `private`, `protected`, `public`, `return`, `short`, `static`, `strictfp`, `super`, `switch`, `synchronized`, `this`, `throw`, `throws`, `transient`, `try`, `void`, `volatile`, and `while`. Whenever possible, use capital letters for constants. It is not necessary, but it makes the code more readable and is a well-established coding practice.

To use special characters within a string, you need to escape them with a backslash, as shown in Table 2-2. With \u followed by up to four hexadecimal digits, you can specify any Unicode character. For example, you can enter the Greek capital letter delta as \u0394.

Table 2-2. *Escaped Special Characters*

Character	Escaped
backslash	\\
backspace	\b
carriage return	\r
double quote	\"
form feed	\f
line feed	\n
single quote	\'
tab	\t

Objects and Arrays

To create an object of a certain type (i.e., to instantiate a class) and allocate memory, use the keyword new. In the following example, a new Java object of type String is created:

```
String newString= new String();
```

This creates an object of type Integer with value 55.

You can have arrays of any object type or primitive data type, as in the following examples of array declarations:

```
int[] intArray1;
int[] intArray2 = {10, 100, 1000};
String[] stringArray = {"a", "bb"};
```

intArray1 is null; intArray2 is an array of length three containing 10, 100, and 1000; and stringArray is an array of length two containing the strings "a" and "bb".

Although arrays look special, they're actually just objects and treated like that. Therefore, you can initialize them with new. For example, the following line of code declares an integer array with ten elements, each initialized to zero:

```
int[] array = new int[10];
```

A two-dimensional table is an array in which each element object is itself an array. This is *not* like in C, where a single block of memory contains all elements of multidimensional tables. For example, this line of code represents a table of two rows, but the first row has three elements, while the second one has only two:

```
int[][] table1 = {{11, 12, 13}, {21, 22}};
```

If you define something like this:

```
int[][] table = new int[2][3];
```

you have a table with two rows and three columns, with all elements initialized to zero.

Operators, Assignments, and Comparisons

There are no surprises with the binary operators—that is, the operators that require two operands. They include the expected addition, subtraction, multiplication, division, and modulus (i.e., the remainder of an integer division) operators. When applied to string, the addition operator concatenates them.

Besides the normal assignment operator represented by the equal sign, there is also an assignment operator for each binary operator. For example, the following line of code means that you take the current value of the variable a, add to it b, and store it back into a:

```
a += b;  // same as a = a + b;
```

The most commonly used unary operators (i.e., operators that require a single operand) include the minus sign, which changes the sign of what follows, and the increment and decrement operators:

```
a = -b;
a++;  // same as a += 1;
a--;  // same as a -= 1;
```

You can assign the value of an expression of one type to a variable of another type, but with some restrictions. With numeric types, you can only assign values to variables that are of the same type or "larger." For example, you can assign an `int` value to a variable of type `long`, but to assign a `long` value to an `int` variable, you'd have to *typecast* (i.e., downcast) the value, as in `int iVar = (int)1234567L;`. Be careful with that, because you might lose precision when downcasting floating-point numbers!

You can assign objects to variables of other types, but only if the type of the variable is a superclass of the class from which you instantiated the object. Similarly to the downcasting of numeric types, you can typecast a value of a superclass into a variable of a subclass type.

Comparison operators are straightforward when applied to primitive data types. You have `==` to check for equality, `!=` to check for inequality, `>` to check for "greater than," `>=` to check for "greater than or equal to," `<` to check for "less than," and `<=` to check for "less than or equal to." Nothing surprising there. However, you have to be careful when you make comparisons between objects, as the following example illustrates:

```
String s1 = "abc";
String s2 = "abc";
String s3 = "abcd".substring(0,3);
boolean b1 = (s1 == "abc");  // parentheses not needed but nice!
boolean b2 = (s1 == s2);
boolean b3 = (s1 == s3);
```

As perhaps you expected, b1 and b2 turn out to be `true`, but b3 is `false`, although s3 was set to `"abc"`! The problem is that comparison operators don't look inside the objects. They only check whether the objects are *the same instance* of a class, not whether they hold the same value. Therefore, as long as you shift around the `"abc"` string, the compiler keeps referring to the same instance of a literal string, and everything behaves as expected. However, when you create a different instance of `"abc"`, the check for equality fails. The lesson to be learned is that if you want to compare the content of objects, you have to use the `equals` method. In this example, `s1.equals(s3)` would have returned `true`.

For objects, you also have the comparison operator `instanceof`, which isn't available for primitive data types like `int`. For example, `("abc" instanceof String)` calculates to `true`. Be aware that an object isn't only an instance of the class it was instantiated from, but it's also an instance of all its superclasses up to and including `Object`, which is the superclass of all classes. It makes sense: a `String` is also an `Object`, even if the reverse often is not true.

With `&&` for *logical and*, `||` for *logical or*, and `!` for *logical not*, you can concatenate comparisons to form more complex conditions. For example, `((a1 == a2) && !(b1 || b2))` calculates to `true` only if `a1` equals `a2` and both `boolean` variables `b1` and `b2` are `false`.

Selections

The following statement assigns to the string variable `s` a different string depending on a condition:

```
if (a == 1) {
  s = "yes";
  }
else {
  s = "no";
  }
```

You can omit the `else` part.

You could have achieved an identical result with a conditional expression and a single assignment:

```
String s = (a== 1) ? "yes" : "no";
```

You could also achieve the same result with the following code:

```
switch(a) {
  case 1:
    s = "yes";
    break;
  default:
    s = "no";
    break;
  }
```

Obviously, the `switch` statement is only useful when there are more than just two alternatives. For example, instead of having a chain of `if`/`else` statements, as in the following example:

```
if (expression == 3) {...}
else if (expression == 10) {...}
else {...}
```

you would gain both in clarity and in conciseness with

```
switch (expression) {
  case (3): ... break;
  case (10): ... break;
  default: ... break;
  }
```

At the very least, you'll calculate the expression only once. Note that if you omit a `break`, execution continues to the following `case`.

The switch variable can be of type `String`. Therefore, you can write switches like the following one:

```
String yn;
...
switch (yn) {
  case ("y"): /* handle the yes case */ break;
  case ("n"): /* handle the no case */ break;
  default: /* is something fishy going on? */ break;
  }
```

Iterations

This statement repeatedly executes the *statements* with increasing values of k, beginning from *init-value*:

```
for (int k = init-value; k < limit; k++) { statements; }
```

The general format is

```
for (initial-assignment; end-condition; iteration-expression) { statements; }
```

The *initial-assignment* is executed only once, before entering the loop. The *statements* are then repeatedly executed as long as the *end-condition* is satisfied. As the *end-condition* is checked before executing the *statements*, they are not executed at all if the *end-condition* is false from the beginning. The *iteration-expression* is executed at the end of each iteration, before the *end-condition* is checked to see whether the loop should be reentered for a new iteration.

You can omit either the *initial-assignment* or the *iteration-expression*. If you omit both, you should replace the for loop with a while loop. The following two lines are equivalent:

```
while (end-condition) { statements; }
for (;end-condition;) { statements; }
```

The do-while statement is an alternative to the while loop:

```
do { statements; } while (end-condition);
```

The do-while statement checks the *end-condition* at the end of an iteration instead of at the beginning, like the for and while loops do. As a result, the statements inside a do-while loop are always executed at least once, even when the *end-condition* is false from the beginning.

The iteration statements described so far are identical to those of C, but Java also supports a variant of the for loop tailored to make the handling of collections easier. Suppose you need a method that produces a concatenation of a set of strings. It might look like this:

```
String concatenate(Set<String> ss) {
  String conc = "";
  Iterator<String> iter = ss.iterator();
  while (iter.hasNext()) {
    conc += iter.next();
  }
  return conc;
  }
```

With the Java for-each variant of the `for` loop, you can drop the definition of the iterator and write clearer code:

```
String concatenate(Set<String> ss) {
  String conc = "";
  for (String s : ss) {
    conc += s;
    }
  return conc;
  }
```

Implicit Objects

The most commonly used implicit objects defined by Tomcat are `out` and `request`, followed by `application` and `session`. But I will go through them in alphabetical order, for ease of reference.

Whether you create objects within JSP pages or Tomcat implicitly creates them for you, you cannot use them properly unless you know in which scope they are available. There are four possible scopes. In order of increasing generality, they are *page*, *request*, *session*, and *application*. You will learn more about them in the following sections.

In general, if you are not sure what class a particular object instantiates, you can always display its name with the following expression:

```
<%=the_misterious_object.getClass().getName()%>
```

The `application` Object

The `application` object is an instance of the class `org.apache.catalina.core.ApplicationContextFacade`, which Tomcat defines to implement the interface `javax.servlet.ServletContext`. It provides access to the resources shared within the web application. For example, by adding an attribute (which can be an object of any type) to `application`, you can ensure that all JSP files that make up your web application have access to it.

Example: Using an Attribute to Enable and Disable Conditional Code

One of the advantages of using JSP is that the web server doesn't need to reinterpret the source file of a page every time a client requests that page. The JSP container translates each JSP page into a Java file and compiles it into a class, but this only happens when you update the JSP source. You might like to be able to switch on or off some particular functionality for debugging or other purposes, without having to edit one or more files and force Tomcat to recompile them when you flip the switch. To achieve this result, you only need to wrap the functionality in question inside a conditional statement, as the following one:

```
if (application.getAttribute("do_it") != null) {
  /* ...place your "switchable" functionality here... */
  }
```

You also need to include two small JSP pages in your application: the first one to set the attribute do_it (see Listing 2-1) and the second one to remove it (see Listing 2-2).

Listing 2-1. do_it.jsp

```
<%@page language="java" contentType="text/html"%>
<html><head><title>Conditional code ON</title></head>
<body>Conditional code
<%
  application.setAttribute("do_it", "");
  if (application.getAttribute("do_it") == null) out.print("not");
  %>
enabled</body></html>
```

Listing 2-2. do_it_not.jsp

```
<%@page language="java" contentType="text/html"%>
<html><head><title>Conditional code OFF</title></head>
<body>Conditional code
```

```
<%
  application.removeAttribute("do_it");
  if (application.getAttribute("do_it") == null) out.print("not");
  %>
enabled</body></html>
```

Create new jsps in the same test Project folder created in Chapter 1 and copy the code or place them in the WebContent folder. At last, start Tomcat in Eclipse and type in your browser the URL when you want to enable the conditional code:

```
http://localhost:8080/test/do_it.jsp
```

Until you disable it by typing the URL

```
http://localhost:8080/test/do_it_not.jsp
```

or by restarting Tomcat, the conditional code will remain enabled in all pages of your application. Notice that in the example do_it.jsp only sets the attribute do_it to an empty string, but you can also define different values to have a finer selection of code to be activated.

Note that you can use the same mechanism to switch on and off HTML code.

The config Object

The config object is an instance of the org.apache.catalina.core. StandardWrapperFacade class, which Tomcat defines to implement the interface javax. servlet.ServletConfig. Tomcat uses this object to pass information to the servlets.

The following config method is the only one you might ever use; its use is trivial:

```
config.getServletName()
```

The exception Object

The exception object is an instance of a subclass of Throwable (e.g., java.lang. NullPointerException) and is only available in error pages.

Listing 2-3 shows you two methods to send the stack trace to the output. The first one, using getStackTrace, gives you access to each trace element as an object of type java.lang.StackTraceElement, which you can then analyze with methods such as getClassName, getFileName, getLineNumber, and getMethodName.

Listing 2-3. stack_trace.jsp

```jsp
<%@page language="java" contentType="text/html"%>
<%@page import="java.util.*, java.io.*"%>
<%@page isErrorPage="true"%>
<html><head><title>Print stack trace</title></head><body>
From exception.getStackTrace():<br/>
<pre><%
  StackTraceElement[] trace = exception.getStackTrace();
  for (int k = 0; k < trace.length; k++) {
    out.println(trace[k]);
    }
  %></pre>
Printed with exception.printStackTrace(new PrintWriter(out)):
<pre><%
  exception.printStackTrace(new PrintWriter(out));
  %></pre>
</body></html>
```

Notice the directive <%@page isErrorPage="true"%>, without which the implicit object exception is not defined.

If you execute this page as if it were a normal page, you will get a NullPointerException. Listing 2-4 shows a simple example of how you can use an error page.

Listing 2-4. cause_exception.jsp

```jsp
<%@page language="java" contentType="text/html"%>
<%@page errorPage="stack_trace.jsp"%>
<html><head><title>Cause null pointer exception</title></head><body>
<%
  String a = request.getParameter("notThere");
  int len = a.length(); // causes a null pointer exception
  %>
</body></html>
```

Notice the `<%@page errorPage="stack_trace.jsp"%>` directive, which links the error page of Listing 2-4 to the occurrence of exceptions. To cause a `NullPointerException`, the page requests a parameter that doesn't exist and then accesses it. If you use `try/catch` to trap the exception, obviously the error page is not executed.

To see the two pages in action, create new jsps in the same test Project folder created in Chapter 1 and copy the code or place them in the WebContent folder. At last, start Tomcat in Eclipse and type in a browser the URL

```
http://localhost:8080/test/cause_exception.jsp.
```

The out Object

You use the `out` object in JSP as you use the `System.out` object in Java: to write to the standard output. The standard output for a JSP page is the body of the HTML response sent back to the client. Therefore, the scriptlet `<%out.print(expression);%>` causes the result of the expression to be displayed in the client's browser. You can achieve the same result by simply typing `<%=expression%>`.

Keep in mind that whatever you write in a JSP page outside scriptlets and other JSP elements is sent to the output anyway. Therefore, the following three lines have exactly the same effect on the response:

```
<% out.print("abc"); %>
<%="abc"%>
abc
```

Clearly, it makes no sense to use the first two formats when you need to write literal values. To decide whether to use a scriptlet delimited by `<%..%>` or an expression delimited by `<%=..%>`, you should look at the surrounding code and decide what makes it as easy to read as possible.

The most useful methods of the object `out` are `print` and `println`. The only difference between the two is that `println` appends a newline character to the output. As an argument, both methods accept a string or any other primitive type variable. In the following example, the `int` value stored in `intVar` is automatically converted to a string:

```
out.print("a string" + intVar + obj.methodReturningString() + ".");
```

Incidentally, you could use either of the following two methods to do the conversion manually:

```
String s = Integer.toString(intVar);
String s = "" + intVar;
```

Be aware that if you try to print an object or an array by sticking its name into a print statement, you *won't* necessarily see its content in the output. If the object doesn't support a toString() method, you'll see a mysterious string representing the reference to the object.

Most manuals state that out is an instance of the javax.servlet.jsp.JspWriter class, which you can use to write into the response. This is not entirely correct, because JspWriter is an abstract class, and as such, it cannot be instantiated. In reality, out is an instance of the nonabstract class org.apache.jasper.runtime.JspWriterImpl, which extends JspWriter. Tomcat defines JspWriterImpl precisely to implement the JspWriter methods. For all practical purposes, this is inconsequential to you, but some of you sharp-eyed readers might have thought that I was talking about instantiating an abstract class. It usually pays to be precise.

The JspWriter class includes the definition of a handful of fields. You won't need them, but mentioning them gives me the opportunity to give you some useful information.

The autoFlush field tells you whether the JspWriter is flushed automatically when its buffer fills up or whether an IOException is thrown upon overflow. The default for out is true, which means that Tomcat will send a partial response to the client if the buffer fills up. You can set it to false with the directive <%@page autoFlush="false"%>, and you should do so if you expect the client to be an application. Sending the response in "chunks" is perfectly OK when the client is a browser, but an application will probably expect the response in a single block. If you expect the client to be an application and set autoFlush to false, you should also use <%@page buffer="size-in-kb"%>, to ensure that the output buffer is large enough to store your largest response. The field autoFlush is protected, but you can obtain its value with the isAutoFlush method.

The bufferSize field is the size in bytes of the output buffer. The default for out is 8192 bytes. It's a protected field, but you can obtain its value with the getBufferSize method.

There are also three constant integer fields (DEFAULT_BUFFER, NO_BUFFER, and UNBOUNDED_BUFFER of type public static final int), but you can safely ignore them. Just for the record, they're respectively used to test whether the JspWriter is buffered (and uses the default buffer size), isn't buffered, or is buffered with an unbounded buffer.

Besides the fact that you have no variable or attribute to check against these values, you're in any case well served by the getBufferSize method (which returns 0 if the output is not buffered).

You've already seen in several examples that you can use print and println to write to the output buffer. As an argument, you can use any of the eight primitive data types of Java (boolean, char, byte, short, int, long, float, and double), an array of characters (char[]), an object (java.lang.Object), or a string (java.lang.String). In practice, you'll usually use a String argument, as in the following example:

```
out.print("fun(" + arg + ") = " + fun(arg));
```

Here, fun(arg) is executed, and both arg and the value returned by fun(arg) are automatically converted to strings to be concatenated with the rest.

The write method, inherited from java.io.Writer, sends a portion of an array of characters or of a string to the output. For example, if cbuf is a variable of type char[], out.write(cbuf, offs, len) will write a portion of cbuf, with offs being the offset of the first character and len being the number of characters to be copied. You could achieve the same result by extracting a part of the array with the following code and then printing it with print:

```
char[] portion = java.util.Arrays.copyOfRange(cbuf, offs, offs+len-1)
```

However, it would be less efficient, because first you would be copying a portion of the original array—an operation you don't need when using write.

You're not likely to use any of the other methods, and you should definitely avoid using close, which closes the output stream. Tomcat closes the stream when it is safe to do so, and you don't want to fiddle with it.

The pageContext Object

Most manuals state that pageContext is an instance of the javax.servlet.jsp. PageContext class to access all objects and attributes of a JSP page. Similar to what I said concerning JspWriter, this is only partly true, because this class, like JspWriter, is also abstract. In reality, pageContext is an instance of the nonabstract class org.apache. jasper.runtime.PageContextImpl, which extends PageContext.

The PageContext class defines several fields, including PAGE_SCOPE, REQUEST_SCOPE, SESSION_SCOPE, and APPLICATION_SCOPE, which identify the four possible scopes.

It also supports more than 40 methods, about half of which are inherited from the javax.servlet.jsp.JspContext class.

You have to pay particular attention when using the removeAttribute method, which accepts either one or two arguments.

For example, pageContext.removeAttribute("attrName") removes the attribute from *all* scopes, while the following code only removes it from the page scope:

```
pageContext.removeAttribute("attrName", PAGE_SCOPE)
```

The request Object

The request variable gives you access within your JSP page to the HTTP request sent to it by the client. It's an instance of the org.apache.catalina.connector. RequestFacade class, which Tomcat defines to implement the javax.servlet.http. HttpServletRequest and javax.servlet.ServletRequest interfaces.

More on Request Parameters and Client Info

In Chapter 1, you have already seen how to list all the parameters of a request. When accessing individual parameters by name, you should use some caution. Typically, you do it with the following line of code:

```
String myPar = request.getParameter("par-name");
```

And then, you do something with the parameter only if it exists—that is, if getParameter returns a non-null value:

```
if (par != null) { ...
```

Note that in the request generated by a URL like this:

```
http://localhost:8080/my_page.jsp?aaa&bbb=&ccc=3
```

the parameters aaa and bbb exist but are set to the empty string. Therefore, getParameter does *not* return null for them.

As you already saw in Chapter 1, the request can include more than one value associated with the same parameter. For example, the following URL generates a request with three values for the parameter aaa:

```
http://localhost:8080/my_page.jsp?aaa&aaa=4&aaa=7
```

If you execute getParameter, you only get the first value, which is the empty string in the example. If you want to get them all, you have to use a different method:

```
String[] ppar = request.getParameterValues("par-name");
```

and this returns an array of strings. To check that the parameter has actually been set only once and to something other than the empty string, you might then perform the following test:

```
if (ppar != null && ppar.length == 1 && ppar[0].length() > 0) { ...
```

In Chapter 1, you also saw how to determine the type of browser that sent the request. Another useful piece of information you can get about the client is its preferred locale. For example, the following line of code could set the variable clientLocale to the string "en_US":

```
String clientLocale = request.getLocale().toString();
```

But if the viewer were in a country where a language other than English is spoken, you might get other locales (e.g., "de_DE" for German). If you had a multilingual site, the locale would tell you the working language of your user. You could check whether you support it and, if you do, set it as a default for the response.

The getRemoteHost method, which returns the client's hostname (or that of its proxy server), could be useful in a similar way, because you could look at the string after the last dot to identify foreign domain names (e.g., it for Italy). Unfortunately, in many cases, the remote address cannot be resolved to a name, and you end up getting only the client's IP address, exactly as if you had called the getRemoteAddress method. Services available on the Internet let you resolve an IP address to the country where the system resides, but you might have to pay for a reliable service.

Caution   You cannot mix methods that handle parameters with methods that handle the request content or methods that access the request content in different ways. For example, if you execute any two of the methods request. getParameter, getReader, and getInputStream when handling a request, the second one you execute will fail.

Example: Listing the Headers

Create new jsp in the same test Project folder created in Chapter 1 and copy the following code or place it in the WebContent folder. Listing 2-5 shows code that displays the request headers.

Listing 2-5. req_headers.jsp

```
<%@page language="java" contentType="text/html"%>
<%@page import="java.util.*"%>
<html><head><title>Request Headers</title></head><body>
<%
  Enumeration headers = request.getHeaderNames();
  int kh = 0;
  while (headers.hasMoreElements()) {
    String hName = (String)headers.nextElement();
    out.println("------- " + hName);
    Enumeration hValues = request.getHeaders(hName);
    while (hValues.hasMoreElements()) {
      out.println("<br/>   " + hValues.nextElement());
      }
    out.println("<br/>");
    }
  %>
</body></html>
```

At last, start Tomcat in Eclipse and type in a browser the URL

```
http://localhost:8080/test/req_headers.jsp
```

Figures 2-1 and 2-2 show the request headers generated, respectively, by Chrome and Firefox. Interesting, aren't they?

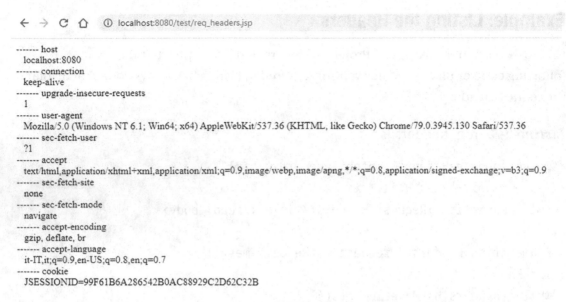

Figure 2-1. *Request headers generated by Google Chrome*

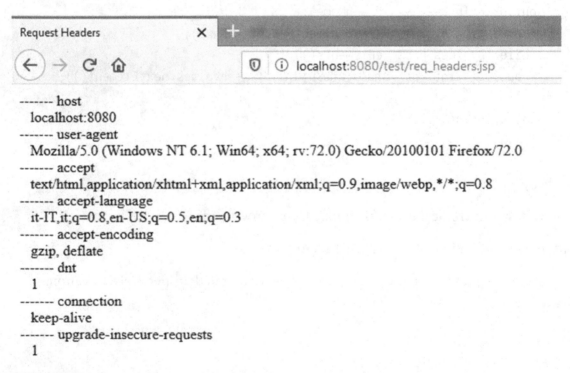

Figure 2-2. *Request headers generated by Mozilla Firefox*

Example: Reading the Request Body

You can read the request content with either getInputStream or getReader (but not both for the same request). Listing 2-6 shows you an example with getInputStream.

Listing 2-6. req_getInputStream.jsp

```
<%@page language="java" contentType="text/html"%>
<%@page import="java.util.*, java.io.*"%>
<%
  int    len = request.getContentLength();
  byte[] buf = null;
  int    n = 0;
  if (len > 0) {
    buf = new byte[len];
    n = request.getInputStream().read(buf);
    }
%>
<html><head><title>Test request.getInputStream</title></head><body>
  <form action="" method="post" enctype="multipart/form-data">
    <input type="hidden" name="oneTwoThree" value="123"/>
    <input type="file" name="fil"/>
    <input type="submit"/>
    </form>
  <table border="1">
    <tr><td>getContentType()</td><td><%=request.getContentType()%></td></tr>
    <tr><td>getContentLength()</td><td><%=len%></td></tr>
<%
    out.print("<tr><td>getInputStream(): " + n + "</td><td><pre>");
    for (int k = 0; k < n; k++) out.print((char)buf[k]);
    out.println("</pre></td></tr>");
  %>
    </table>
</body></html>
```

Listing 2-7 shows you an example with getReader. There are several methods to read the content, but the important thing to keep in mind is that getInputStream returns data in binary form and unbuffered, while getReader returns buffered characters.

Listing 2-7. req_getReader.jsp

```
<%@page language="java" contentType="text/html"%>
<%@page import="java.util.*, java.io.*"%>
<%
  int    len = request.getContentLength();
  String s = "";
  if (len > 0) {
    char[] cbuf = new char[len];
    int    n = request.getReader().read(cbuf, 0, len);
    s = new String(cbuf);
    }
  %>
<html><head><title>Test request.getReader</title></head><body>
  <form action="" method="post">
    <input type="hidden" name="oneTwoThree" value="123"/>
    <input type="hidden" name="fourFiveSix" value="456"/>
    <input type="submit"/>
    </form>
  <table border="1">
    <tr><td>getContentType()</td><td><%=request.getContentType()%></td></tr>
    <tr><td>getContentLength()</td><td><%=len%></td></tr>
    <tr><td>getReader(): <%=s.length()%></td><td><pre><%=s%></pre></td></tr>
    </table>
</body></html>
```

Now, create new jsps in the same test Project folder created in Chapter 1 and copy the code or place them in the WebContent folder. At last, start Tomcat in Eclipse and type in a browser the URL

```
http://localhost:8080/test/req_getInputStream.jsp
```

Figure 2-3 shows the output of req_getInputStream.jsp.

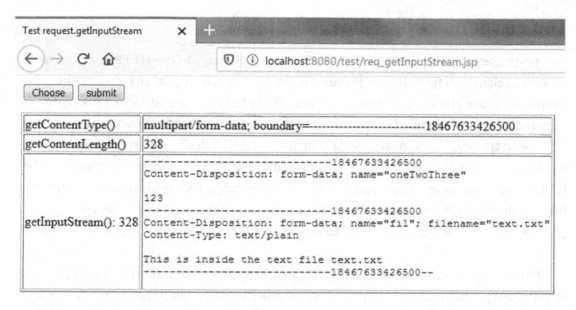

Figure 2-3. *Output of req_getInputStream.jsp*

I've uploaded the file named `text.txt`, which only contains the text `This is inside the test file text.txt`. In the real world, the file would perhaps contain a formatted document, an image, or a video clip. With this example, you can also get an idea of the multipart format. As you can see, the content type actually contains a definition of the boundary, which is then used inside the request body to separate its parts. Each part consists of a header, followed by an empty line and its content. Figure 2-4 shows the output of `req_getReader.jsp`.

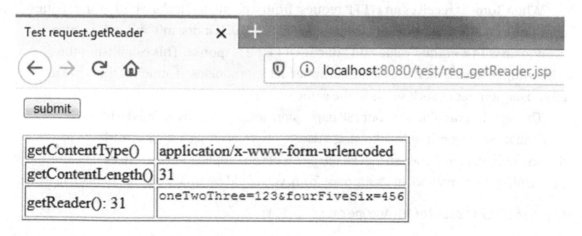

Figure 2-4. *Output of req_getReader.jsp*

The `response` Object

The `response` variable gives you access within your JSP page to the HTTP response to be sent back to the client. It is an instance of the `org.apache.catalina.connector.ResponseFacade` class, which Tomcat defines to implement the interfaces `javax.servlet.http.HttpServletResponse` and `javax.servlet.ServletResponse`.

The `HttpServletResponse` interface includes the definition of 41 status codes (of type `public static final int`) to be returned to the client as part of the response. The HTTP status codes are all between 100 and 599. The range 100–199 is reserved to provide information, 200–299 to report successful completion of the requested operation, 300–399 to report warnings, 400–499 to report client errors, and 500–599 to report server errors.

The normal status code is `SC_OK (200)`, and the most common error is `SC_NOT_FOUND (404)`, which occurs when the client requests a page that doesn't exist. Working with Tomcat, the most common server error is `SC_INTERNAL_SERVER_ERROR (500)`. You get it when there is an error in a JSP. You can use these constants as arguments of the `sendError` and `setStatus` methods.

The `session` Object

The term *session* refers to all the interactions a client has with a server from the moment the user views the first page of an application to the moment they quit the browser (or the session expires because too much time has elapsed since the last request).

When Tomcat receives an HTTP request from a client, it checks whether the request contains a cookie that by default is named `JSESSIONID`. If it doesn't find it, it creates the cookie with a unique value and attaches it to the response. This establishes the beginning of a session. If the client's browser accepts cookies, it attaches that cookie to all subsequent requests it sends to the same server.

The `session` variable lets your JSP pages store information associated with each individual user. For example, following a user login, you can set a session attribute to the access level of that user, so that all the pages of your application can check it before performing their function. In its simplest form, you could set up such a mechanism like this:

```
session.setAttribute("MyAppOperator", "");
```

Then, you can use the following code to check it:

```
boolean isOperator = (session.getAttribute("MyAppOperator")  != null);
if (isOperator) { ...
```

You can save in a session-scoped attribute much more than a simple access level. You only need to define a class to hold the preferences (e.g., UserPrefs), fill in an object of that type (named, say, preferences) when the user logs in, and save it as a session's attribute, like in the following example:

```
session.setAttribute("upref", preferences);
```

In all the pages of your application, you can then retrieve that information with something like this:

```
UserPrefs preferences = (UserPrefs)session.getAttribute("upref");
```

By doing so, as long as the user keeps his or her browser running and the session doesn't timeout, you don't need to reload the user's preferences from a database.

The variable session is an instance of the org.apache.catalina.session. StandardSessionFacade class, which Tomcat defines to implement the javax.servlet. http.HttpSession interface.

The session object supports a dozen methods, including setMaxInactiveInterval, which lets you specify the timeout in seconds (the default is 1800 s = 30 minutes). You can also set the timeout for your application to a given number of minutes by inserting a <session-config> element in your application's \WEB-INF\web.xml file. To do so, you need to place the following code inside the <web-app> element:

```
<session-config>
  <session-timeout>write here the timeout in minutes</session-timeout>
  </session-config>
```

Alternatively, you can also change Tomcat's default timeout by inserting the <session-config> element in the \conf\web.xml file you find inside the Tomcat home directory.

Directive Elements

JSP pages use directive elements to pass to Tomcat data about themselves. This data influences the translation process from a script file to a Java servlet class. As directives only play a role when a JSP page is recompiled after you modify it, they have no specific effect on the individual HTML responses.

There are three directives that you can use in JSP pages: `page`, `include`, and `taglib`. Their syntax is as follows:

```
<%@directive-name attr1="value1" [attr2="value2"...] %>
```

The `page` Directive

The `page` directive defines several page-dependent properties expressed through attributes. These properties should appear only once in a JSP page (unless the multiple instances all have the same value, but why should you do that?). You can write more than one `page` directive in a JSP page, and they will all apply. Their order or position within the page is generally irrelevant.

This directive is used in all JSP pages. Typically, a JSP page starts with a `page` directive to tell Tomcat that the scripting language is Java and that the output is to be HTML:

```
<%@page language="java" contentType="text/html"%>
```

This is almost always followed by one or more further `page` directives to tell Tomcat which external class definitions your code needs, for example:

```
<%@page import="java.util.ArrayList"%>
<%@page import="java.util.Iterator"%>
<%@page import="myBeans.OneOfMyBeans"%>
```

It is *not* good coding practice to import whole class libraries, as in

```
<%@page import="java.util.*"%>
```

because any relaxation of control, sooner or later, creates problems. In any case, as you can see in the following example, you don't need to write a separate directive for each class you need to include:

```
<%@page import="java.util.ArrayList, java.util.Iterator"%>
```

In addition to `language`, `contentType`, and `import`, the page directive also supports `autoFlush`, `buffer`, `errorPage`, `extends`, `info`, `isELIgnored`, `isErrorPage`, `isScriptingEnabled`, `isThreadSafe`, `pageEncoding`, `session`, and `trimDirectiveWhitespaces`.

Listing 2-8 shows you a simple program that utilizes the isThreadSafe attribute to test concurrency. Create new jsps in the same test Project folder created in Chapter 1 and copy the code or place them in the WebContent folder. At last, start Tomcat in Eclipse and type in a browser the URL

```
http://localhost:8080/test/concurrency.jsp
```

Listing 2-8. concurrency.jsp

```
<%@page language="java" contentType="text/html"%>
<%@page isThreadSafe="false"%>
<%! int k = 0;%>
<html><head><title>Concurrency</title></head><body>
<%
  out.print(k);
  int j = k + 1;
  Thread.sleep(5000);
  k = j;
  out.println(" -> " + k);
%>
</body></html>
```

The program declares the instance variable k, copies it to the variable j, increments j, waits for five seconds, and copies the incremented j back to k. It also displays k at the beginning and at the end.

If you reload the page several times, you'll see that k is increased every time the page refreshes. Now view the page in another browser (not just another browser window, because caching plays funny tricks); for example, view it in Chrome if you normally use Firefox. If you keep reloading the page in the two browsers, you'll see the k keeps increasing regardless of which browser you're looking at. This is because k is an instance variable.

Now reload the page in the first browser and then immediately in the second browser. Do you notice how the second browser takes longer to refresh? This is because you've set isThreadSafe="false", and Tomcat doesn't execute the servlet code for the two requests at the same time. However, k keeps increasing across the browsers with each page refresh.

Now remove the `page` directive that sets `isThreadSafe` to `false` and repeat the test. When you reload the page on both browsers almost simultaneously, they refresh the page at the same time but with the same value of k! This is because the second execution of the servlet starts while the first one is "holding" for five seconds.

I introduced the five-second delay to be sure that you would see the problem. Without the delay, the time interval between incrementing j and saving it back to k would be vanishingly small. Therefore, you might keep trying for years and never see the problem. Nevertheless, to rely on "it will never happen" when developing code, especially when concurrency plays a role, is a very bad practice. Other factors might influence the timing, and suddenly you might start seeing a problem once a day or even more rarely. It could have a damaging effect on how users consider your website.

The price paid for playing it safe with `isThreadSafe` is that it can slow down execution significantly. Fortunately, there's a better way to make the threads safe than relying on Tomcat. Look at Listing 2-9 that you can configure as Listing 2-8 and then type in a browser the URL

```
http://localhost:8080/test/concurrency2.jsp
```

Listing 2-9. concurrency2.jsp

```
<%@page language="java" contentType="text/html"%>
<%!
  int k = 0;
  Object syncK = new Object();
  %>
<html><head><title>Concurrency</title></head><body>
<%
  synchronized(syncK) {
    out.print(k);
    int j = k + 1;
    Thread.sleep(5000);
    k = j;
    out.println(" -> " + k);
    }
  %>
</body></html>
```

You protect the critical part of the code by enclosing it in a synchronized block. The syncK variable, being defined in a declaration element, is an instance variable shared like k among all the requests. I haven't used k because synchronized requires an object. In this simple case, instead of creating a new object specifically to protect the code, I could have used this, representing the servlet itself. But in general, if there were more than one block of code to protect, it wouldn't be a good idea. The best strategy to maximize efficiency, besides staying locked as little as possible, is to use specific locks.

Caution   I spent a bit of time on the attribute isThreadSafe because concurrency often is not well understood or implemented and causes intermittent bugs that are devilish to eliminate. Therefore, avoid implementing concurrency in the UI layer and delegate as much as possible its handling to the container running the web application. In fact, Tomcat automatically manages scheduling and synchronization of jobs and it is also possible to configure Tomcat concurrency, but it is over the scope of this book.

Earlier in this chapter, you have already seen how to use errorPage and isErrorPage (in "The Exception Object") and trimDirectiveWhitespaces, autoFlush, and buffer (in "The Out Object"). Here is a brief description of the remaining attributes of the page directive:

- **extends** tells Tomcat which class the servlet should extend.

- **info** defines a string that the servlet can access with its getServletInfo() method.

- **isELIgnored** tells Tomcat whether to ignore EL expressions.

- **isScriptingEnabled** tells Tomcat whether to ignore scripting elements.

- **pageEncoding** specifies the character set used in the JSP page itself.

- **session** tells Tomcat to include or exclude the page from HTTP sessions.

The bottom line is that, in most occasions, you can leave these additional attribute sets to their default values.

The `include` **Directive**

The `include` directive lets you insert into a JSP page the unprocessed content of another text file. For example, the following line of code includes a file named `some_jsp_code` with the extension `jspf`:

```
<%@include file="some_jsp_code.jspf"%>
```

JSPF stands for *JSP Fragment*, although, more recently, chunks of JSP code have been called *JSP Segments*, rather than Fragments. In fact, any text file with any extension will do.

As Tomcat does the merging before any translation, the raw content of the included file is pasted into the page without any check. All the HTML tags and JSP variables defined before the line containing the directive are available to the included code. This directive can be very useful, but use it sparingly, because it can easily lead to unmaintainable code, with bits and pieces spread all over the place.

The `taglib` **Directive**

You can extend the number of available JSP tags by directing Tomcat to use external self-contained tag libraries. The `taglib` directory identifies a tag library and specifies what prefix you use to identify its tags. For example, this code

```
<%@taglib uri="http://mysite.com/mytags" prefix="my"%>
```

makes it possible for you to write the following line as part of your JSP page:

```
<my:oneOfMyTags> ... </my:oneOfMyTags>
```

The following code includes the core JSP Standard Tag Library:

```
<%@taglib uri="http://java.sun.com/jsp/jstl/core" prefix="c"%>
```

You will find the description of JSTL and how to use it in the next chapters. In section "JSP's Tag Extension Mechanism" of the same chapter, I'll explain the possible advantages of creating your own libraries of tags and how to do it. For the time being, simply remember that the `taglib` directive tells Tomcat what libraries to load and where they are.

Summary

In this chapter, you learned all scripting and directive JSP elements.

I started by explaining the Java syntax used in scriptlets and the implicit objects defined by Tomcat, with several examples showing how to use them.

After that, I described the JSP directives.

In the next chapter, you will learn how to build complex JSP applications.

CHAPTER 3

JSP Application Architectures

In the first two chapters, you learned a large portion of JSP's components through brief examples. In this chapter, I will tell you how everything fits together in complex applications.

The insertion of Java code into HTML modules opens up the possibility of building dynamic web pages, but to say that it is possible doesn't mean you can do it efficiently and effectively. If you start developing complex applications exclusively by means of scripting elements, you'll rapidly reach the point where the code will become difficult to maintain. The key problem with mixing Java and HTML, as in "Hello World!", is that the application logic and the way the information is presented in the browser are mixed. Often, the business application designers and the web-page designers are different people with complementary and only partially overlapping skills. While application designers are experts in complex algorithms and databases, web designers focus on page composition and graphics. The architecture of your JSP-based applications should reflect this distinction. The last thing you want to do is blur the roles within the development team and end up with everybody doing what somebody else is better qualified to do. And even if you develop everything yourself, by keeping presentation and application logic separate, you will build more stable and more maintainable applications.

The Model 1 Architecture

The simplest way to separate presentation and logic is to move the bulk of the application logic from JSP to Java classes (i.e., Java beans), which can then be used within JSP (see Figure 3-1). This is called the JSP Model 1 architecture.

L. Manelli and G. Zambon, *Beginning Jakarta EE Web Development*,
https://doi.org/10.1007/978-1-4842-5866-8_3

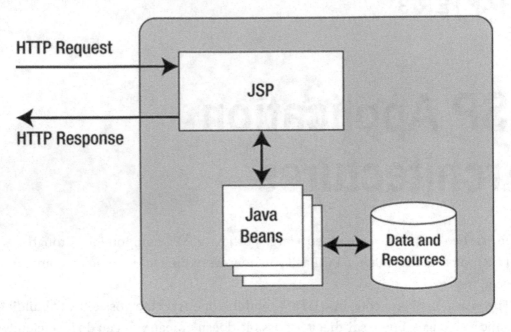

Figure 3-1. *JSP Model 1 architecture*

Although Model 1 is acceptable for applications containing up to a few thousand lines of code, the JSP pages still have to handle the HTTP requests, and this can cause headaches for the page designers.

The Model 2 Architecture

A better solution, more suitable for larger applications, is to split the functionality further and use JSP exclusively to format the HTML pages. This solution comes in the form of the JSP Model 2 architecture, also known as the model view controller (MVC) design pattern (see Figure 3-2).

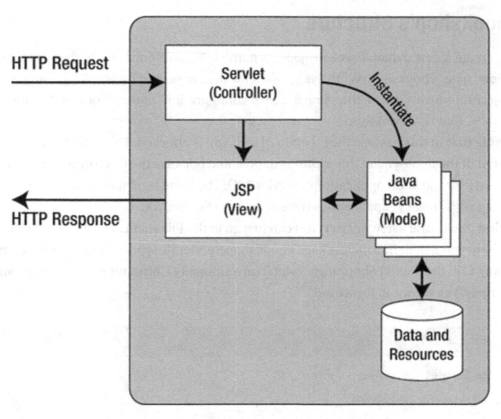

Figure 3-2. *JSP Model 2 architecture*

With this model, a servlet processes the request, handles the application logic, and instantiates Java beans. JSP obtains data from the beans and can format the response without having to know anything about what's going on behind the scenes.

E-bookshop

To illustrate this model, I will describe a sample application called *E-bookshop*, a small application to sell books online. E-bookshop is not really functional, because the list of books is hard-coded in the application rather than stored in a database. Also, nothing happens once you confirm the order. However, this example serves the purpose of showing you how Model 2 lets you completely separate business logic and presentation. Later in this chapter, I will introduce a better version of an online bookshop application that will accompany us through the rest of the book.

E-bookshop's Structure

Now, create a new dynamic web project. Its name is "ebookshop", and in the next dialog window, type "ebookshop\WEB-INF\classes" as default output folder. When the next dialog comes up, associate the same name of configuration "context root" to "context directory", that is, "ebookshop".

Note that in this passage the creation of web.xml is checked. The automatic creation of the deployment descriptor is deprecated because the descriptor is no longer necessary for the latest applications (Servlet 3.X). The issue is related to the ability of working with "legacy" applications developed with Servlet 2.X.

Now, we create a new Servlet! You can just go to the File menu ➤ New ➤ Servlet.

Then, you can define the package ebookshop.Servlet (it is possible to insert different folders). Call the Servlet ShoppingServlet (conventionally Class and Servlet names are capitalized) as shown in Figure 3-3.

Figure 3-3. *Eclipse, servlet name, and package configuration*

Finally, it is important to check the methods init and destroy in a Servlet.

We can immediately see that Eclipse generates the following annotation by default:

```
@WebServlet("/ShoppingServlet")
You can change it with /eshop:
@WebServlet("/eshop")
```

The annotation tells Tomcat that the requests will refer to the servlet as /eshop. As the root folder of this application (i.e., the folder immediately inside webapps) is ebookshop, Tomcat will then route to this servlet all the requests it will receive for the URL

```
http://servername:8080/ebookshop/eshop.
```

A little tip: if you want to indent file, select everything with Ctrl+A and then type Ctrl+I.

Now, you can copy the Servlet code or overwrite the file in the folder. I leave to you the choice.

Now, create a Java Class. To create a new class, right-click the ebookshop project and select "New ➤ Class" and give the name MyLog and package myclasses, as shown in Figure 3-4.

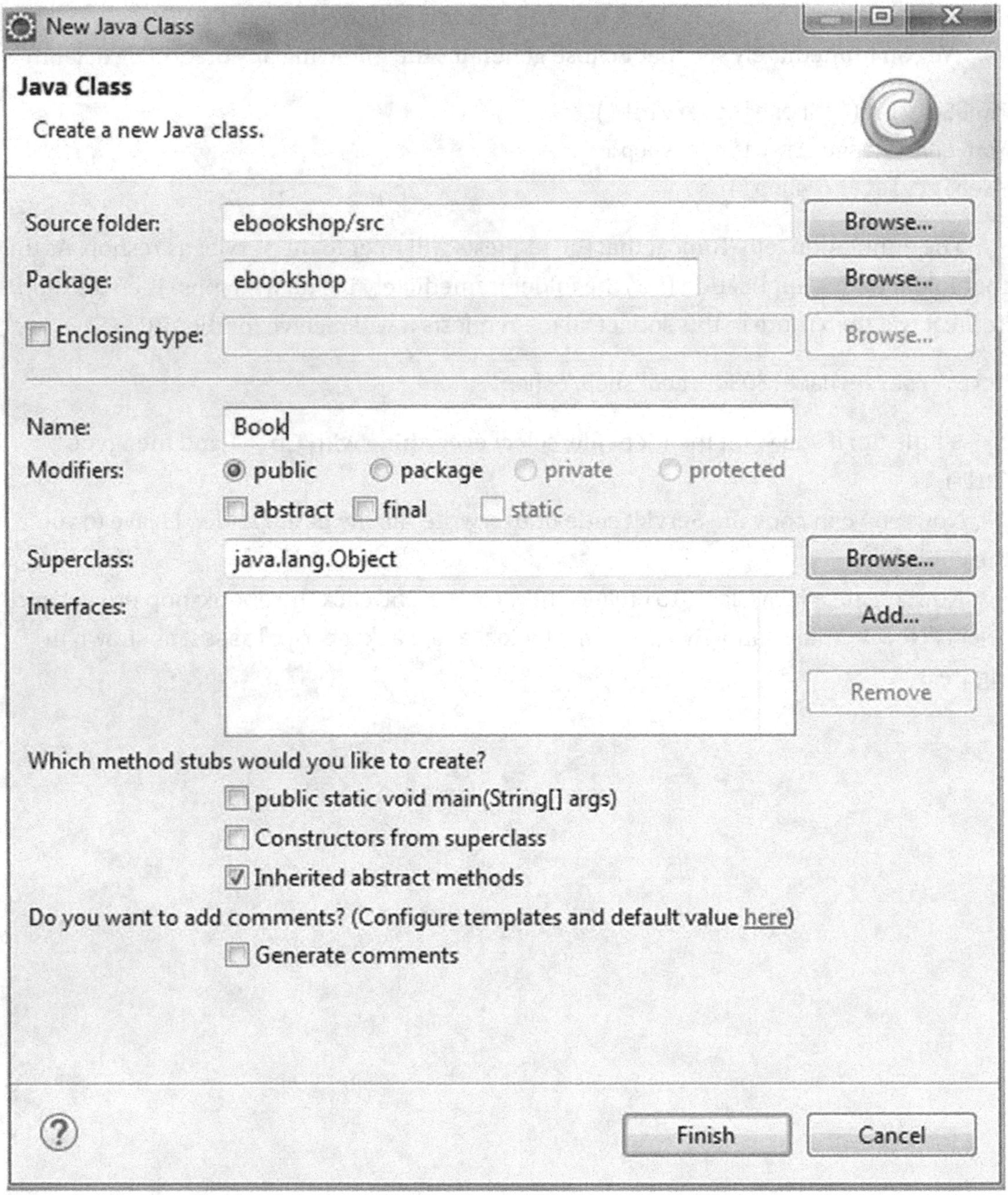

Figure 3-4. *Eclipse—creating a Java Class*

Now, you can insert the other source files in your folder:

- index.jsp, Checkout.jsp in workspace\ebookshop\ebookshop

- Book.java, in workspace\ebookshop\src

At last, refresh the project (position the cursor on the ebookshop project folder shown in the Project Explorer ➤, right-click, and select Refresh).

To get the application to work, you first need to compile it: it is simple with Eclipse, more than from the command line with `javac`! `Build is automatic, but you can also use the clean option to refresh the project build (from main menu select project` ➤, clean and select the ebookshop project`)`.

After deploying the project (Run on Server), you can now open a browser and type `http://localhost:8080/ebookshop/`; you should see the application's home page. If you want to export the project, use the WAR file; that is the best way to deploy your applications to more than one server: copy them into `webapps`, and Tomcat will do the rest for you. What could be easier than that?

Figure 3-5 shows the E-bookshop's home page, which you see when you type `http://localhost:8080/ebookshop` in your browser's address field.

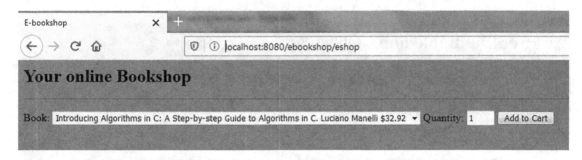

Figure 3-5. *The E-bookshop home page*

You can select a book by clicking the drop-down list, as shown in Figure 3-5, type in the number of copies you need, and then click the `Add to Cart` button. Every time you do so, the content of your shopping cart appears at the bottom of the window, as shown in Figure 3-6.

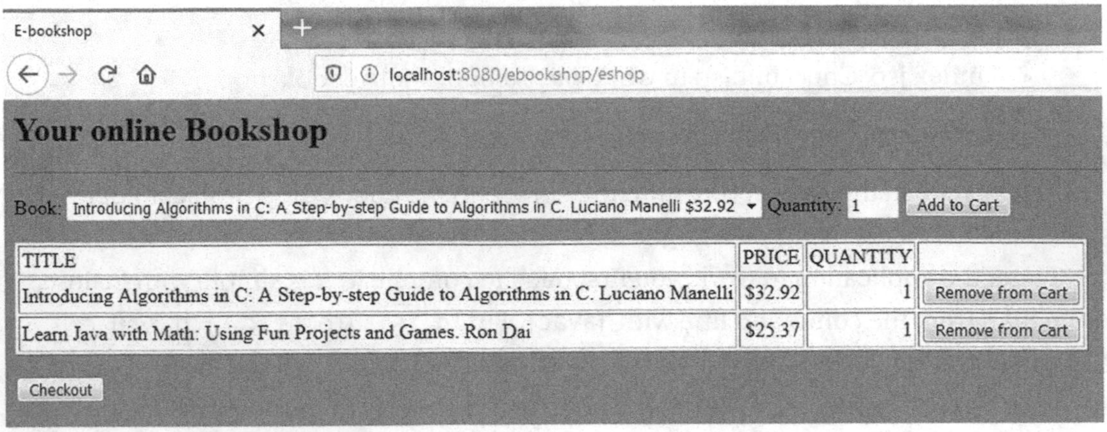

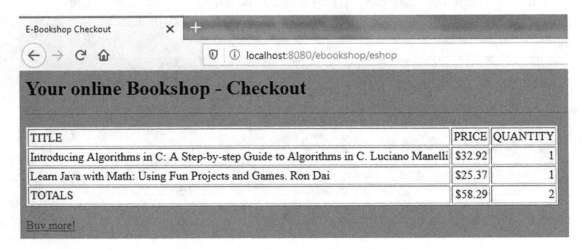

Figure 3-6. *The E-bookshop home page displaying the shopping cart*

You can remove an item from the shopping cart or go to the checkout. If you add additional copies of a book to the cart, the quantity in the cart increases accordingly.

If you click the Checkout button, you'll see the page shown in Figure 3-7.

Figure 3-7. *The E-bookshop checkout page*

If you click the Buy more! link, you'll go back to the home page with an empty shopping cart, ready for more shopping.

The E-bookshop Home Page

Listing 3-1 shows the home page http://localhost:8080/ebookshop/index.jsp. For
ease of reading, I've highlighted the JSP directives and scriptlets in bold. The JSP index.
jsp represents the V (view) component of the MVC design pattern.

Listing 3-1. The E-bookshop Home Page index.jsp

```
<%@page language="java" contentType="text/html"%>
<%@page trimDirectiveWhitespaces="true"%>
<%@page session="true" import="java.util.Vector, ebookshop.Book"%>
<html>
<head>
  <title>E-bookshop</title>
  <style type="text/css">
    body {background-color:gray; font-size=10pt;}
    H1 {font-size:20pt;}
    table {background-color:white;}
  </style>
  </head>
<body>
  <H1>Your online Bookshop</H1>
  <hr/><p/>
<%  // Scriptlet 1: check whether the booklist is ready
  Vector<ebookshop.Book> booklist =
      (Vector<ebookshop.Book>)session.getValue("ebookshop.list");
  if (booklist == null) {
    response.sendRedirect("/ebookshop/eshop");
    }
  else {
  %>
    <form name="addForm" action="eshop" method="POST">
      <input type="hidden" name="do_this" value="add">
      Book:
      <select name=book>
<%  // Scriptlet 2: copy the booklist to the selection control
```

```jsp
            for (int i = 0; i < booklist.size(); i++) {
                out.println("<option>" + (String)booklist.elementAt(i) +
                "</option>");
                }
    %>
            </select>
        Quantity: <input type="text" name="qty" size="3" value="1">
        <input type="submit" value="Add to Cart">
        </form>
        <p/>
<%  // Scriptlet 3: check whether the shopping cart is empty
    Vector shoplist =
            (Vector<ebookshop.Book>)session.getAttribute("ebookshop.cart");
    if (shoplist != null  &&  shoplist.size() > 0) {
    %>
        <table border="1" cellpadding="2">
        <tr>
        <td>TITLE</td>
        <td>PRICE</td>
        <td>QUANTITY</td>
        <td></td>
        </tr>
<%  // Scriptlet 4: display the books in the shopping cart
        for (int i = 0; i < shoplist.size(); i++) {
            Book aBook = shoplist.elementAt(i);
    %>
            <tr>
              <form name="removeForm" action="eshop" method="POST">
                <input type="hidden" name="position" value="<%=i%>">
                <input type="hidden" name="do_this" value="remove">
                <td><%=aBook.getTitle()%></td>
                <td align="right">$<%=aBook.getPrice()%></td>
                <td align="right"><%=aBook.getQuantity()%></td>
                <td><input type="submit" value="Remove from Cart"></td>
                </form>
```

```
        </tr>
<%
        } // for (int i..
  %>
        </table>
        <p/>
        <form name="checkoutForm" action="eshop" method="POST">
            <input type="hidden" name="do_this" value="checkout">
            <input type="submit" value="Checkout">
            </form>
<%
        } // if (shoplist..
      } // if (booklist..else..
  %>
        </body>
</html>
```

First, `index.jsp` (as shown in Scriptlet 1) checks whether the list of books to be sold is available, and if it isn't, it passes the control to the servlet, which then must initialize the book list. In a real online bookshop, the book list would be very long and kept in a database. Note that JSP doesn't *need to know* where the list is kept. This is the first hint at the fact that application logic and presentation are separate. You'll see later how the servlet fills in the book list and returns control to `index.jsp`. For now, let's proceed with the analysis of the home page.

If Scriptlet 1 discovers that the book list exists, it copies it into the `select` control one by one (as shown in Scriptlet 2). Notice how JSP simply creates each `option` by writing to the `out` stream. When the buyer clicks the `Add to Cart` button after selecting a title and possibly changing the number of copies, the home page posts a request to the `eshop` servlet with the hidden parameter `do_this` set to `add`. Once more, the servlet takes care of updating or creating the shopping cart by instantiating the class `Book` for each new book added to the cart. This is application logic, not presentation of information.

Scriptlet 3 checks whether a shopping cart exists. `index.jsp`, being completely data-driven, doesn't remember what has happened before, so it runs every time from the beginning. Therefore, it checks for the presence of a shopping cart even when the buyer sees the book list for the very first time.

Scriptlet 4 displays the items in the shopping cart, each one with its own form. If the buyer decides to delete an entry, `index.jsp` sends a request to the servlet with the hidden parameter `do_this` set to `remove`.

The sole purpose of the last two scriptlets is to close the curly brackets of `if`s and `for`s. However, notice that the form to ask the servlet to do the checkout is only displayed to the buyer when the shopping cart isn't empty. This is possible because Tomcat, when converting a JSP page into a Java servlet, processes all scriptlets together, without expecting each one of them individually to contain a complete block of code. HTML elements can then be enclosed within a Java block statement spanning two scriptlets.

If the buyer clicks the `Checkout` button, `index.jsp` will send a request to the servlet with the hidden parameter `do_this` set to `checkout`.

Finally, notice the use of the expression elements `<%=i%>`, `<%=aBook.getTitle()%>`, `<%=aBook.getPrice()%>`, and `<%=aBook.getQuantity()%>`. The first expression, `<%=i%>`, is the position of the book within the shopping cart. The other three are the execution of methods of an object of type `Book`, which the servlet instantiated for each new book added to the cart.

You've probably noticed that the address shown in the browser is `http://localhost:8080/ebookshop/eshop`. This is actually the address of the Java servlet that controls the application.

The E-bookshop Servlet

Listing 3-2 shows the source code of the servlet. In this section and in the following one, I will explain how the code works. The servlet ShoppingServlet.java represents the C (controller) component of the MVC design pattern.

Listing 3-2. ShoppingServlet.java

```
package ebookshop;
import java.util.Vector;
import java.io.IOException;
import javax.servlet.ServletException;
import javax.servlet.ServletConfig;
import javax.servlet.ServletContext;
import javax.servlet.RequestDispatcher;
import javax.servlet.http.HttpServlet;
```

```java
import javax.servlet.http.HttpServletRequest;
import javax.servlet.http.HttpSession;
import javax.servlet.http.HttpServletResponse;
import ebookshop.Book;

public class ShoppingServlet extends HttpServlet {

  public void init(ServletConfig conf) throws ServletException  {
    super.init(conf);
    }

  public void doGet (HttpServletRequest req, HttpServletResponse res)
      throws ServletException, IOException {
    doPost(req, res);
    }

  public void doPost (HttpServletRequest req, HttpServletResponse res)
      throws ServletException, IOException {
    HttpSession session = req.getSession(true);
    @SuppressWarnings("unchecked")
    Vector<Book> shoplist =
      (Vector<Book>)session.getAttribute("ebookshop.cart");
    String do_this = req.getParameter("do_this");

    // If it is the first time, initialize the list of books, which in
    // real life would be stored in a database on disk
    if (do_this == null) {
      Vector<String> blist = new Vector<String>();
      blist.addElement("Learn HTML5 and JavaScript for iOS. Scott Preston
      $39.99");
      blist.addElement("Java 7 for Absolute Beginners. Jay Bryant $39.99");
      blist.addElement("Beginning Android 4. Livingston $39.99");
      blist.addElement("Pro Spatial with SQL Server 2012. Alastair
      Aitchison $59.99");
      blist.addElement("Beginning Database Design. Clare Churcher $34.99");
      session.setAttribute("ebookshop.list", blist);
      ServletContext sc = req.getSession().getServletContext();
      RequestDispatcher rd = sc.getRequestDispatcher("/");
```

```
        rd.forward(req, res);
      }
    else {

      // If it is not the first request, it can only be a checkout request
      // or a request to manipulate the list of books being ordered
      if (do_this.equals("checkout")) {
        float dollars = 0;
        int   books = 0;
        for (Book aBook : shoplist) {
          float price = aBook.getPrice();
          int   qty = aBook.getQuantity();
          dollars += price * qty;
          books += qty;
        }
        req.setAttribute("dollars", dollars+""));
        req.setAttribute("books", books+"");
        ServletContext sc = req.getSession().getServletContext();
        RequestDispatcher rd = sc.getRequestDispatcher("/Checkout.jsp");
        rd.forward(req, res);
      } // if (..checkout..

      // Not a checkout request - Manipulate the list of books
      else {
        if (do_this.equals("remove")) {
          String pos = req.getParameter("position");
          shoplist.removeElementAt (Integer.parseInt(pos));
        }
        else if (do_this.equals("add")) {
          boolean found = false;
          Book aBook = getBook(req);
          if (shoplist == null) {  // the shopping cart is empty
            shoplist = new Vector<Book>();
            shoplist.addElement(aBook);
          }
```

```
        else {  // update the #copies if the book is already there
          for (int i = 0; i < shoplist.size() && !found; i++) {
            Book b = (Book)shoplist.elementAt(i);
            if (b.getTitle().equals(aBook.getTitle())) {
              b.setQuantity(b.getQuantity() + aBook.getQuantity());
              shoplist.setElementAt(b, i);
              found = true;
            }
          } // for (i..
          if (!found) {  // if it is a new book => Add it to the shoplist
            shoplist.addElement(aBook);
          }
        } // if (shoplist == null) .. else ..
      } // if (..add..

      // Save the updated list of books and return to the home page
      session.setAttribute("ebookshop.cart", shoplist);
      ServletContext sc = getServletContext();
      RequestDispatcher rd = sc.getRequestDispatcher("/");
      rd.forward(req, res);
      } // if (..checkout..else
    } // if (do_this..
  } // doPost

private Book getBook(HttpServletRequest req) {
  String myBook = req.getParameter("book");
  int    n = myBook.indexOf('$');
  String title = myBook.substring(0, n);
  String price = myBook.substring(n+1);
  String qty = req.getParameter("qty");
  return new Book(title, Float.parseFloat(price), Integer.parseInt(qty));
  } // getBook
}
```

As you can see, the init() method only executes the standard servlet initialization, and the doGet() method simply executes doPost(), where all the work is done. If you were to remove the doGet() method, you would effectively forbid the direct call of the servlet. That is, if you typed `http://localhost:8080/ebookshop/eshop` in your browser, you would receive an error message that says the requested resource isn't available. As it is, you can type the URL with or without trailing `eshop`.

The highlighted line shows that I suppressed a warning. Normally, a warning tells you that something might be wrong. Therefore, it is not good to have spurious warnings, because they might distract you from noticing warnings you should fix. The use of `@suppressWarnings` is in general bad practice and encourages you to use a sloppy programming style. In this particular case, the compiler complained about the typecasting of a generic `Object` to a `Vector`, but I knew that the attribute `ebookshop.cart` was of type `Vector<book>`.

When you analyze `index.jsp`, you can see that it passes control to the servlet on four occasions, as listed here from the point of view of the servlet:

1. **If no book list exists**: This happens at the beginning, when the buyer types `http://localhost:8080/ebookshop/`. The servlet executes without any parameter, initializes the book list, and passes control straight back to `index.jsp`.

2. **When the buyer clicks `Add to Cart`**: The servlet executes with `do_this` set to `add` and a parameter containing the book description. Normally, this would be done more elegantly with a reference to the book rather than the whole description, but we want to keep things as simple as possible. The servlet creates a cart if necessary and adds to it a new object of type `Book` or, if the same book is already in the cart, updates its quantity. After that, it passes the control back to `index.jsp`.

3. **When the buyer clicks `Remove from Cart`**: The servlet executes with `do_this` set to `remove` and a parameter containing the position of the book within the cart. The servlet removes the book in the given position by deleting the object of type `Book` from the vector representing the cart. After that, it passes the control back to `index.jsp`.

4. **When the buyer clicks `Checkout`**: The servlet executes with `do_this` set to `checkout`. The servlet calculates the total amount of money and the number of books ordered, adds them as attributes to the HTTP request, and passes the control to `Checkout.jsp`, which has the task of displaying the bill.

More on E-bookshop

By now, it should be clear to you how the servlet is in control of the application and how JSP is only used to present the data. To see the full picture, you only need to see Book. java, the Java bean used to represent a book, and Checkout.jsp, which displays the bill. Listing 3-3 shows the code for Book.java that represents the M (model) component of the MVC design pattern.

Listing 3-3. Book.java

```
package ebookshop;
public class Book {
  String title;
  float  price;
  int    quantity;
  public Book(String t, float p, int q) {
    title    = t;
    price    = p;
    quantity = q;
    }
  public String getTitle()         { return title; }
  public void   setTitle(String t) { title = t; }
  public float  getPrice()         { return price; }
  public void   setPrice(float p)  { price = p; }
  public int    getQuantity()      { return quantity; }
  public void   setQuantity(int q) { quantity = q; }
  }
```

In a more realistic case, the class Book would contain much more information, which the buyer could use to select the book. Also, the class attribute title is a misnomer, as it also includes the author names, but you get the idea. Listing 3-4 shows the code for Checkout.jsp.

Listing 3-4. Checkout.jsp

```jsp
<%@page language="java" contentType="text/html"%>
<%@page session="true" import="java.util.Vector, ebookshop.Book" %>
<html>
<head>
  <title>E-Bookshop Checkout</title>
  <style type="text/css">
  body {background-color:gray; font-size=10pt;}
  H1 {font-size:20pt;}
  table {background-color:white;}
  </style>
</head>
<body>
  <H1>Your online Bookshop - Checkout</H1>
  <hr/><p/>
  <table border="1" cellpadding="2">
    <tr>
      <td>TITLE</td>
      <td align="right">PRICE</td>
      <td align="right">QUANTITY</td>
    </tr>
<%
    Vector<Book> shoplist =
        (Vector<Book>)session.getAttribute("ebookshop.cart");
    for (Book anOrder : shoplist) {
%>
      <tr>
        <td><%=anOrder.getTitle()%></td>
        <td align="right">$<%=anOrder.getPrice()%></td>
        <td align="right"><%=anOrder.getQuantity()%></td>
      </tr>
<%
    }
    session.invalidate();
  %>
```

```
    <tr>
      <td>TOTALS</td>
      <td align="right">$<%=(String)request.getAttribute("dollars")%></td>
      <td align="right"><%=(String)request.getAttribute("books")%></td>
      </tr>
    </table>
  <p/>
  <a href="/ebookshop/eshop">Buy more!</a>
  </body>
</html>
```

Checkout.jsp displays the shopping cart and the totals precalculated by the servlet, and it invalidates the session so that a new empty shopping cart will be created if the application is restarted from the same browser window.

Note that you could have included the checkout logic in index.jsp and made its execution dependent on the presence of the two totals. However, I wanted to show you a more structured application. It's also better design to keep different functions in different JSP modules. In fact, I could have also kept the shopping cart in a separate JSP file. In real life, I would have certainly done so. In addition, I would have saved the styles in a Cascading Style Sheets (CSS) file rather than repeating them in all JSP sources. Finally, there is close to no error checking and reporting. You could easily crash this application. In a real case, you would add an error page as explained in the previous chapter.

Before we move on, you'll certainly find it interesting to see the dynamic HTML page that actually reaches the browser after adding one item to the shopping cart (see Listing 3-5).

Listing 3-5. HTML Generated by index.jsp

```
<html>
<head>
  <title>E-bookshop</title>
  <style type="text/css">
    body {background-color:gray; font-size=10pt;}
    H1 {font-size:20pt;}
    table {background-color:white;}
    </style>
  </head>
```

```html
<body>
  <H1>Your online Bookshop</H1>
  <hr/><p/>
<form name="addForm" action="eshop" method="POST">
     <input type="hidden" name="do_this" value="add">
     Book:
     <select name=book>
<option>Learn HTML5 and JavaScript for iOS. Scott Preston $39.99</option>
<option>Java 7 for Absolute Beginners. Jay Bryant $39.99</option>
<option>Beginning Android 4. Livingston $39.99</option>
<option>Pro Spatial with SQL Server 2012. Alastair Aitchison $59.99</
option>
<option>Beginning Database Design. Clare Churcher $34.99</option>
</select>
     Quantity: <input type="text" name="qty" size="3" value="1">
     <input type="submit" value="Add to Cart">
     </form>
   <p/>
<table border="1" cellpadding="2">
     <tr>
     <td>TITLE</td>
     <td>PRICE</td>
     <td>QUANTITY</td>
     <td></td>
     </tr>
<tr>
         <form name="removeForm" action="eshop" method="POST">
           <input type="hidden" name="position" value="0">
           <input type="hidden" name="do_this" value="remove">
           <td>Pro Spatial with SQL Server 2012. Alastair Aitchison </td>
           <td align="right">$59.99</td>
           <td align="right">1</td>
           <td><input type="submit" value="Remove from Cart"></td>
           </form>
         </tr>
</table>
```

```
    <p/>
    <form name="checkoutForm" action="eshop" method="POST">
      <input type="hidden" name="do_this" value="checkout">
      <input type="submit" value="Checkout">
      </form>
</body>
</html>
```

Neat, isn't it?

You now have in your hands the full code of a nontrivial Java/JSP application, but you still need to know how to make these four modules work together.

Summary

In this chapter, I described the application architectures suitable for web applications and provided the example E-bookshop to explain how the Model-View-Controller architecture works.

You then learned how to create a Servlet and a Class in the Eclipse IDE. It was necessary at this point because, with E-bookshop, we had reached the limit of what was reasonable to do without an IDE.

In the next chapters, I'll introduce the Eshop project, which, in different versions, I will use to complete the description of JSP and to explain JSF and take you through the remaining functionality of JSP. To do that, I will use simple dedicated examples and the relevant aspects of the eshop application.

CHAPTER 4

Databases

In many cases, a web application is nothing more than a front end for a database (DB). In fact, what makes web pages dynamic is precisely the fact that there is a significant amount of data behind them. In this chapter you will learn to working with databases and SQL.

A database consists of organized data, that is, the data itself and a *schema* that provides data structures. Nowadays, most databases are organized in *tables* consisting of *rows* and *columns*. This is a natural way of organizing data, and you're probably familiar with it through the use of spreadsheets. You can define the table characteristics independently of the actual data you're going to store into it. This is another instance of the separation of formatting and content, which you've already encountered in Chapter 3, when we discussed web applications. For example, a table of employees would probably include columns named `FirstName`, `LastName`, and `SocialSecurityNumber` containing strings of text; columns named `EmployeeNumber` and `YearSalary` would contain numbers; and columns named `DateOfBirth` and `EmployedSince` would contain dates. The data associated with each employee would then all be stored into a row.

A *field* is an individual data item within a table, corresponding to the intersection of a row and a column. One or more columns can be specified as *unique keys*, used to identify each individual employee. For this purpose, you could use either one of the columns mentioned previously (e.g., `EmployeeNumber`) or the combination of first and last name and date of birth. The unique key used in preference over the others is called the *primary key* of a table.

An additional type of key is the *foreign key*. In this case, the column is defined as a reference to a unique key of another table. Besides avoiding duplication of data, this type of constraint increases the consistency of the database. For example, a table containing customer contracts could include a column referring to the column of employee numbers defined in the employee table. This would ensure that each contract would be associated with an existing salesperson.

Sometimes it's useful to present only some columns and rows, as if they were a table in their own right. Such virtual tables are called *views*.

© Luciano Manelli and Giulio Zambon 2020
L. Manelli and G. Zambon, *Beginning Jakarta EE Web Development*,
https://doi.org/10.1007/978-1-4842-5866-8_4

An important property is the *transaction* that represents a key concept in DBMSs in terms of concurrent access to the same tables and indicates a series of operations that have to be performed without interruption, that is, without any other operation "sneaking in" between them. A transaction is characterized by four properties—atomicity, consistency, isolation, and durability (ACID):

- **Atomicity**: It guarantees that either all the individual steps of an operation are performed or none at all. You must not be able to perform partial transactions.

- **Consistency**: It refers to the fact that a transaction is not supposed to violate the integrity of a database.

- **Isolation**: It means that concurrent operations cannot see intermediate values of a transaction.

- **Durability**: It refers to the capacity of a database to guarantee that a transaction, once completed, is never going to be "forgotten," even after a system failure.

DBMS

A database management system (DBMS), such as MySQL, is a software package that lets you create, read, update, and delete (CRUD) both items of data and elements of the schema.

Therefore, when talking about a database, you need to distinguish between three aspects:

- The data it contains

- The structure you impose on the data in order to CRUD it efficiently

- The software that allows you to manipulate both the data itself and the database structure (the DBMS)

Working with a database means that you're interacting with its DBMS. You can do that through a command-line interface (CLI), through graphical user interfaces (GUIs) provided by the DBMS vendor and third parties, or programmatically through an API.

The DBMS can build an *index* for each key, so that the data can be retrieved more quickly. This will obviously slow down insertion and deletion of rows (i.e., of new records), because the DBMS will have to spend time updating the indexes, but most databases are more frequently interrogated than modified. Therefore, it usually pays to define indexes, at least those that can speed up the most common queries.

In this chapter's examples and in the book as Eshop database, I'll use *MySQL* as the DBMS of choice, because, first, it's available for free and, second, it's the most widely used of the freely available DBMSs. As such, it has been proven to work reliably in all sorts of environments.

Structured Query Language

Structured Query Language (SQL) is the most widely used language to interact with DBMSs. Most DBMSs don't support the whole SQL standard. Moreover, vendors sometimes add nonstandard elements that, in practice, prevent full portability across DBMSs. In general, regardless of whether we're talking about database organization, table structure, or actual data, you'll need to perform four CRUD operations. The corresponding SQL statements begin with a keyword that identifies the operation (e.g., INSERT, SELECT, UPDATE, or DELETE), followed when necessary by a keyword specifying on what type of entity the operation is to be performed (e.g., DATABASE, TABLE, or INDEX) and by additional elements. You use the SELECT statement for retrieving information.

You can create databases, tables, and indexes with the CREATE statement, update them with ALTER, and delete them with DROP. Similarly, you can create and delete views with CREATE and DROP, but you cannot update them once you've created them. You use INSERT to create new rows within a table, and you use DELETE to delete them. The UPDATE statement lets you modify entire rows or one or more individual fields within them.

The statements that let you modify the structures are collectively referred to as Data Definition Language (DDL), while those that let you modify the content are called Data Manipulation Language (DML).

In many applications, the structure of databases, tables, indexes, and views, once initially defined, remains unchanged. Therefore, you'll often need within your applications only the statements operating on rows and fields. In any case, you'll certainly need SELECT, which you use to interrogate databases both in terms of their structure and the data they contain. Finally, to complete the list of statements you're likely to need when developing applications, there are START TRANSACTION, COMMIT, and ROLLBACK, which you need to use transactions.

When you want to retrieve, update, or delete rows, you obviously have to identify them. You do this with the WHERE keyword followed by a <where_condition>.

INSERT

INSERT stores one or more rows in an existing table or view. See Listing 4-1 for a description of its format.

Listing 4-1. The SQL Statement INSERT

```
INSERT INTO {tbl_name | view_name} [(col_name [, col_name ...])]
    {VALUES (<val> [, <val> ...]) | <select>};
    ;
<select> = A SELECT returning the values to be inserted into the new rows
```

You can use INSERT to create one row in a table (or a single-table view) from scratch or to create one or more rows by copying data from other tables.

UPDATE

UPDATE modifies the content of one or more existing rows in a table (or single-table view). See Listing 4-2 for a description of its format.

Listing 4-2. The SQL Statement UPDATE

```
UPDATE {tbl_name | view_name} SET col_name = <val> [, col_name = <val> ...]
    [WHERE <where_condition>];
```

DELETE

DELETE removes one or more rows from an existing table or a view that is not read-only. See Listing 4-3 for a description of its format.

Listing 4-3. The SQL Statement DELETE

```
DELETE FROM {tbl_name | view_name} [WHERE <where_condition>];
```

SELECT

In particular, SELECT (that can be used also to obtain the result of applying a function to the data) retrieves data from one or more tables and views.

Listing 4-4 shows how you use SELECT to obtain data.

Listing 4-4. SELECT to Obtain Data

```
SELECT [ALL | DISTINCT ] {* | <select_list>}
    [FROM <table_references> [WHERE <where_condition>]]
    [ORDER BY <order_list>]
    ;
<select_list> = col_name [, <select_list>]
<table_references> = one or more table and/or view names separated by
commas
<order_list> = col_name [ASC | DESC] [, <order_list> ...]
```

Conceptually, it is simple: SELECT one, some, or all columns FROM one or more tables or views WHERE certain conditions are satisfied; then present the rows ORDERed as specified. Some examples will clarify the details:

- SELECT * is the simplest possible SELECT, but you'll probably never use it. It returns everything you have in your database.

- SELECT * FROM table is the simplest practical form of SELECT. It returns all the data in the table you specify.

- SELECT a_col_name, another_col_name FROM table still returns all the rows of a table, but for each row, it returns only the values in the columns you specify. Use the keyword DISTINCT to tell the DBMS that it should *not* return any duplicate row.

- SELECT * FROM table WHERE condition only returns the rows for which the condition you specify is satisfied.

- SELECT * FROM table ORDER BY col_name returns all the rows of a table ordered on the basis of a column you specify.

The SQL standard has been widely adopted, and, as a result, most of what I'm going to say concerning SQL actually applies to all DBMSs. As you can imagine, there are still proprietary additions and variations that, in some cases, make SQL less portable than what it could and should be, but it won't affect us. The SQL standard specifies a lot of reserved words as keywords; therefore, it should be clear that in this chapter, I couldn't possibly give you more than a small introduction to SQL and DBMS.

At last, to write comments in an SQL script, you enclose them between /* and */, like Java's block comments.

Introducing eshop application

Now, in this section, I will introduce the eshop application, which will remain with us through the rest of the book.

The first thing is to create a simple database, which we will use in the eshop application you will encounter in the next chapter. It is important to emphasize on design of database, because a good design ensures elimination of data redundancy, consistent data, and high-performance application.

Taking an object-oriented approach, I'll begin by specifying the objects that the application needs to handle, the operations which those objects support, and the roles of the people who perform those operations.

Each role corresponds to a separate user interface, and the two main roles are the administrator and the customer. The administrators manage products, orders, and customer records, but for our purposes, it is sufficient to implement the public interface of a customer buying from a catalog.

Entities and Operations

In eshop we won't keep track of orders and customers. Once the customer goes to the checkout, enters credit-card information, and checks out, we'll save the order, but we won't do anything with it. In the real world, we'd have to process the purchase by charging the credit-card account and dispatching the order.

Product Categories

It makes sense to group the products into categories, especially if the catalog is diversified and substantial. As eshop only sells books, its categories refer to broad book subjects, such as Historical Mysteries, Science Fiction, and Web Development.

Each category has a *name* and an *identifier*. The identifier is guaranteed to be unique, thereby allowing us to refer to each category without ambiguity. Normally, a category would have additional attributes, like description, status, date of creation, and so on. To implement the customer interface, the only operation you need with such a bare-bones category definition is obtaining a category name given its ID.

Books

Each book has a *title*, an *author*, a *price*, a unique *identifier*, a *category ID*, and an image of the *front cover*. Customers must be able to select books from a category, search for books, display the book details, and put books into a shopping cart.

Shopping Cart

The minimum amount of information stored in a shopping cart is a list of items, each consisting of a book identifier and the number of ordered copies. I decided to duplicate in the shopping cart title, description, and price of the books instead of using their book IDs. Besides simplifying the application, this also protects the customer from book updates that might occur while he or she is still shopping. In a more sophisticated application, when some book attributes change, you might want to inform the customers who've placed the book in their cart but haven't yet completed the checkout. You wouldn't be able to do so without saving the original information. Obviously, this only avoids a problem due to concurrent access of data. To protect the information from more serious occurrences like server failures, you would have to implement more general solutions, like saving session data on non-volatile storage and server clustering.

Customers must be able to change the number of copies of each book in the cart, remove a book altogether, and go to the checkout. They should also be able to display the shopping cart at any time.

Order

Although this sample application doesn't cover orders, it's useful to specify the structure of an order. You need two separate classes: one to represent the ordered items and one with the customer's data.

For each ordered item, you need to save the book data obtained from the shopping cart. Additionally, for each order, you need to save the customer data and a unique order number.

Creating MySQL Schema and Tables

Now we will create and populate our database. First, define the DB "shop". Once we create the DB, it is possible to create the tables following from the entities discussed in previous section, which are

- **categories** table
- **books** table
- **orders** table
- **order_details** table

The logic design of the database is shown in the following tables (Table 4-1, Table 4-2, Table 4-3, and Table 4-4), characterized by name, length, type of data, and constraints (i.e., a field is a primary key and another must be not null).

Table 4-1. *Categories Table*

Field Name	Length	Type	Constraints
category_id	–	INT	Primary Key Not null Index
category_name	70	VARCHAR	Not Null

Table 4-2. *Books Table*

Field Name	Length	Type	Constraints
book_id	–	INT	Primary Key Not null Index
title	70	VARCHAR	Not Null
author	70	VARCHAR	–
price	–	DOUBLE	Not Null
category_id	–	INT	Foreign Key of categories table Not null

Table 4-3. *Orders Table*

Field Name	Length	Type	Constraints
order_id	–	BIGINT	Primary Key Not null Index
delivery_name	70	VARCHAR	Not Null
delivery_address	70	VARCHAR	Not Null
cc_name	70	VARCHAR	Not Null
cc_number	32	VARCHAR	Not Null
cc_expiry	10	VARCHAR	Not Null

Table 4-4. *Order_details Table*

Field Name	Length	Type	Constraints
id	–	BIGINT	Primary Key Not null Index
book_id	–	INTEGER	Foreign Key of books table Not null
title	70	VARCHAR	Not Null
author	70	VARCHAR	
quantity	–	INT	Not Null
price	–	DOUBLE	Not Null
order_id	–	BIGINT	Foreign Key of categories table Not null

The *Index* speeds up the search of an element in a table.

I use VARCHAR data type for cc_number and cc_expire to simplify controls for these fields. In an application ready for production, you should use a numeric data type for cc_number and date data type for cc_expire. Note that I used INT for book id and categories, while I used BIGINT for orders and order details, because I supposed a number of orders bigger than the books.

119

Listing 4-5 shows the SQL script for the creation of the 'shop' database.

Listing 4-5. shop_create.sql

```
01  DROP DATABASE IF EXISTS `shop`;
02  CREATE DATABASE `shop`;
03  CREATE TABLE `shop`.`categories` (
04  `category_id` int NOT NULL AUTO_INCREMENT,
05  `category_name` varchar(70) NOT NULL,
06  PRIMARY KEY (`category_id`),
07  KEY `category_id_key` (`category_id`)
08  );
09  CREATE TABLE `shop`.`books` (
10  `book_id` int NOT NULL AUTO_INCREMENT,
11  `title` varchar(70) NOT NULL,
12  `author` varchar(70) DEFAULT NULL,
13  `price` double NOT NULL,
14  `category_id` int NOT NULL,
15  PRIMARY KEY (`book_id`),
16  KEY `book_id_key` (`book_id`),
18  CONSTRAINT `category_id` FOREIGN KEY (`category_id`) REFERENCES
`categories` (`category_id`)
19  );
20  CREATE TABLE `shop`.`orders` (
21  `order_id` bigint NOT NULL AUTO_INCREMENT,
22  `delivery_name` varchar(70) NOT NULL,
23  `delivery_address` varchar(70) NOT NULL,
24  `cc_name` varchar(70) NOT NULL,
25  `cc_number` varchar(32) NOT NULL,
26  `cc_expiry` varchar(20) NOT NULL,
27  PRIMARY KEY (`order_id`),
28  KEY `order_id_key` (`order_id`)
29  );
30  CREATE TABLE `order_details` (
31  `id` bigint NOT NULL AUTO_INCREMENT,
32  `book_id` int NOT NULL,
```

```
33  `title` varchar(70) NOT NULL,
34  `author` varchar(70) DEFAULT NULL,
35  `quantity` int NOT NULL,
36  `price` double NOT NULL,
37  `order_id` bigint NOT NULL,
38  PRIMARY KEY (`id`),
39  KEY `order_details_id_key` (`id`),
42  CONSTRAINT `book_id` FOREIGN KEY (`book_id`) REFERENCES `books` (`book_id`),
43  CONSTRAINT `order_id` FOREIGN KEY (`order_id`) REFERENCES `orders`
    (`order_id`)
44  );
```

Line 01 removes the database. The IF EXISTS option allows you to delete it only if it already exists. This option is used to prevent the reported error when you use the creation script the first time if the database does not exist. The DROP statement deletes the database and the physical disk files, so you should have a backup of the database if you want to restore it in the future.

Line 02 creates a blank database named shop.

Lines 03 to 08 create a table to store book *categories*.

Lines 09 to 19 create a table to store book *records*.

Lines 20 to 29 create a table to store book *orders*.

Lines 30 to 44 create a table to store book *order_details*.

Lines 06, 15, 27, and 38 set the *primary keys* in the tables.

Lines 18, 42, and 43 set the *foreign keys* in the tables.

To execute the SQL script, you can use the command-line client you see in Chapter 1. You will find the script in the software package for this chapter.

Open the command-line client. Open shop_create.sql with a text editor, copy everything, and paste it onto the command-line client. Listing 4-6 shows what you will get.

Listing 4-6. Log of shop_create.sql

```
Enter password: ****
Welcome to the MySQL monitor.  Commands end with ; or \g.
Your MySQL connection id is 334
Server version: 8.0.19 MySQL Community Server - GPL
```

Type 'help;' or '\h' for help. Type '\c' to clear the current input statement.

```
mysql> DROP DATABASE IF EXISTS `shop`;
Query OK, 4 rows affected (4.45 sec)

mysql> CREATE DATABASE `shop`;
Query OK, 1 row affected (0.18 sec)

mysql> CREATE TABLE `shop`.`categories` (
    ->    `category_id` int NOT NULL AUTO_INCREMENT,
    ->    `category_name` varchar(70) NOT NULL,
    ->    PRIMARY KEY (`category_id`),
    ->    KEY `category_id_key` (`category_id`)
    ->    );
Query OK, 0 rows affected (1.55 sec)

mysql> CREATE TABLE `shop`.`books` (
    ->    `book_id` int NOT NULL AUTO_INCREMENT,
    ->    `title` varchar(70) NOT NULL,
    ->    `author` varchar(70) DEFAULT NULL,
    ->    `price` double NOT NULL,
    ->    `category_id` int NOT NULL,
    ->    PRIMARY KEY (`book_id`),
    ->    KEY `book_id_key` (`book_id`),
    ->    CONSTRAINT `category_id` FOREIGN KEY (`category_id`) REFERENCES
           `categories` (`category_id`)
    -> );
Query OK, 0 rows affected (1.30 sec)

mysql> CREATE TABLE `shop`.`orders` (
    ->    `order_id` bigint NOT NULL AUTO_INCREMENT,
```

```
    ->    `delivery_name` varchar(70) NOT NULL,
    ->    `delivery_address` varchar(70) NOT NULL,
    ->    `cc_name` varchar(70) NOT NULL,
    ->    `cc_number` varchar(32) NOT NULL,
    ->    `cc_expiry` varchar(20) NOT NULL,
    ->    PRIMARY KEY (`order_id`),
    ->    KEY `order_id_key` (`order_id`)
    -> );
Query OK, 0 rows affected (1.54 sec)

mysql> CREATE TABLE `shop`.`order_details` (
    ->    `id` bigint NOT NULL AUTO_INCREMENT,
    ->    `book_id` int NOT NULL,
    ->    `title` varchar(70) NOT NULL,
    ->    `author` varchar(70) DEFAULT NULL,
    ->    `quantity` int NOT NULL,
    ->    `price` double NOT NULL,
    ->    `order_id` bigint NOT NULL,
    ->    PRIMARY KEY (`id`),
    ->    KEY `order_details_id_key` (`id`),
    ->    CONSTRAINT `book_id` FOREIGN KEY (`book_id`) REFERENCES `books`
          (`book_id`),
    ->    CONSTRAINT `order_id` FOREIGN KEY (`order_id`) REFERENCES `orders`
          (`order_id`)
    -> );
Query OK, 0 rows affected (1.51 sec)

mysql>
```

Now that the database is in place, insert book categories and book records using the script shop_populate.sql by copying everything and pasting onto the console. The file is shown in Listing 4-7.

Listing 4-7. shop_populate.sql

```
INSERT INTO `shop`.`categories` (`category_id`, `category_name`) VALUES
('1', 'Web Development');
INSERT INTO `shop`.`categories` (`category_id`, `category_name`) VALUES
('2', 'Science Fiction');
INSERT INTO `shop`.`categories` (`category_id`, `category_name`) VALUES
('3', 'Historical Mysteries');
INSERT INTO `shop`.`books` (`book_id`, `title`, `author`, `price`,
`category_id`) VALUES ('1', 'MYSQL 8 Query Performance Tuning', 'Jesper
Wisborg Krogh', '34.31', '1');
INSERT INTO `shop`.`books` (`book_id`, `title`, `author`, `price`,
`category_id`) VALUES ('2', 'JavaScript Next', 'Raju Gandhi', '36.70', '1');
INSERT INTO `shop`.`books` (`book_id`, `title`, `author`, `price`, `category_
id`) VALUES ('3', 'The Complete Robot', 'Isaac Asimov', '12.13', '2');
INSERT INTO `shop`.`books` (`book_id`, `title`, `author`, `price`,
`category_id`) VALUES ('4', 'Foundation and Earth', 'Isaac Asimov',
'11.07', '2');
INSERT INTO `shop`.`books` (`book_id`, `title`, `author`, `price`,
`category_id`) VALUES ('5', 'The Da Vinci Code', 'Dan Brown', '7.99', '3');
INSERT INTO `shop`.`books` (`book_id`, `title`, `author`, `price`,
`category_id`) VALUES ('6', 'A Column of Fire', 'Ken Follett', '6.99', '3');
```

To execute the SQL script, you can also use the Workbench introduced in Chapter 1. The first thing is to launch Workbench and go to SCHEMAS tab. Now, as shown in Figure 4-1, right-click and select "Create Schema…" on the context menu. If the "shop" database exists, right-click it, select "Drop Schema…", and delete it.

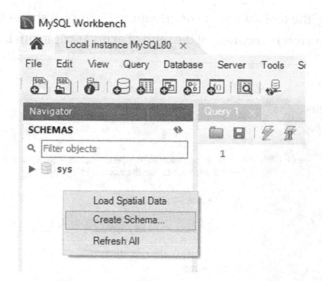

Figure 4-1. *MySQL workbench—how to create a new schema*

Now create the Schema. Type "shop" in the name input and click "apply", as shown in Figure 4-2.

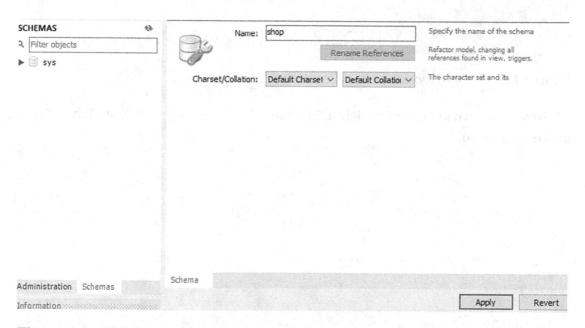

Figure 4-2. *MySQL workbench—creating a new schema*

Before applying, the tool asks for a confirmation. Figure 4-3 shows the final window that confirms the (correct) execution of the (and of every) script with its log.

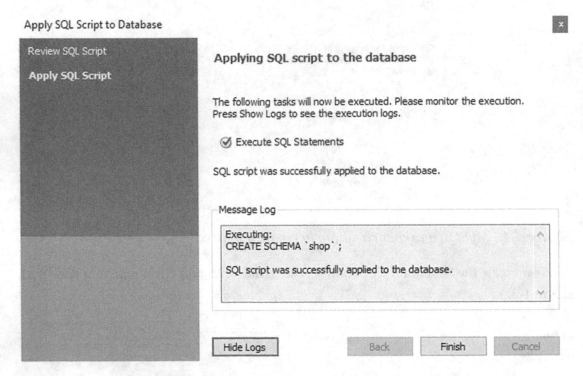

Figure 4-3. *MySQL workbench—execution of a script*

Now, as shown in Figure 4-4, right-click "Tables" label and select "Create Table..." in the context menu.

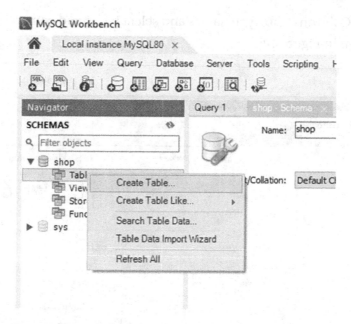

Figure 4-4. *MySQL workbench—how to create a new table*

Type "categories" in the name input as shown in Figure 4-5.

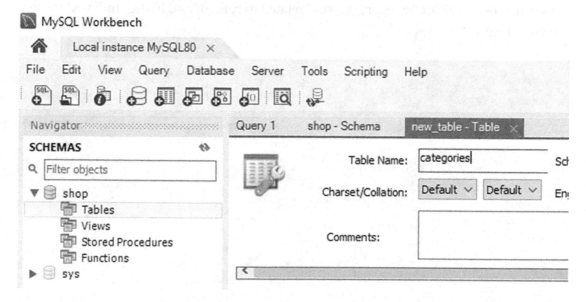

Figure 4-5. *MySQL workbench—creating a new table*

Now, in the "Columns" tab, type names and select types and constraints in the input columns as shown in Figure 4-6.

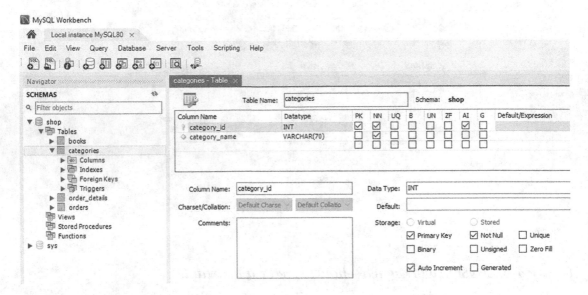

Figure 4-6. *MySQL workbench—creating columns in a table*

Then, type the index "category_id_key" related to category_id in the "Indexes" tab as shown in Figure 4-7.

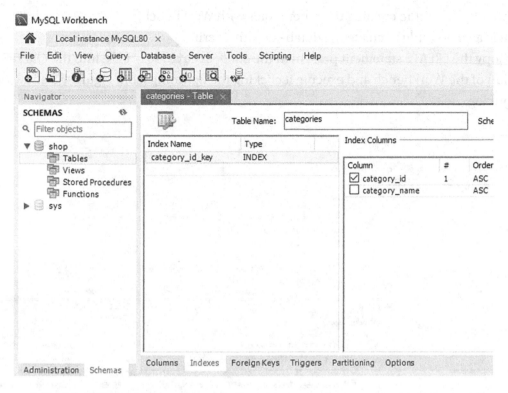

***Figure 4-7.** MySQL workbench—creating a new index*

At the end, click "apply" for applying SQL script to the database. Then, after a control, the script is executed. It is possible to create the other tables in this way.

Figure 4-8 shows how to create a foreign key (in this case, for *books* table): type the name "category_id"—related to categories table—in the "Foreign Keys" tab.

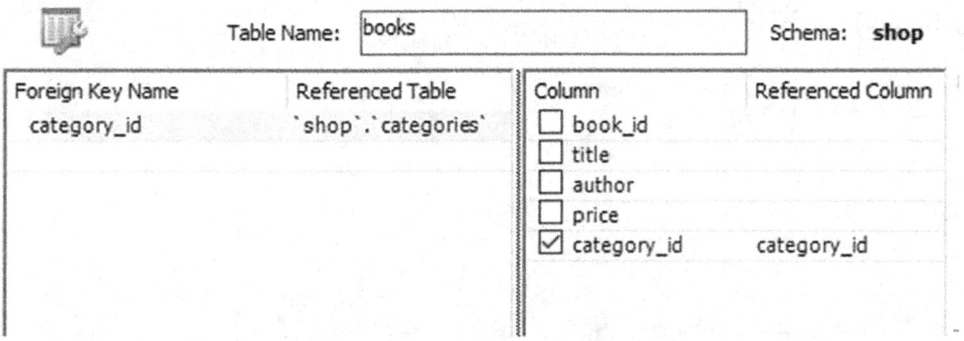

***Figure 4-8.** MySQL workbench—creating a foreign key*

You can continue creating the other tables with Workbench.

It is also possible to create the database with a script.

Copy the CREATE statement present in the shop_create.sql file into the *Query* section of the Workbench and execute it clicking the lightning icon. Figure 4-9 shows the output log.

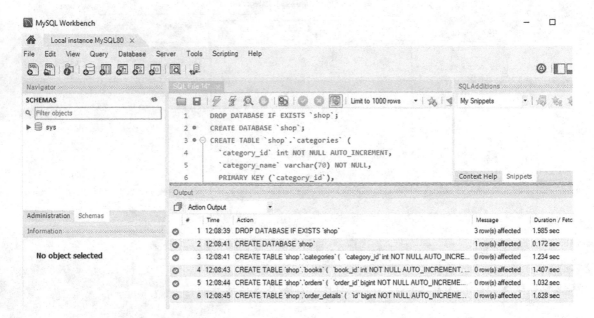

Figure 4-9. *MySQL workbench—creating the shop database*

Now that the database is in place, insert book categories and book records by using the MySQL Workbench, as shown in Figure 4-10. Select the table categories ➤, click the grid icon ➤, and insert category *names* and *id* in the new lines of the result grid (as in spreadshetets).

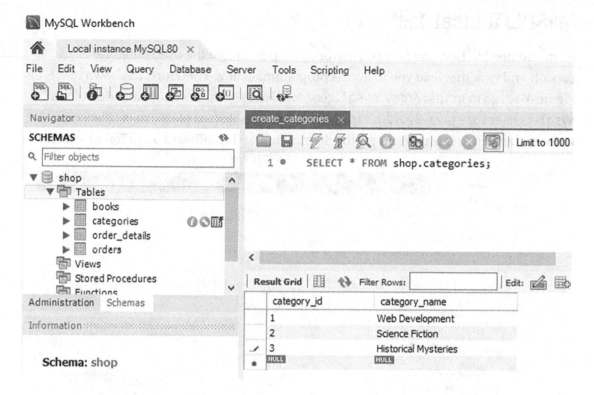

Figure 4-10. *Workbench—list of all categories*

Do the same for books table. At last, the query "select * from books;" will list all the books you have inserted, as shown in Figure 4-11.

book_id	title	author	price	category_id
1	MYSQL 8 Query Performance Tuning	Jesper Wisborg Krogh	34.31	1
2	JavaScript Next	Raju Gandhi	36.7	1
3	The Complete Robot	Isaac Asimov	12.13	2
4	Foundation and Earth	Isaac Asimov	11.07	2
5	The Da Vinci Code	Dan Brown	7.99	3
6	A Column of Fire	Ken Follett	6.99	3
NULL	NULL	NULL	NULL	NULL

Figure 4-11. *List of all books*

MySQL/Tomcat Test

First, you need to have the Java connector corresponding to the used database version and type that lead you to access programmatically. Therefore, as shown in Figure 4-12, go to `https://dev.mysql.com/downloads/connector/j/` and download `mysql-connector-java-8.0.20.zip`. Ensure that the selected platform is "Platform Independent": this is important for the distribution of the software on different systems.

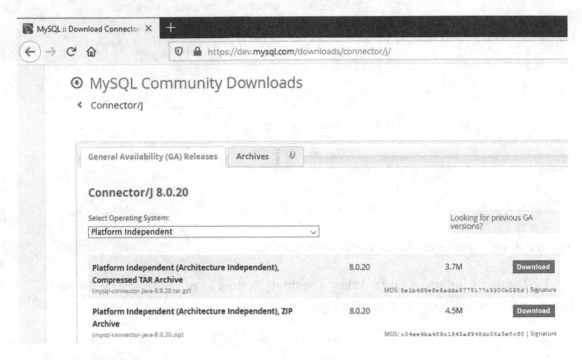

Figure 4-12. *MySQL Connector download page*

To install a JDBC, you can copy the JAR file in the lib folder of your web application, or better, you can copy its JAR file (mysql-connector-java-8.0.19.jar) into `%CATALINA_HOME%\lib\`. In the second case, you avoid an eventually memory lack of the server, while in the first case, you can use the application in different environments, without updating the lib folder of the servers.

To be sure that everything works, you still need to check that you can access the database from Tomcat using JSP. That is, the Tomcat is able to use the JDBC connector. To do so, you can use the JSP page shown in Listing 4-8, which lists all books in the database.

Listing 4-8. jdbc.jsp

```
01   <%@page language="java" contentType="text/html"%>
02   <%@page import="java.sql.*"%>
03   <html><head><title>JDBC test</title></head><body>
04   <%
05     Class.forName("com.mysql.cj.jdbc.Driver");
06     Connection conn = DriverManager.getConnection(
07         "jdbc:mysql://localhost:3306/shop", "root", "root");
08     Statement stmt = conn.createStatement();
09     ResultSet rs = stmt.executeQuery("select * from books");
10   %><table border= "1"><%
11     ResultSetMetaData resMetaData = rs.getMetaData();
12     int nCols = resMetaData.getColumnCount();
13   %><tr><%
14     for (int kCol = 1; kCol <= nCols; kCol++) {
15       out.print("<td><b>" + resMetaData.getColumnName(kCol) +
         "</b></td>");
16     }
17   %></tr><%
18     while (rs.next()) {
19       %><tr><%
20       for (int kCol = 1; kCol <= nCols; kCol++) {
21         out.print("<td>" + rs.getString(kCol) + "</td>");
22       }
23       %></tr><%
24     }
25   %></table><%
26     conn.close();
27   %>
28   </body></html>
```

Here is how `jdbc.jsp` obtains the list of books from the database and then displays them:

05:	Load JDBC to connect to the database server.
06-07:	Connect to the database.
08:	Create an empty statement to query the database.
09:	Execute the query to list all books and store the result set into a local variable.
11:	Obtain information on the structure of the result set.
12:	Obtain the number of columns of the result set.
13-17:	Display the column names.
18-23:	List the books one per row.
26:	Close the connection to the database server.

Don't worry if things are not completely clear. Later in the next chapter, I will explain in detail how you access a database from Java. For the time being, I just want to give you an example of how you can test database connectivity with a simple JSP page.

To execute the page, create a simple web project "conn" as shown in Chapter 1: copy the code in a new jsp page and the jdbc driver in the lib directory. Figure 4-13 shows how the generated page appears in a web browser.

book_id	title	author	price	category_id
1	MYSQL 8 Query Performance Tuning	Jesper Wisborg Krogh	34.31	1
2	JavaScript Next	Raju Gandhi	36.7	1
3	The Complete Robot	Isaac Asimov	12.13	2
4	Foundation and Earth	Isaac Asimov	11.07	2
5	The Da Vinci Code	Dan Brown	7.99	3
6	A Column of Fire	Ken Follett	6.99	3

Figure 4-13. *jdbc.jsp output*

In a more realistic situation, you would replace the category identifiers with the category names, but I want to keep this first example as simple as possible.

There is one thing, though, that deserves a comment: it is bad practice to hard-code in a page the name of the database, of the user ID, and of the access password. Sooner or later, you might need to change one of those parameters, and the last thing you want to do is to go through all your pages to do it. The initialization parameters exist precisely to avoid such error-prone procedure.

First, you need to include the parameter definitions in the web.xml file that's inside the WEB-INF folder of your application's root directory. You need to insert the lines shown in Listing 4-9 within the body of the web-app element.

Listing 4-9. web.xml Fragment to Define Initialization Parameters

```
<context-param>
  <param-name>dbName</param-name>
  <param-value>my-database-name</param-value>
  </context-param>
<context-param>
  <param-name>dbUser</param-name>
  <param-value>my-userID</param-value>
  </context-param>
<context-param>
  <param-name>dbPass</param-name>
  <param-value>my-password</param-value>
  </context-param>
```

In the example, my-database-name would be jdbc:mysql://localhost:3306/shop, and my-userID and my-password would be root.

To access the parameters from within any JSP page, you then just need to type something like the following:

```
String dbName = application.getInitParameter("dbName");
String dbUser = application.getInitParameter("dbUser");
String dbPass = application.getInitParameter("dbPass");
```

After that, you can replace lines 6 and 7 of the example with

```
Connection conn = DriverManager.getConnection(dbName, dbUser, dbPass);
```

You can modify the jdbc.jsp or create a new file (I created a new jdbcParam.jsp).

Database Architecture

In some cases, a database might contain a small amount of data, have a simple structure, and reside together with the application software on a home PC. In other cases, at the higher end of the scale, it might hold millions of records, have a data structure of great complexity, and run on a cluster of powerful servers.

In any case, regardless of size, environment, and complexity, the DBMS is organized around the client/server architecture. The system on which your DB resides is the *server*, and the system from which you need to access your DB is the *client*, even when they're one and the same PC. Therefore, in order to be able to work with data and a data structure, you first have to establish a connection from the client to the database on the server. To be able to do so, you need the following three pieces of information:

- The URL of your server

- A user ID that allows you to access the DB

- The password that goes together with the user ID

Once you establish the connection, you can then begin to manipulate the DB structure and its content via SQL statements. Be aware that although you need to provide a user ID and password when you connect to the server, this doesn't automatically mean that a user has access to all databases on the same server. You can (and, in most cases, should) allow access to specific databases to some users and not others. In fact, you can define one or more new users for each new database you create and group them according to the capabilities they are required to have (i.e., database administrators, developers, etc.). This ensures total confidentiality of data when several users share a database server. It's good practice to define different users for different applications so that you don't risk "cross-polluting" data.

To design a web application for the created database, you basically associate each Java class to a table that represents the data you need to store permanently. Each column of your table then becomes an attribute of your class. In a sense, to express it in OO terminology, each row corresponds to an instantiation of your class containing different data. For example, the Java class shown in Listing 4-10 is modeled to reflect book categories.

Listing 4-10. Category.java

```java
package eshop.beans;

public class Category {
  private int id;
  private String name;

  public Category(int id, String name) {
    this.id = id;
    this.name = name;
    }

  public int getId() { return id; }
  public void setId(int id) { this.id = id; }

  public String getName() { return name; }
  public void setName(String name) { this.name = name; }
  }
```

Accordingly, to store data in the shop database, you can use different SQL insert statements. Each SQL statement consists of a verb that defines the operation to be done, the identifier of the object operated on, and one or more operation parameters, often enclosed in parentheses. For example, use this code, which stores a new record in the database:

```sql
INSERT INTO `shop`.`categories` (`category_id`, `category_name`) VALUES
('3', 'Historical Mysteries');
```

Incidentally, be aware that SQL, contrary to Java, is not case-sensitive.

Use the powerful select SQL statement to read data. It lets you create complex queries that include sorting the data. Here's a simple example:

```sql
SELECT category_id,category_name FROM shop.categories WHERE category_id=
```

To retrieve all columns of a table, you replace the comma-separated list of columns with an asterisk. The WHERE clause can consist of several conditions composed by means of logical operators.

You use the UPDATE statement to modify row contents:

```sql
UPDATE shop.categories SET category_name='Science Fiction'    WHERE
category_id=2
```

Using DELETE, you can remove rows:

```
DELETE FROM shop.categories WHERE category_id > '3';
```

You can also operate on the data structure. To do so, you use the alter statement, as in the following example:

```
alter table categories add new_column_name column-definition;
```

This lets you add a column to an existing table. If you replace add with modify or drop, the alter statement will let you redefine a column or remove it.

In general, the SQL statements are grouped depending on their purposes. Table 4-5 gives you a summary of their classification.

Table 4-5. *Classification of SQL Statements*

Group	Description
Data Definition Language (DDL)	Statements used to define the DB structure (e.g., create, alter, drop, and rename)
Data Manipulation Language (DML)	Statements used to manage data (e.g., select, insert, update, and delete)
Data Control Language (DCL)	Statements used to control access to the data (e.g., grant, used to give access rights to a user, and revoke, used to withdraw them)
Transaction ControL (TCL)	Statements used to group together DML statements into logical transactions (e.g., commit and rollback)

In the next chapter, I'll explain how to execute any SQL statement, but we'll concentrate mainly on DML.

Summary

In this chapter, I introduced you to working with databases and SQL. Then I introduced you to Eshop application and I guided you to the design of its database and to its creation with MySQL tools. At last, I explained how to access databases from a simple JSP.

CHAPTER 5

Eshop Application

In the first three chapters, you learned a large portion of JSP's components through brief examples, while in the fourth chapter you were introduced to the Eshop application and implemented the database. In this chapter, I will tell you how everything fits together in complex applications.

The insertion of Java code into HTML modules opens up the possibility of building dynamic web pages, but to say that it is possible doesn't mean you can do it efficiently and effectively. If you start developing complex applications exclusively by means of scripting elements, you'll rapidly reach the point where the code will become difficult to maintain. The key problem with mixing Java and HTML, as in "Hello World!", is that the application logic and the way the information is presented in the browser are mixed. Often, the business application designers and the web-page designers are different people with complementary and only partially overlapping skills. While application designers are experts in complex algorithms and databases, web designers focus on page composition and graphics. The architecture of your JSP-based applications should reflect this distinction. The last thing you want to do is blur the roles within the development team and end up with everybody doing what somebody else is better qualified to do. And even if you develop everything yourself, by keeping presentation and application logic separate, you will build more stable and more maintainable applications.

A Better Online Bookshop

The online bookshop you saw in Chapter 3 was a good introduction to the MVC architecture, but in order to explore the use of the database created in Chapter 4, other JSP features, and JSF, we need an example with more substance.

© Luciano Manelli and Giulio Zambon 2020
L. Manelli and G. Zambon, *Beginning Jakarta EE Web Development*,
https://doi.org/10.1007/978-1-4842-5866-8_5

Importing Eshop WAR File into Eclipse

You will find the code of the whole project in the software package for this chapter, and the easiest way to work on the application is to import it into Eclipse.

The first step is to select the menu item Import... in the File menu. When the Select dialog opens, scroll down to the folder named Web, open it, select WAR file, and click Next >, as shown in Figure 5-1.

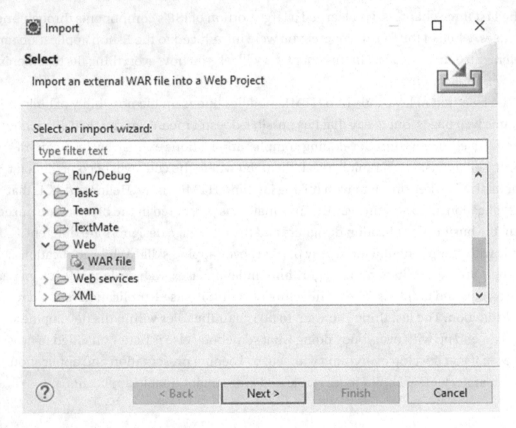

Figure 5-1. *Eclipse—selecting to import a WAR file*

When the next dialog comes up, browse to select eshop.war and click Finish. Eclipse will create the eshop project for you.

The Customer Interface

To launch the application, start Tomcat from Eclipse and view on your browser the URL http://localhost:8080/eshop/shop. Figure 5-2 shows eshop's home page. The top section includes a link to the shopping cart, while the sidebar on the left features a search box and a list of categories. The other pages only differ in the central panel, which in the home page contains a welcome message.

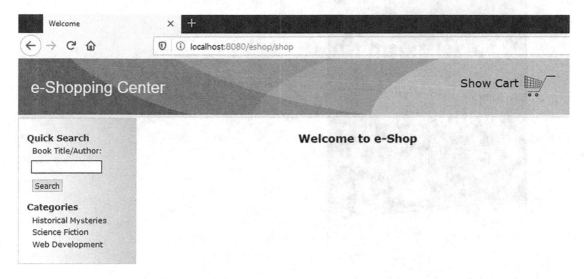

Figure 5-2. *E-shop's home page*

Figure 5-3 shows the panel containing the list of books in a category.

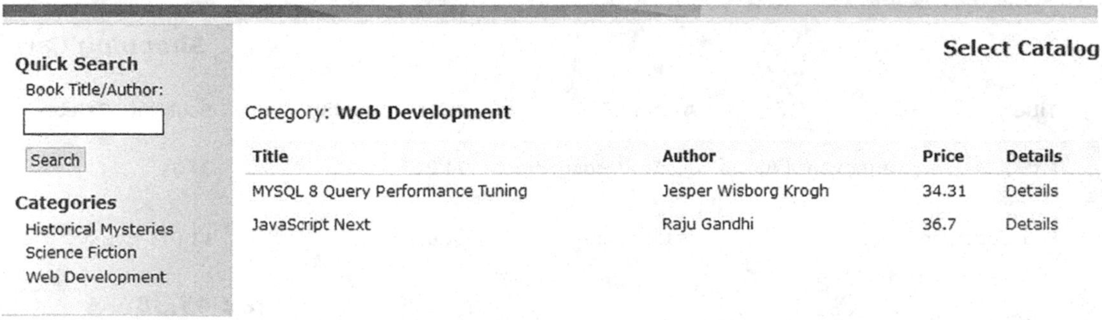

Figure 5-3. *A book category on E-shop*

Figure 5-4 shows the details of a book.

Figure 5-4.   *A book's details on E-shop*

Figure 5-5 shows the shopping cart with a couple of items.

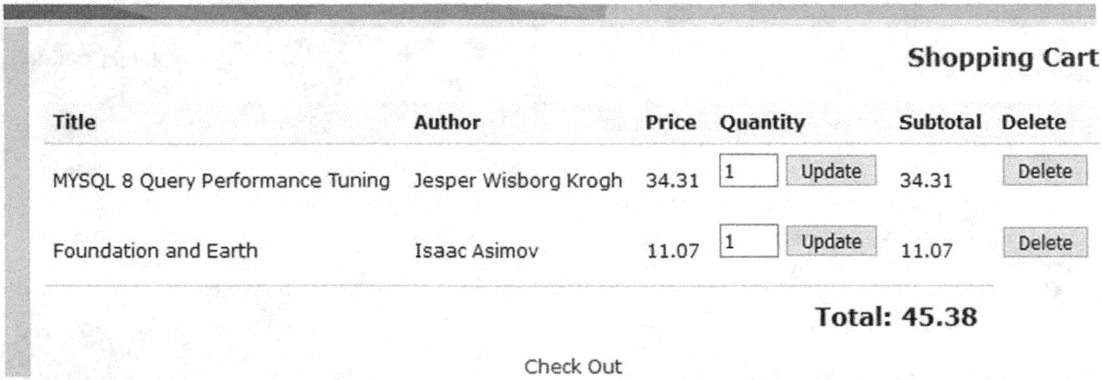

Figure 5-5.   *E-shop's shopping cart*

Pretty straightforward, isn't it?

The E-shop Architecture

E-shop is an MVC application. The data and the business logic (the model) reside in a database and Java classes; the user interface (the view) is implemented in JSP; and the handler of client requests (the controller) is an HTTP Java servlet.

When the servlet receives a client HTTP request, it instantiates the model's central class and forwards the request to the appropriate JSP page. The JSP page obtains data from the model and generates the HTML response. The model isn't aware of what the JSP pages do with the data it provides, and the JSP pages aren't aware of where and how the model keeps the data.

The Model

The central model class is called DataManager. Its purpose is to hide all database operations from the JSP pages. DataManager supports some methods that have to do with initialization and connecting to the database. Table 5-1 lists the methods that implement the business logic of the application.

Table 5-1. *DataManager Methods*

Type	Method
String	getCategoryName(int categoryId)
Hashtable	getCategories()
ArrayList	getSearchResults(String keyword)
ArrayList	getBooksInCategory(String categoryId)
Book	getBookDetails(int bookId)
long	insertOrder(String contactName, String deliveryAddress, String ccName, String ccNumber, String ccExpiryDate, Hashtable shoppingCart)

Their purpose should be pretty clear. I would just like to make a couple of points concerning `insertOrder`. First, the value it returns is the order ID to be given back to the client. Second, in a more realistic case, all parameters, with the exception of the shopping cart, would be replaced by a customer ID, typically the customer's email address. In this simple application, however, as it doesn't keep track of the customers, there are no permanent customer records and customer IDs.

The Controller

The controller servlet is named ShopServlet and extends javax.servlet.http.HttpServlet. As I introduced in Chapter 3, the @*WebServlet* annotation on top of the class declares the servlet under the name of eshop.ShopServlet, where eshop is the package of the servlet and the context of the application, with a URL mapping of http://<server>:<port>/eshop/shop:

```
@WebServlet(name = "ShopServlet", urlPatterns = {"/shop/*"})
```

Annotations were introduced in the Servlet API 3.0 (javax.servlet.annotation package) and make your life easier, because everything regarding a servlet is mapped in the servlet class (i.e., configuration and source code in the same place): if you use annotations, the deployment descriptor (web.xml) could be not required. First, when you create a servlet, you want to map it to some URL without going to another file to add the mapping. Moreover, using annotations, you do not need repeating same names in different files making mistakes, or renaming a servlet class forgetting to rename it in the web.xml: in these cases, you only discover the mistake at deployment time.

It is also possible to use annotations to set init parameters, but I suggest you do not, because if you use annotations to set up init parameters, you need to recompile your application every time a parameter is changed. In this case, the use of a deployment descriptor is better. Moreover, these two approaches are not mutually exclusive: for example, you can use annotations on servlet to define URL patterns or others fixed parameters and define database configuration in the web.xml (changing them without having to modify the code).

Servlet Initialization

Tomcat executes the servlet method `init` immediately after instantiating the servlet (see Listing 5-1).

Listing 5-1. ShopServlet.java—init Method

```
public void init(ServletConfig config) throws ServletException {
  System.out.println("*** initializing controller servlet.");
  super.init(config);

  DataManager dataManager = new DataManager();
  dataManager.setDbUrl(config.getInitParameter("dbUrl"));
  dataManager.setDbUserName(config.getInitParameter("dbUserName"));
  dataManager.setDbPassword(config.getInitParameter("dbPassword"));

  ServletContext context = config.getServletContext();
  context.setAttribute("base", config.getInitParameter("base"));
  context.setAttribute("imageUrl", config.getInitParameter("imageUrl"));
  context.setAttribute("dataManager", dataManager);

  try {  // load the database JDBC driver
    Class.forName(config.getInitParameter("jdbcDriver"));
    }
  catch (ClassNotFoundException e) {
    System.out.println(e.toString());
    }
  }
```

As you can see, the initialization consists of three main activities: instantiating and configuring the data manager, saving some parameters for later use by the JSP pages (remember that JSP can access the servlet context via the implicit variable `application`), and loading the driver necessary to access the database—JDBC stands for Java DataBase Connector.

Notice that all these activities are done by setting servlet context attributes to values obtained through this method:

```
config.getInitParameter("init-parameter-name")
```

These values are stored in the `WEB-INF\web.xml` file, as shown in Listing 5-2.

Listing 5-2. Partial web.xml

```
<web-app ...>
  ...
  <servlet>
    ...
    <init-param>
      <param-name>dbUrl</param-name>
      <param-value>jdbc:mysql://localhost:3306/shop</param-value>
      </init-param>
    ...
    </servlet>
  ...
  <web-app ...>
```

Table 5-2 shows the initialization parameters defined for this application.

Table 5-2. *Servlet Initialization Parameters*

Name	Value
base	/eshop/shop
imageUrl	/eshop/images/
jdbcDriver	com.mysql.jdbc.Driver
dbUrl	jdbc:mysql://localhost:3306/shop
dbUserName	root
dbPassword	root

The initialization parameter values associated with the database are explained in Chapter 4.

From Chapter 2, you know that Tomcat makes available to JSP the servlet context by defining the implicit object `application`. Therefore, for example, the value set in `ShopServlet.init()` with `context.setAttribute("imageUrl", ...)` is available to JSP as the value returned by `application.getAttribute("imageUrl")`.

Request Handling

Depending on what the user does, the page currently being displayed in the browser sends to the servlet a request with a specific value of the `action` parameter. The servlet then forwards each request to a JSP page determined by that value. For example, the page that shows the shopping cart also includes a button to check out. If the user clicks it, the page will send to the servlet a request with the `action` parameter set to `"checkOut"`.

The View

Table 5-3 shows the list of all JSP pages in the application. I will explain them in the next chapters, as we look at the different aspects of the application.

Table 5-3. *JSP Pages*

Name	Function	Mode of Access
index.jsp	The initial page welcoming a new user	
LeftMenu.jsp	Standard page sidebar	Included in all non-menu pages
TopMenu.jsp	Standard page header	Included in all non-menu pages
SelectCatalog.jsp	Lists books of a category	LeftMenu.jsp
SearchOutcome.jsp	Lists books selected through a search	LeftMenu.jsp
BookDetails.jsp	Shows the details of one book	SelectCatalog.jsp and SearchOutcome.jsp
ShoppingCart.jsp	Displays the shopping cart	TopMenu.jsp and ShoppingCart.jsp
Checkout.jsp	Requests a customer's payment data	ShoppingCart.jsp
OrderConfirmation.jsp	Confirms acceptance of an order	Checkout.jsp

Additionally, you have a style-sheet file named `eshop.css`.
A typical user session proceeds as follows:

1. The user starts by accessing `http://your-web-site/eshop/shop` and sees the welcome page with a left-side menu containing a search box and a list of book categories. The user then can

   - Type a word in the search box and hit the `Search` button, or select a book category.

   - Select one of the books by clicking the corresponding `Details` link. The application then replaces the list of books with an image of the front cover of the book and all the information available in the database about that book.

   - Add the book to the shopping cart. The application then automatically takes the user to the shopping cart, where it is possible to update the number of copies or delete the book entry.

   - Repeat the previous steps until the user is ready to submit the order. From the shopping cart page, the user can then click the `Check Out` link.

2. The checkout page asks the user to provide his or her personal and financial data. When the user clicks the `Confirm Order` button, the page tells the application to memorize the order.

At any time, the user can add books through the left-side menu or go to the shopping cart through the top-side menu to modify the order.

The E-shop Database Access

You operate on databases by executing SQL statements. To do so from within Java/JSP, you need an API consisting of several interfaces, classes, and method definitions included in the class libraries of JDK. Additionally, you also need a driver that implements that API for the specific DBMS (i.e., MySQL) in the native code of your system (i.e., a Windows PC).

Connecting to the Database

The first step to access a database from Java is to load the driver, without which nothing will work. To do so, you execute the method `Class.forName("com.mysql.jdbc. Driver")` in the `init` method of the servlet (see Listing 5-1).

To be able to switch from MySQL to other DBMSs without much effort, I stored the driver name in an `init` parameter defined in `WEB-INF\web.xml` as follows:

```
<init-param>
  <param-name>jdbcDriver</param-name>
  <param-value>com.mysql.cj.jdbc.Driver</param-value>
</init-param>
```

This way, you can load it as follows when initializing the servlet:

```
java.lang.Class.forName(config.getInitParameter("jdbcDriver"));
```

Once you load the driver, you also need to connect to the database before you can access its content. In the E-shop application, you do this by executing a data manager (of type `DataManager`, defined in `WEB-INF\classes\eshop\model\DataManager.java`) method, as shown in the following line of code:

```
java.sql.Connection connection = dataManager.getConnection();
```

The data manager's `getConnection` method, in turn, obtains the connection from the JDBC driver, as shown in the fragment in Listing 5-3.

Listing 5-3. The DataManager.getConnection Method

```
public Connection getConnection() {
  Connection conn = null;
  try {
    conn = DriverManager.getConnection(getDbURL(), getDbUserName(),
    getDbPassword());
    }
  catch (SQLException e) {
    System.out.println("Could not connect to DB: " + e.getMessage());
    }
  return conn;
  }
```

To be able to change the database, the user ID, or the password without having to rebuild the application, you define them in servlet initialization parameters as you did for the name of the JDBC driver and as I showed earlier in this chapter:

```
dbURL: jdbc:mysql://localhost:3306/shop
dbUserName: root
dbPassword: root
```

Port 3306 is the default for MySQL and can be configured differently. Obviously, in real life, you would use a different user and, most importantly, define a secure password.

Once you finish working with a database, you should always close the connection by executing `connection.close()`. E-shop does it via another data manager's method, as shown in Listing 5-4.

Listing 5-4. The DataManager.putConnection Method

```
public void putConnection(Connection conn) {
  if (conn != null) {
    try { conn.close(); }
    catch (SQLException e) { }
    }
  }
```

Before you can start hacking at your database, you still need to create an object of type `java.sql.Statement`, as it is through the methods of that object that you execute SQL statements. Use this code to create a statement:

```
Statement stmt = connection.createStatement();
```

Once you're done with one statement, you should release it immediately with `stmt.close()`, because it takes a non-negligible amount of space, and you want to be sure that it doesn't hang around while your page does other things.

Accessing Data

The `Statement` class has many methods, plus some more inherited ones. Nevertheless, two methods are likely to satisfy most of your needs: `executeQuery` and `executeUpdate`.

The executeQuery Method

You use this method to execute a `select` SQL statement, like this:

```
String sql = "select book_id, title, author from books where category_id=1"
    + " order by author, title";
ResultSet rs = stmt.executeQuery(sql);
```

In the example, the method returns in the variable `rs` of type `java.sql.ResultSet` all the books in category 1, sorted by author name and title. The rows in the result set only contain the columns specified in the `select` statement, which in this example are `book_id`, `title`, and `author`.

At any given time, you can only access the row of the result set pointed to by the so-called *cursor*, and by default you can only move the cursor forward. The usual way of accessing the rows of the result set is to start from the first one and "go down" in sequence. For example, with the `shop` database, the following code:

```
while (rs.next()) {
  out.println(rs.getString(3) + ", " + rs.getString(2) + "<br/>");
  }
```

would produce the following output:

```
Jesper Wisborg Krogh, MYSQL 8 Query Performance Tuning
Raju Gandhi, JavaScript Next
```

The `next` method moves the cursor down one row. After the cursor goes past the last row, `next()` returns `false`, and the `while` loop terminates. Initially, the cursor is positioned *before* the first row. Therefore, you have to execute `next()` once in order to access the very first row.

Besides `next()`, there are other methods that let you reposition your cursor. Five of them return a `boolean` such as `next()`, which returns `true` if the cursor points to a row. They are `absolute(`*row-position*`)`, `first()`, `last()`, `previous()`, and `relative(`*number-of-rows*`)`. The `beforeFirst()` and `afterLast()` methods also move the cursor but are of type `void`, because they always succeed. The `isBeforeFirst()`, `isFirst()`, `isLast()`, and `isAfterLast()` methods check whether the cursor is in the corresponding positions, while `getRow()` returns the position of the row currently pointed to by the cursor.

Keep in mind that in order to be able to move the cursor around, you have to specify a couple of attributes when you create the statement, that is, *before* you actually execute the query. This is how you do it:

```
Statement stmt = connection.createStatement(
  ResultSet.TYPE_SCROLL_INSENSITIVE,
  ResultSet.CONCUR_READ_ONLY
  );
```

`ResultSet.TYPE_SCROLL_INSENSITIVE` is what allows you to move the cursor forth and back within the result set. This parameter can only have one of the following two other values: `ResultSet.TYPE_FORWARD_ONLY` (the default) and `ResultSet.TYPE_SCROLL_SENSITIVE`. The difference between `SENSITIVE` and `INSENSITIVE` is that with `INSENSITIVE`, you're not affected by changes made to the result set while you're working with it (more about this in a moment). This is probably what you want.

`ResultSet.CONCUR_READ_ONLY` states that you don't want to modify the result set. This is the default, and it makes sense in most cases. The alternative is to specify `ResultSet.CONCUR_UPDATABLE`, which allows you to insert, delete, and modify result rows. Now you can see why you might like to use `ResultSet.TYPE_SCROLL_SENSITIVE` as the first parameter: it lets you see the modifications made to the result set after you started working with it, rather than showing how it was before those changes. On the other hand, in a complex application with several threads operating on the same result set, you'll probably prefer to ignore the changes made in other threads. In such a situation, it would have to be 100 percent clear which thread would be allowed to modify which rows; otherwise, you'd end up with a mess.

`ResultSet` provides several methods for retrieving a column value in different formats, given a column position or its label. For example, the following two methods will return the same value:

```
long bookID = rs.getLong(1);
long bookID = rs.getLong("book_id");
```

The column position refers to the columns specified in the `select` statement. Notice that the column numbering begins with 1, not with 0 as is customary in Java. There are many available types (Array, BigDecimal, Blob, boolean, byte, int, long, ecc.), for most of which exists a corresponding update method, which lets you modify a column.

For example, the following code writes "Joe Bloke" in the author column of the current row of the result set:

```
rs.updateString("author", "Joe Bloke");
```

Note that there are no update methods for the types InputStream, Reader, and URL. You can also set a column to null with the methods updateNull(*column-index*) and updateNull(*column-label*).

ResultSet provides more than two dozen additional methods that let you do things such as transfer changes from an updated result set to the actual database or refresh a row that somebody else might have modified in the actual database after you performed the query. One method that you might find useful returns the column position in your result set given its name:

```
int findColumn(column-label)
```

The result set is automatically disposed of when the corresponding statement is closed. Therefore, you don't really need to execute rs.close(), as long as you immediately close the statement when you no longer need it.

The executeUpdate Method

You can use this method to execute the SQL statements insert, update, and delete. For example, if you want to add a new book category to the E-shop example, you do something like this:

```
String sql = "insert into categories (category_id, category_name)"
    + " values (4, 'Comic Books')";
stmt.executeUpdate(sql);
```

You don't need to define all the columns, because the undefined fields are set automatically to their corresponding default values. That said, as I haven't specified any default in the definition of the categories table, the following statement would result in the field category_name being set to null:

```
stmt.executeUpdate("insert into categories (category_id) values (4)");
```

To avoid this occurrence, I could have defined the category_name column with a default:

```
category_name varchar(70) default 'Miscellanea'
```

Transactions

In E-shop, I have defined two separate tables for data associated with a book order: one for the customer data and one for the individual books ordered. It would be bad if you completely lost an order, but perhaps it would be even worse if you lost some items and only processed a partial order. It would also be a problem if you saved the order details in the database but failed to save the customer data. That would leave some "orphaned" book items with no information concerning the buyer. You don't need to worry about this if you save the customer data first: then, by the time you start saving the order details, the customer record is already on disk. But how do you ensure that the database only contains complete orders?

Normally, when you execute an SQL `insert`, the data is immediately stored into the database. To ensure the completion of orders, you could keep track of the updates you've already successfully executed and reverse them if you cannot complete the whole order. However, this would be very complicated, and there would be no guarantee of success. Moreover, in a more complex application, there might be several operations proceeding simultaneously and causing the same database records to be accessed concurrently. The solution is a built-in, foolproof mechanism capable of ensuring that some complex transactions are done "in one shot" or not at all.

This mechanism is actually quite simple. It works like this:

1. Immediately after connecting to the DB with `conn = DriverManager.getConnection(...)`, execute `conn.setAutoCommit(false)`. This tells MySQL not to make permanent changes to the database until you confirm them.

2. Perform all the updates that form your complex transaction. Be sure that you place them inside a `try` block as part of a `try/catch` construct.

3. In the `catch` block, include the statement `conn.rollback()`. If one of the updates fails, an `SQLException` will be thrown, and when the `catch` block is executed, the `rollback` will cause MySQL to "forget" the uncommitted updates.

4. When all the updates have completed without being interrupted by any exception, execute `conn.commit()` to tell MySQL that it can finalize the updates.

The E-shop Data Model

All database operations are concentrated in the data model of an MVC architecture. JSP modules interact with the database by executing methods of the DataManager class, which accept and/or return data in the form of Java beans. By mediating DB access via the data manager and Java beans, you ensure that the view and the model can be developed independently.

Figure 5-6 shows the structure of the model.

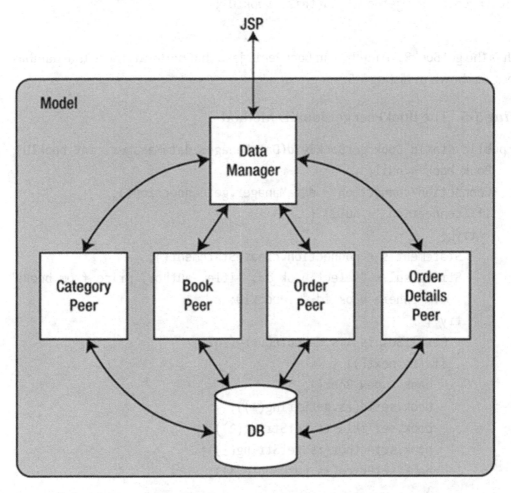

Figure 5-6. *The data model structure*

The DataManager class sets up and closes connections to the database; however, concerning table access, it only acts as a clearinghouse. Specific classes perform the actual operations on individual tables. In this way, you ensure that changes to individual tables have the minimum impact on the application. This is actually an example of the Java Enterprise Edition pattern called Data Access Object (DAO).

For example, the JSP page that displays the book details obtains the information concerning the requested book by executing the following method of the data manager:

```
public Book getBookDetails(int bookID) {
  return BookPeer.getBookById(this, bookID);
  }
```

It is the getBookByID method in BookPeer.java that performs the actual database access, as shown in Listing 5-5.

Listing 5-5. The BookPeer.getBookID Method

```
01: public static Book getBookById(DataManager dataManager, int bookID) {
02:    Book book = null;
03:    Connection connection = dataManager.getConnection();
04:    if (connection != null) {
05:      try {
06:        Statement s = connection.createStatement();
07:        String sql = "select book_id, title, author, price from books"
08:           + " where book_id=" + bookID;
09:        try {
10:          ResultSet rs = s.executeQuery(sql);
11:          if (rs.next()) {
12:            book = new Book();
13:            book.setId(rs.getString(1));
14:            book.setTitle(rs.getString(2));
15:            book.setAuthor(rs.getString(3));
16:            book.setPrice(rs.getDouble(4));
17:          }
18:        }
19:        finally { s.close(); }
20:      }
```

```
21:     catch (SQLException e) {
22:        System.out.println("Could not get book: " + e.getMessage());
23:        }
24:     finally {
25:        dataManager.putConnection(connection);
26:        }
27:     } return book;
28:   }
```

In line 03, you open the database connection by invoking a method of the data manager that also reports an error in case of failure. Then you start a `try` block where you do the actual work. In the corresponding `catch` block, you display an error message (line 22), and in the `finally` block (line 25), you close the DB connection. Remember that the `finally` block is executed whether the `try` succeeds or not. In this way, you ensure that the connection is closed in case of failure.

Inside the outermost `try` (lines 05–20), you create a statement and set up the query string before starting a second `try` block (lines 09–17). Similar to what you did concerning the connection, you use the `finally` block to close the statement (line 19).

This is a technique of general applicability: every time you do something that needs to be undone, take care of it immediately inside a `try` block by placing the "undoing" statement in the corresponding `finally`. In this way, you'll be sure not to leave any "ghosts" behind you. It's true that Java's garbage-collection mechanism should take care of removing unreferenced objects, but it's good practice to clean up behind yourself as you go, especially when you're dealing with databases and potentially large objects, such as statements and result sets. At the very least, your application will work more efficiently. And it feels good to write "clean" code.

Line 10 is where you actually execute the query. You know that you're not going to get more than one row in the result set, because the `book_id` is a unique key of the book table.

You might be thinking, "Why should I go through the data manager at all? Couldn't I simply execute the `BookPeer` method from JSP?" Well, you could, but it wouldn't be clean, and dirtiness sooner or later causes problems.

Furthermore, consider the more complex case in which you want to save an order. From the JSP point of view, you only want to call a method of the data manager that takes care of both the customer's data and the shopping cart. Behind the scenes, though, two different tables need to be updated: one for the orders and one for the order details.

Therefore, it makes a lot of sense to execute the overall transaction in the data manager (see Listing 5-6) while leaving the updates of individual tables to the peer classes.

Listing 5-6. The DataManager.insertOrder Method

```
public long insertOrder(Customer customer, Hashtable shoppingCart) {
  long returnValue = 0L;
  long orderId = System.currentTimeMillis();
  Connection connection = getConnection();
  if (connection != null) {
    Statement stmt = null;
    try {
      connection.setAutoCommit(false);
      stmt = connection.createStatement();
      try {
        OrderPeer.insertOrder(stmt, orderId, customer);
        OrderDetailsPeer.insertOrderDetails(stmt, orderId, shoppingCart);
        try { stmt.close(); }
        finally { stmt = null; }
        connection.commit();
        returnValue = orderId;
      }
      catch (SQLException e) {
        System.out.println("Could not insert order: " + e.getMessage());
        try { connection.rollback(); }
        catch (SQLException ee) { }
      }
    }
    catch (SQLException e) {
      System.out.println("Could not insert order: " + e.getMessage());
    }
    finally {
      if (stmt != null) {
        try { stmt.close(); }
        catch (SQLException e) { }
      }
```

```
    putConnection(connection);
    }
  }
  return returnValue;
}
```

The two lines in bold show you how the data manager asks the peer classes of the tables orders and order_details to do the update. Notice that you pass to them the same statement and order ID. Listing 5-7 shows insertOrder, one of the two methods that do the updates.

Listing 5-7. The OrderPeer.insertOrder Method

```
public static void insertOrder(Statement stmt, long orderId,
    Customer customer) throws SQLException {
  String sql = "insert into orders (order_id, delivery_name,"
      + " delivery_address, cc_name, cc_number, cc_expiry) values ('"
      + orderId + "','" + customer.getContactName() + "','"
      + customer.getDeliveryAddress() + "','"
      + customer.getCcName() + "','" + customer.getCcNumber()
      + "','" + customer.getCcExpiryDate() + "')"
      ;
  stmt.executeUpdate(sql);
}
```

Listing 5-8 shows the other method, insertOrderDetails.

Listing 5-8. The OrderDetailsPeer.insertOrderDetails Method

```
public static void insertOrderDetails(Statement stmt, long orderId,
    Hashtable shoppingCart) throws SQLException {
  String sql;
  Enumeration enumList = shoppingCart.elements();
  while (enumList.hasMoreElements()) {
    CartItem item = (CartItem)enumList.nextElement();
```

```
    sql = "insert into order_details (order_id, book_id, quantity,"
        + " price, title, author) values ('" + orderId + "','"
        + item.getBookID() + "','" + item.getQuantity() + "','"
        + item.getPrice() + "','" + item.getTitle() + "','"
        + item.getAuthor() + "')"
        ;
    stmt.executeUpdate(sql);
    }
}
```

The methods throw the SQL exception rather than catch it locally, so that the data manager's method catches it.

Summary

In this chapter, I described the E-shop project, which, in different versions, I will use to complete the description of JSP and to explain JSF. I showed you how to establish a connection, insert data, and perform queries. To complete the summary of essential DB operations, I also described how to group elementary updates into transactions.

In the next two chapters, I'll take you through the remaining functionality of JSP. In particular, the next chapter will be dedicated to the action elements. To do that, I will use simple dedicated examples and the relevant aspects of the eshop application.

CHAPTER 6

JSP in Action

In Chapter 2, you learned that there are three types of JSP elements: scripting, directives, and actions. I described the first two types directly in Chapter 2, and the time has come to look at JSP actions. Actions, like scriptlets, are processed when a page is requested. In this chapter, you will learn how to use JSP standard actions, how to create actions of your own design, and how to use some of the actions contained in the JSP Standard Tag Library. Besides small specific examples, you will also learn the role of actions in the eshop application that I introduced in the previous chapter. Actions can do everything that scripting elements can do, as you will see at the end of the next chapter, when I will tell you how to write JSP code without any scripting element at all.

JSP Standard Actions

While Tomcat executes directive elements when translating a page, it executes action elements when processing a client's HTTP request.

JSP actions specify activities to be performed when a page is requested and can therefore operate on objects and affect the response. They normally take the following form:

```
<jsp:action-name attr1="value1" [attr2="value2"...]> ... </jsp:action-name>
```

However, actions can also have a body, like in the following example:

```
<jsp:action-name attribute-list>
  <jsp:subaction-name subaction-attribute-list/>
  </jsp:action-name>
```

There are eight JSP standard actions (forward, include, useBean, setProperty, getProperty, element, text, and plugin) and five additional actions that can only appear in the body of other actions (param, params, attribute, body, and fallback).

© Luciano Manelli and Giulio Zambon 2020
L. Manelli and G. Zambon, *Beginning Jakarta EE Web Development*,
https://doi.org/10.1007/978-1-4842-5866-8_6

There are also two additional action elements—invoke and doBody—that you cannot invoke from within JSP pages. There is also a further standard action—root—that I will explain at the end of the next chapter.

Actions: forward, include, and param

The forward action lets you abort execution of the current page and transfer the request to another page:

```
<jsp:forward page="myOtherPage.jsp">
  <jsp:param name="newParName" value="newParValue"/>
  </jsp:forward>
```

The include action is similar to forward, the main difference being that it returns control to the including page after the included page has completed execution. The output of the included page is appended to the output generated by the including page up to the point where the action is executed.

As shown in the example, jsp:param lets you define a new parameter for the invoked page, which also has access to the parameters already available to the invoking page.

Here is another example of a forward action:

```
<% String dest = "/myJspPages/" + someVar; %>
<jsp:forward page="<%=dest%>">
  <jsp:param name="newParName" value="newParValue"/>
  </jsp:forward>
```

This is 100 percent equivalent to the following scriptlet:

```
<%
  String dest = "/myJspPages/" + someVar;
  RequestDispatcher rd = application.getRequestDispatcher(dest +
  "?newParName=newParValue");
  rd.forward(request, response);
%>
```

Tomcat clears the output buffer upon executing the forward action. Therefore, the HTML code generated up to that point by the current page is lost. But if the current page has already filled the response buffer by the time it is aborted with forward, that part of the response will have already left the server. This will probably result in a bad page sent to the client. Therefore, you have to be very careful when invoking forward from within a page that generates a large output.

You don't have to worry about such a problem with include, because Tomcat doesn't clear the output buffer when it executes that action.

With both forward and include, the destination page must be a well-formed and complete JSP page. The forward action must satisfy the additional requirement of generating a complete and valid HTML page, because the output of the destination page is what goes back to the client's browser in the HTML response. The destination page of an include action might even generate only a single character, although in most cases it provides HTML code. For example, the top bar of the eshop application is generated in the page TopMenu.jsp (see Listing 6-1) and included in seven JSP pages with this code:

```
<jsp:include page="TopMenu.jsp" flush="true"/>
```

The flush attribute (default false) ensures that the HTML generated so far by the including page is sent to the client before executing the included page. Note that the included page is not allowed to change the response headers or the status code.

Listing 6-1. TopMenu.jsp

```
<%@page language="java" contentType="text/html"%>
<%
  String base = (String)application.getAttribute("base");
  String imageUrl = (String)application.getAttribute("imageUrl");
  %>
<div class="header">
  <div class="logo">
    <p>e-Shopping Center</p>
    </div>
  <div class="cart">
    <a class="link2" href="<%=base%>?action=showCart">Show Cart
      <img src="<%=imageUrl%>/cart.gif" border="0"/></a>
    </div>
  </div>
```

TopMenu.jsp generates the HTML code in Listing 6-2 (shown after I removed the empty lines).

Listing 6-2. HTML Generated by TopMenu.jsp

```
<div class="header">
  <div class="logo">
    <p>e-Shopping Center</p>
    </div>
  <div class="cart">
    <a class="link2" href="/eshop/shop?action=showCart">Show Cart
      <img src="/eshop/images/cart.gif" border="0"/></a>
    </div>
  </div>
```

Notice that TopMenu.jsp uses styles (such as class="header") that aren't loaded or defined within the same file. If you're wondering how that's possible, you probably don't clearly understand the distinction between source JSP and output HTML. The JSP code in TopMenu.jsp is executed on the server, and it produces HTML code, which is then appended to the output buffer. JSP *doesn't need* style sheets. It is the generated HTML that needs them when it's interpreted by the client's browser.

You might think that <jsp:include page="..."/> is the same as <%@include file="..."%>, but this is definitely not the case. The most important difference is that while the include directive includes the content of a file without any processing, the include action includes the *output* of the included resource. If the resource is a JSP page, this makes a big difference. In practical terms, this also explains why JSP pages to be included with jsp:include must be well-formed and complete pages rather than simply JSP fragments.

To illustrate a subtle consequence of the different mechanisms of inclusion, I have prepared a small test page (see Listing 6-3). To try it out, you can copy to the tests Tomcat folder (webapps\ROOT\tests\) the folder named jsp_include that you will find in the software package for this chapter, or better, you can create a new web project "tests" in Eclipse and copy the same jsp_include folder in the WebContent folder (you can do this by simply copying the folder from the software package and pasting it in the folder in Eclipse environment).

Then type http://localhost:8080/tests/jsp_include/includes.jsp in a web browser.

Listing 6-3. includes.jsp

```
<%@page language="java" contentType="text/html"%>
<html><head><title>A</title></head><body>
<table border="1">
  <tr><th>incl B</th><th>incl C</th><th>C contains</th></tr>
  <tr><td>jsp:include</td><td>jsp:include</td><td><jsp:include
  page="d/b_act.jsp"/></td></tr>
  <tr><td>jsp:include</td><td>@include</td><td><jsp:include
  page="d/b_dir.jsp"/></td></tr>
  <tr><td>@include</td><td>jsp:include</td><td><%@include
  file="d/b_act.jsp"%></td></tr>
  <tr><td>@include</td><td>@include</td><td><%@include
  file="d/b_dir.jsp"%></td></tr>
  </table>
</body></html>
```

As you can see, I first included the d/b_act.jsp and d/b_dir.jsp files with an include action and then with an include directive. The two files contain these lines, respectively:

```
<%@page language="java" contentType="text/html"%><jsp:include page="c.txt"/>
<%@page language="java" contentType="text/html"%><%@include file="c.txt"%>
```

I placed a c.txt file (only containing the letter A) in the directory of includes.jsp and a second c.txt file (only containing the letter B) in the d directory. Figure 6-1 shows the result of running includes.jsp.

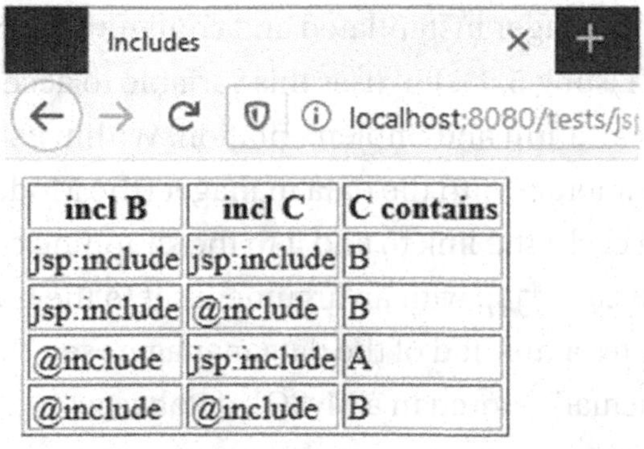

incl B	incl C	C contains
jsp:include	jsp:include	B
jsp:include	@include	B
@include	jsp:include	A
@include	@include	B

Figure 6-1. *The output of includes.jsp*

As you can see, `includes.jsp` displays the letter B in all cases except when you implement the outer inclusion with the directive and the inner inclusion with the action. This means that only with that particular combination of file inclusions, `includes.jsp` accesses the `c.txt` file that is in the same directory. In the other three cases, `includes.jsp` accesses the `c.txt` file that is in the d directory, together with `b_act.jsp` and `b_dir.jsp`. To understand these results, you have to know that when Tomcat translates a JSP page into a Java class, it replaces `<jsp:include page="fname"/>` with an execution of the method `org.apache.jasper.runtime.JspRuntimeLibrary.include(request, response, "fname", out, false)`, while `<%@include file="fname"%>` results in the copying of the *content* of the fname file. Therefore, in the third case of the example, the `<jsp:include page="c.txt"/>` inside `b_act.jsp` is replaced with an `include(request, response, "c.txt", out, false)`, and then the whole `b_act.jsp` is copied into `includes.jsp`. That's why the servlet picks up the file in the directory of `includes.jsp`. The fact that `b_act.jsp` was in a different directory was lost when its `include` directive was replaced by the file content.

I decided to spend a bit of time on this issue because the inclusion mechanism is often misunderstood and causes many people to knock their heads against the wall when files seem to disappear.

Action: useBean

The `useBean` action declares a new JSP scripting variable and associates a Java object to it. For example, the following code declares the variable `dataManager` of type `eshop.model.DataManager`:

```
<jsp:useBean id="dataManager" scope="application" class="eshop.model.DataManager"/>
```

This is the same data manager instantiated and configured in `ShopServlet.java` as you saw in Chapter 5 (Listing 5-1). JSP uses this variable to access the data without having to worry about its location and implementation. Within `eshop`, this is the only way for JSP (the View) to interact with the data manager (the Model). For example, when a user selects a book and clicks the link to add it to the shopping cart, the controller servlet executes `ShoppingCart.jsp` with an argument set to the book identifier. Then, `ShoppingCart.jsp` executes a method of the data manager (see Table 5-1) to obtain the book details, which are actually stored in a MySQL database:

```
Book book = dataManager.getBookDetails(bookId);
```

The result is stored in an object of type book, from which JSP can obtain individual book attributes by executing simple get methods such as book.getTitle() and book.getAuthor().

jsp:useBean accepts the attributes beanName, class, id, scope, and type, of which only id is mandatory.

If you type <jsp:useBean id="objName"/>, Tomcat will check whether an object named objName exists in pageContext. If it exists, Tomcat will create a variable named objName of the same type as the object, so that you can access the object in subsequent JSP scripting elements. If the object doesn't exist, Tomcat will throw a java.lang.InstantiationException.

If you type <jsp:useBean id="objName" scope="*aScope*"/> with *aScope* set to one of the words page, request, session, or application, Tomcat will behave as described in the previous paragraph, but it will look for the objName object in the given scope rather than in the page context. In other words, page is the default scope.

Also jsp:useBean can create new objects. Whether useBean does it and what type of variable it makes available for JSP scripting depends on the three remaining attributes: class, type, and beanName.

If you specify class and set it to a fully qualified class name (i.e., with its package, as in java.lang.String) but specify neither type nor beanName, Tomcat will instantiate an object of the given class in the scope you specify with the attribute scope (or in the page scope by default).

If together with class you also specify type, Tomcat will set the data type of the new object to the value of the type attribute. You can set the type attribute to the same class as the class attribute (which is equivalent to omitting type), to a superclass of class, or to an interface implemented by class.

If instead of class you specify the beanName attribute, Tomcat will behave as if you had specified class, but only after attempting to find a serialized bean of that class. Serializing a bean means that the object's data is converted to a byte stream and saved in a file with the extension ser. Tomcat expects to find serialized objects in the same folder containing the application classes. For example, a serialized bean of the xxx.yyy.Zzz class is expected to be in the WEB-INF\classes\xxx\yyy\Zzz.ser file. This mechanism lets you save an object in a file and then load it into your JSP page. You can actually have several serialized beans of the same class (e.g., Zzz.ser, Zzz_tests.ser, Zzz25.ser, and Abc.ser). Fortunately, the designers of JSP have thought this issue through and allowed you to set the value of beanName at request time (the other attributes must be hard-coded), so that you can parameterize your page for what concerns loading serialized objects.

Finally, pay attention that the servlet creates the objects in the correct scope. In the previous chapter, the initialization method of the eshop servlet (see Listing 5-1) first instantiated the dataManager object and then saved it in the application scope.

Caution   Don't confuse the scope of a bean as specified with the useBean attribute scope with the scope of the scripting variable that Tomcat associates to the bean.

As an example of useBean scopes, the following code instantiates a MyClass object that remains available as long as the session remains valid:

```
<jsp:useBean class="myPkg.MyClass" id="myObj" scope="session"/>
```

You'll be able to access it via a scripting variable named myObj in any page within the same session with the following statement:

```
<jsp:useBean id="myObj" type="myPkg.MyClass" scope="session"/>
```

However, the scope of the scripting variable myObj is determined by where within your page you execute useBean, as with the declaration of any other scripting variable. If you find this confusing, consider this: in the page containing the second useBean, you don't have access to the scripting variable myObj until you execute the useBean action. Before that, the scripting variable is undefined, although the bean called myObj already exists, as it was instantiated by the first useBean in a previously executed page. This tells you that the scripting variable referring to the object and the actual object are two different things with two different scopes, even if they share the same name.

Incidentally, the first useBean (with class, id, and scope) is completely equivalent to this:

```
<%
MyClass myName = new MyClass();
session.setAttribute("myObj", myObj);
%>
```

and the second useBean (with id, type, and scope) is the same as this:

```
<%
MyClass myObj = (MyClass)session.getAttribute("myObj");
%>
```

168

This representation should make completely clear that the object and the scripting variable are two different entities. In the second scriptlet, you could even decide to call the scripting variable with a different name.

Because of all the options implemented by combining its attributes, as I said at the beginning, useBean is somewhat tricky to use. But you can always come back to this page in case of doubt!

Actions: setProperty and getProperty

A bean property is nothing else than an attribute of a bean's class, but only when you define for that attribute the standard get and set methods. To make it completely clear, both get and set must be there. Otherwise, that class attribute is *not* a bean property.

Additionally, you must name the two methods respectively get and set, followed by the full name of the attribute with the first letter capitalized. For example, if you define the attribute named myAttr, you must name the two attributes getMyAttr and setMyAttr. Otherwise, again, Tomcat will not recognize the attribute as a bean property.

An example from the eshop application will convince you that you are better off if Tomcat recognizes an attribute as a property. The JSP page OrderConfirmation.jsp has the following two elements:

```
<jsp:useBean id="customer" class="eshop.beans.Customer"/>
<jsp:setProperty property="*" name="customer"/>
```

The useBean action instantiates an object of type Customer and assigns it to the variable named customer. The action is equivalent to

```
Customer customer = new Customer();
```

By defining property="*", the setProperty action tells Tomcat to set all bean properties of the newly created object. What setProperty does *not* say is to what values they should be set. This is because the values come from request parameters named *exactly* like the properties. Check out the definition of the Customer class, shown in Listing 6-4.

Listing 6-4. Customer.java

```java
package eshop.beans;

public class Customer {
  private String contactName = "";
  private String deliveryAddress = "";
  private String ccName = "";
  private String ccNumber = "";
  private String ccExpiryDate = "";

  public String getContactName() {
    return contactName;
    }
  public void setContactName(String contactName) {
    this.contactName = contactName;
    }

  public String getDeliveryAddress() {
    return deliveryAddress;
    }
  public void setDeliveryAddress(String deliveryAddress) {
    this.deliveryAddress = deliveryAddress;
    }

  public String getCcName() {
    return ccName;
    }
  public void setCcName(String ccName) {
    this.ccName = ccName;
    }

  public String getCcNumber() {
    return ccNumber;
    }
  public void setCcNumber(String ccNumber) {
    this.ccNumber = ccNumber;
    }
```

```
public String getCcExpiryDate() {
  return ccExpiryDate;
  }
public void setCcExpiryDate(String ccExpiryDate) {
  this.ccExpiryDate = ccExpiryDate;
  }
}
```

As you can see, the Customer class defines private attributes and then the methods to access them, so that they can be recognized as properties.

It is interesting the setProperty action

```
<jsp:setProperly property-"*" namc-"customer"/>
```

is equivalent to the following code:

```
customer.setContactName(request.getParameter("contactName");
customer.setDeliveryAddress(request.getParameter("deliveryAddress");
customer.setCcName(request.getParameter("ccName");
customer.setCcNumber(request.getParameter("ccNumber"));
customer.setCcExpiryDate(request.getParameter("ccExpiryDate"));
```

The implementation with the action is more compact and, most importantly, it remains valid regardless of whether you add or remove customer attributes. And that's what makes setProperty worthwhile.

Also jsp:getProperty is useful, because it sends the value of a property to the output. For example, suppose you define MyClass as shown in Listing 6-5.

Listing 6-5. MyClass.java

```
package tests.mclasses;
import java.io.Serializable;
public class MyClass implements java.io.Serializable {
  public static final long serialVersionUID = 1L;
  private int i;
  public MyClass() {i = 0;}
  public void setI(int i) {this.i = i;}
  public int getI() {return i;}
  }
```

As you can see, the integer attribute i is a property. Listing 6-6 shows the JSP page that uses both getProperty and setProperty.

Listing 6-6. myObj.jsp

```
<%@ page language="java" contentType="text/html;
charset=ISO-8859-1"  pageEncoding="ISO-8859-1"%>
<%@page import=" java.util.*, tests.myclasses.MyClass"%>
<%@page trimDirectiveWhitespaces="true"%>
<html><head><title>myObj</title></head><body>
<jsp:useBean id="obj" class=" tests.myclasses.MyClass" scope="session">
    <jsp:setProperty name="obj" property="i" value="11"/>
</jsp:useBean>
<jsp:getProperty name="obj" property="i"/>
<jsp:setProperty name="obj" property="i" value="22"/>
<jsp:getProperty name="obj" property="i"/>
</body></html>
```

To try it out, create a new class "MyClass" in the created Eclipse project "tests" unsder the package tests.myclasses and then copy the code in the folder named jsp_getProperty that you will find in the software package for this chapter. Do the same thing for the JSP page. Type in a browser http://localhost:8080/tests/myObj.jsp.

As you can see, myObj.jsp instantiates the bean object with useBean and initializes its attribute by executing setProperty within the body of useBean. The advantage of doing it that way is that Tomcat only attempts to execute the sub-action setProperty if the instantiation of the bean succeeds.

The two executions of getProperty send the value of i to the output. As a result, myObj.jsp generates the following HTML page:

```
<html><head><title>myObj</title></head><body>
1122</body></html>
```

The example also shows that in setProperty you can replace the value attribute with param. Then, Tomcat sets the attribute to the value of the identically named request parameter. Notice how the page directive with trimDirectiveWhitespaces set to true only leaves a single newline, after <body>, because it is in the HTML template. It results in 11 and 22 being "fused" into 1122. Not necessarily what you would like to have.

Actions: element, attribute, and body

With the actions `element`, `attribute`, and `body`, you can define XML elements dynamically within a JSP page. One reason why you might like to define XML elements dynamically is that your JSP page, instead of generating a web page to be displayed in a browser, might need to generate an XML file used to exchange data with other modules and applications. The word *dynamically* is important, because it means that you can generate the XML elements at request time rather than statically at compile time.

The JSP page shown in Listing 6-7 generates the HTML output shown in Listing 6-8. It is a meaningless page, only designed to show you how to use these actions. Don't look for a meaning that doesn't exist!

Listing 6-7. actel_element_attribute.jsp

```
<%@page language="java" contentType="text/html"%>
<html>
<head><title>Action elements: element, attribute</title></head>
<body>
<jsp:element name="myElem">
  <jsp:attribute name="myElemAttr">myElemAttr's   value</jsp:attribute>
  <jsp:body>myElem's body</jsp:body>
</jsp:element>
<br/>
<jsp:include page="text.txt"/>
<br/>
<jsp:include>
  <jsp:attribute name="page">text.txt</jsp:attribute>
  </jsp:include>
</body>
</html>
```

Listing 6-8. The Output of actel_element_attribute.jsp

```
<html>
<head><title>Action elements: element, attribute</title></head>
<body>
<myElem myElemAttr="myElemAttr's value">myElem's body</myElem>
<br/>
```

```
This is inside the test file text.txt
<br/>
```
This is inside the test file text.txt
```
</body>
</html>
```

You can test it at http://localhost:8080/tests/actel_element_attribute.jsp.

I have highlighted two parts of the listings. The first highlight shows how to use the actions element, attribute, and body to generate an XML element. Be aware that if you drop the action body, the XML element generated by element will have an empty body, as in the following example:

```
<myElem myElemAttr="myElemAttr's value"/>
```

The second highlight shows how you can use attribute to move the page attribute of include to be inside the body of the include action. The content of the file text.txt is unimportant. You'll find a one-line file in the jsp_element folder of the software package for this chapter (you can copy it in the Eclipse project named "tests").

Action: text

You can use the jsp:text action to write template text. Its syntax is straightforward:

```
<jsp:text>Template data</jsp:text>
```

Its body cannot contain other elements; it can only contain text and EL expressions.

Actions: plugin, params, and fallback

These three actions let you embed an object in a web page when there is a need of a plug-in to run. Its syntax is straightforward:

```
<jsp:plugin type="applet/bean" code="objectcode" codebase="objectcodebase">
  <jsp:params>
     <jsp:param name="name" value="value"/>
  </jsp:params>
     <jsp:fallback>Unable to start plugin</jsp:fallback>
</jsp:plugin>
```

Here the type specifies either an object or a bean, code specifies the class name of the object, and at last the codebase specifies the URL containing the files of the class. The syntax shows also how to pass params and how to inform the user with fallback if the object fails to start.

Comments and Escape Characters

The comment delimiters `<%-- .. --%>` have in JSP the same function as `/* .. */` in Java. You can also use them to "switch off" JSP elements, as shown here:

```
<%-- <jsp:include page="whatever.jsp"/> --%>
```

They can also span over several lines.

Note   Regular HTML comments such as `<!-- ... -->` won't work with JSP.

JSP comments have the advantage over HTML comments in that they are not sent to the client. Their content is therefore invisible to the user.

To include the sequence of characters `<%` and `%>` in template text, you have to "break" them with a backslash, like in `<\%` and `%\>`, so that the JSP engine doesn't interpret them as the beginning and end of scripting elements. Alternatively, you can replace the inequality signs with their corresponding HTML entities, as in `<%` and `%>`.

JSP's Tag Extension Mechanism

You can define your own actions to replace lengthy scriptlets. By "hiding" functions behind custom tags, you can increase modularity and maintainability of your pages.

To write in a JSP page a statement like

```
<myPrefix:myActionTag attributeName="myAttributeName"/>
```

you need to follow the following steps:

1. Define Java classes that provide the functionality of the new actions, including the definition of their attributes (e.g., myAttributeName). These classes are called *tag handlers*.

2. Provide a formalized description of your action elements, so that Tomcat knows how to handle them. For example, you need to specify which actions can have a body and which attributes can be omitted. Such a description is called a tag library descriptor (TLD).

3. In the JSP pages, tell Tomcat that the pages need your *tag library* and specify the prefix that you want to identify those custom tags with.

I will take you through these steps, beginning with bodyless actions, which are simpler to implement.

Bodyless Custom Actions

A bodyless action is an element that, not having an end tag, cannot enclose a body between start and end tags. As an example, let's say you want to develop an action that prints the day of the week of any given date:

```
<wow:weekday date="date"/>
```

with the date attribute accepting values in the form yyyy-mm-dd and defaulting to the current date. All the examples of this section on bodyless actions and the following section of bodied actions are in the software package for this chapter. To test them, import the project tldtest in Eclipse.

Step 1: Define the Tag Handler

A tag handler for a bodyless custom tag is a class that implements the interfaces java.io.Serializable and javax.servlet.jsp.tagext.Tag. Remember that to satisfy an interface, you have to implement all the methods it defines.

To satisfy Serializable, you only need to define a unique identifier, like this:

```
static final long serialVersionUID = 1L;
```

The value identifies the version of your class and the objects you instantiate from it. It is then used when deserializing objects to check that class and object match. As long as you don't have several versions of the class and swap objects between JVMs, you don't really need to worry about it. However, to satisfy the Tag interface, you have to define the methods listed in Table 6-1.

Table 6-1. *The Methods of the Tag Interface*

Method	Description
int doEndTag()	Processes the end tag
int doStartTag()	Processes the start tag
Tag getParent()	Provides a reference to the closest enclosing tag handler
void release()	Removes all the references to objects
void setPageContext(PageContext pc)	Sets the current page context
void setParent(Tag t)	Sets the closest enclosing tag handler

Fortunately, the `javax.servlet.jsp.tagext.TagSupport` class makes life easier by implementing the Tag interface with default methods and other useful methods. Therefore, you only need to extend TagSupport and overwrite the methods you need for your weekday action. You certainly don't need getParent, because the action isn't going to be used in the body of other actions. You don't need doStartTag either, because the action is bodyless, and, as a consequence, you don't have separate start and end tags. In conclusion, you only need to overwrite doEndTag with a method containing all the functionality of the weekday tag.

Listing 6-9 shows you the code of the whole tag handler.

Listing 6-9. WeekdayTag.java

```java
package tags;

import javax.servlet.jsp.JspException;
import javax.servlet.jsp.tagext.TagSupport;
import java.util.Date;
import java.text.SimpleDateFormat;
import java.util.Calendar;
import java.util.GregorianCalendar;

public class WeekdayTag extends TagSupport {
  static final long serialVersionUID = 1L;
  static final String[] WD = {"","Sun","Mon","Tue","Wed","Thu","Fri","Sat"};
  private String date;
```

```
public void setDate(String date) {
  this.date = date;
  }

public int doEndTag() throws JspException {
  GregorianCalendar cal = new GregorianCalendar();
  SimpleDateFormat fmt = new SimpleDateFormat("yyyy-MM-dd");
  fmt.setLenient(true);
  if (date != null && date.length() > 0) {
    Date d = new Date();
    try {
      d = fmt.parse(date);
      }
    catch (Exception e) {
      throw new JspException("Date parsing failed: " + e.getMessage());
      }
    cal.setTime(d);
    }
  try {
    pageContext.getOut().print(WD[cal.get(Calendar.DAY_OF_WEEK)]);
    }
  catch (Exception e) {
    throw new JspException("Weekday writing failed: " + e.getMessage());
    }
  return EVAL_PAGE;
  }
}
```

You need the setDate method because Tomcat uses it to pass the value of the action's date attribute to the tag handler. The corresponding getDate method isn't present, because it is never used and can be omitted. That said, you might argue that working with incomplete Java beans, sooner or later, will get you into trouble. If the action is executed without the date attribute, the date variable defined in doEndTag remains set to null, and the calendar cal, which is used to determine the day of the week, remains set to the current date. On the other hand, if a date attribute is specified in the action, its value is parsed and used to set the calendar.

Notice that the tag handler is named like the tag but with the first letter capitalized and with the Tag suffix. This is a good practice to follow, although you can name your handlers whatever you like. You'll see in a moment how to make the association between a tag and its handler.

The return value EVAL_PAGE means that execution should continue with the page code following the custom action. Use SKIP_PAGE to abort the page.

Step 2: Define the TLD

The TLD is an XML file that describes your tags so that Tomcat knows how to deal with them. Listing 6-10 shows the full TLD for the custom-tag library.

Listing 6-10. wow.tld

```xml
<?xml version="1.0" encoding="UTF-8"?>
<taglib xmlns="http://java.sun.com/xml/ns/javaee"
      xmlns:xsi="http://www.w3.org/2001/XMLSchema-instance"
      xsi:schemaLocation="http://java.sun.com/xml/ns/javaee
      http://java.sun.com/xml/ns/javaee/web-jsptaglibrary_2_1.xsd"
      version="2.1">
<description>Example of a simple tag library</description>
  <tlib-version>1.0</tlib-version>
  <short-name>wow</short-name>
  <tag>
    <description>Displays the day of the week</description>
    <display-name>weekday</display-name>
    <name>weekday</name>
    <tag-class>tags.WeekdayTag</tag-class>
    <body-content>empty</body-content>
    <attribute>
      <name>date</name>
      <rtexprvalue>true</rtexprvalue>
      <type>java.lang.String</type>
      </attribute>
    </tag>
  </taglib>
```

As you can see, the outermost element is `taglib`, which contains a `tag` element for each custom action (in this case, only `weekday`). Apart from `tag`, all `taglib` sub-elements in the example are for information purposes or to be used by tools and can be omitted.

The `tag` element contains an `attribute` sub-element for each action attribute (in this case, only `date`). Of the `tag` sub-elements in the example, you can omit `description` and `display name`. The sub-element `name` defines the custom action name; `tag class` specifies the fully qualified class name of the tag handler; and `body content` specifies the action to be bodyless.

The sub-element `tag class` is what gives you the freedom to name your tag handlers anything you like. The sub-element `body content` is mandatory and can only have one of the following three values: `empty`, `scriptless`, or `tagdependent`. The value `scriptless` is the default and means that the body cannot contain scripting elements, while EL expressions and JSP actions are accepted and processed normally. The value `tagdependent` means that the body content is passed to the tag handler as it is, without any processing. This is useful if the body contains character sequences, such as `<%`, that would confuse Tomcat.

The attribute element in the example has three sub-elements: `name`, which sets the action attribute name; `type`, which sets the class name of the attribute value; and `rtexprvalue`, which decides whether the attribute accepts values at request time.

If you had used a type other than `String`, the value passed to the tag handler would have been of that type. For example, with an attribute defined like this:

```
<attribute>
  <name>num</name>
  <type>java.lang.Integer</type>
</attribute>
```

you would have included the following code in the tag handler:

```
private int num;
public void setNum(Integer num) {
  this.num = num.intValue();
  }
```

When processing the start tag of the custom action, Tomcat would have parsed the string passed to the action (as in `num="23"`) to obtain the `Integer` value for the tag handler.

If you had omitted the rtexprvalue sub-element or set it to false, you would have been forced to pass to the date attribute only constant values, such as "2007-12-05", instead of runtime values such as "<%=aDate%>" (rtexpr stands for real-time expression).

Inside WEB-INF, create a folder named tlds and place wow.tld there.

Step 3: Use the Custom Action

Listing 6-11 shows you a simple JSP page to test the weekday custom action.

Listing 6-11. weekday.jsp

```
1: <%@page language="java" contentType="text/html"%>
2: <%@taglib uri="/WEB-INF/tlds/wow.tld" prefix="wow"%>
3: <% String d = request.getParameter("d"); %>
4: <html><head><title>weekday bodyless tag</title></head><body>
5: weekday today: <wow:weekday/><br/>
6: weekday <%=d%>: <wow:weekday date="<%=d%>"/>
7: </body></html>
```

Line 2 contains the taglib directive, line 4 uses weekday without the date attribute, and line 6 passes the request parameter d to the action. It's as simple as that.

If you type in your browser http://localhost:8080/tldtest/weekday.jsp?d=2012-12-25, you get two lines, such as Today: Wed and 2012-12-25: Tue. If you type the URL without the query, the second line of the output becomes null: Wed. You can execute the example by typing in your browser http://localhost:8080/tldtest/weekday.jsp.

On the other hand, if you type a query with a bad date, such as d=2012-1225, Tomcat shows you an error page with a back trace that begins as follows:

```
org.apache.jasper.JasperException: javax.servlet.ServletException: ➥
  javax.servlet.jsp.JspException: ➥
   Date parsing failed: Unparseable date: "2012-1225"
```

You can execute the example by typing in your browser http://localhost:8080/tldtest/weekday.jsp?d=2012-1225.

Bodied Custom Actions

To show you the differences from the bodyless action, I will implement a version of the weekday action that expects the date in its body instead of in an attribute:

```
<wow:weekdayBody>date</wow:weekdayBody>
```

Step 1: Define the Tag Handler

Similar to bodyless actions, the tag handlers for bodied actions need to implement an interface, only this time it's javax.servlet.jsp.tagex.BodyTag instead of Tag. Again, similarly to bodyless actions, the API provides a convenient class that you can use as a basis: javax.servlet.jsp.tagext.BodyTagSupport. However, as opposed to what you did in the tag handler for a bodyless action, you cannot simply replace the doEndTag method, because the action body will have come and gone by the time you reach the end tag. You first have to overwrite doAfterBody.

An additional complication concerns the default date: if you write the action with an empty body, as follows:

```
<wow:weekdayBody></wow:weekdayBody>
```

the method doAfterBody won't be executed at all. How can you then print out the default day?

The answer is simple: you have to overwrite the doEndTag method and write the default date from there in case there is no body. Listing 6-12 shows the end result.

Listing 6-12. WeekdayBodyTag.java

```java
package tags;

import javax.servlet.jsp.JspException;
import javax.servlet.jsp.tagext.BodyTagSupport;
import java.util.Date;
import java.text.SimpleDateFormat;
import java.util.Calendar;
import java.util.GregorianCalendar;

public class WeekdayBodyTag extends BodyTagSupport {
  static final long serialVersionUID = 1L;
```

```
static final String[] WD = {"","Sun","Mon","Tue","Wed","Thu","Fri","Sat"};
private boolean bodyless = true;  /* 1 */

public int doAfterBody() throws JspException {
  String date = getBodyContent().getString();  /* 2 */
  if (date.length() > 0) {
    GregorianCalendar cal = new GregorianCalendar();
    Date d = new Date();
    SimpleDateFormat fmt = new SimpleDateFormat("yyyy-MM-dd");
    fmt.setLenient(true);
    try {
      d = fmt.parse(date);
      }
    catch (Exception e) {
      throw new JspException("Date parsing failed: " + e.getMessage());
      }
    cal.setTime(d);
    try {
        getPreviousOut().print(WD[cal.get(Calendar.DAY_OF_WEEK)]);  /* 3 */
        }
      catch (Exception e) {
        throw new JspException("Weekday writing failed: " +
        e.getMessage());
        }
    bodyless = false;  /* 4 */
    }
  return SKIP_BODY;
  }

public int doEndTag() throws JspException {
  if (bodyless) {  /* 5 */
    GregorianCalendar cal = new GregorianCalendar();
    try {
      pageContext.getOut().print(WD[cal.get(Calendar.DAY_OF_WEEK)]);
      }
```

```
      catch (Exception e) {
        throw new JspException("Weekday writing failed: " +
        e.getMessage());
        }
      }
    return EVAL_PAGE;
    }
  }
```

Lines 1, 4, and 5 implement the mechanism to ensure that you write the default date but only when the body is empty. In line 1, you define a `boolean` instance variable called `bodyless` and set it to `true`. If there is no body to process, `doAfterBody` does not run, and `doEndTag` in line 5 prints the default day of the week. If, on the other hand, there is a body to process, `doAfterBody` in line 4 sets `bodyless` to `false`, and `doEndTag` does nothing.

Line 2 shows you how to get the body content and line 3 how to get the method to print the date while processing the body. The method has been named `getPreviousOut` to remind you that there can be actions within actions, in which case you'll want to append the output of an inner action to that of an outer one.

Step 2: Define the TLD

To define the new action, you only need to add the `<tag>` shown in Listing 6-13 after the `<tag>` for the bodyless weekday action.

Listing 6-13. The tag Element for weekdayBody

```
<tag>
  <description>Displays the day of the week</description>
  <display-name>weekdayBody</display-name>
  <name>weekdayBody</name>
  <tag-class>tags.WeekdayBodyTag</tag-class>
  <body-content>scriptless</body-content>
  </tag>
```

Notice that you define the `body-content` sub-element as `scriptless` even though it is the default. The purpose is to make the code more readable. It's just a matter of taste.

Step 3: Use the Custom Action

Listing 6-14 shows a modified version of `weekday.jsp` to handle the bodied tag.

Listing 6-14. weekday_b.jsp for the Bodied Action

```
<%@page language="java" contentType="text/html"%>
<%@taglib uri="/WEB-INF/tlds/wow.tld" prefix="wow"%>
<html><head><title>weekday bodied tag</title></head><body>
weekdayBody today: <wow:weekdayBody></wow:weekdayBody><br/>
weekdayBody ${param.d}: <wow:weekdayBody>${param.d}</wow:weekdayBody><br/>
</body></html>
```

Notice that I replaced the `request.getParameter("d")` logic with the simpler and more elegant EL expression `${param.d}`. You have to use an EL expression in any case, because scripting elements aren't allowed in the body of an action. Therefore, you couldn't have used `<%=d%>`. You will learn how to use EL in the next section of this chapter.

Tag Files

Tag files are special JSP files that replace tag handlers written in Java. After all, JSP basically *is* Java.

Do you remember when I told you in Chapter 2 that the only available directive elements are `page`, `include`, and `taglib`? Well, I lied. There are three more directives: `tag`, `attribute`, and `variable`. The reason I didn't mention them is that you can only use them in tag files. Now that you know how to develop custom-tag libraries with Java, I can tell you how to develop them using the JSP syntax and the newly revealed directives. The examples of this section are in the folder `tagtest` of the software package for this chapter. To install them, import the package into Eclipse.

Bodyless Tag

Listing 6-15 shows the tag-file version of the tag handler `WeekdayTag.java` that you saw in Listing 6-9.

Listing 6-15. weekday.tag

```
<%@tag import="java.util.Date, java.text.SimpleDateFormat"
       import="java.util.Calendar, java.util.GregorianCalendar"%>
<%@attribute name="date" required="false"%>
<%
  final String[] WD = {"","Sun","Mon","Tue","Wed","Thu","Fri","Sat"};
  GregorianCalendar cal = new GregorianCalendar();
  if (date != null && date.length() > 0) {
    SimpleDateFormat fmt = new SimpleDateFormat("yyyy-MM-dd");
    fmt.setLenient(true);
    Date d = fmt.parse(date);
    cal.setTime(d);
    }
  out.print(WD[cal.get(Calendar.DAY_OF_WEEK)]);
  %>
```

The `tag` directive of a tag file replaces the `page` directive of a JSP page, and the `attribute` directive lets you define an input parameter. As Tomcat handles the tag exceptions for us, I removed the `try`/`catch` constructs, which certainly makes the code more readable. Another simplification is in sending the result to the output, because in the tag file the implicit variable `out` makes it unnecessary to invoke `pageContext.getOut()`.

Listing 6-16 shows how you modify `weekday.jsp` of Listing 6-11 to use the tag file.

Listing 6-16. weekday_t.jsp

```
<%@page language="java" contentType="text/html"%>
<%@taglib tagdir="/WEB-INF/tags" prefix="wow"%>
<% String d = request.getParameter("d"); %>
<html><head><title>weekday bodyless tag</title></head><body>
weekday today: <wow:weekday/><br/>
weekday <%=d%>: <wow:weekday date="<%=d%>"/><br/>
</body></html>
```

As you can see, the only difference is that the attribute `uri="/WEB-INF/tlds/wow.tld"` of the `taglib` directive has become `tagdir="/WEB-INF/tags"`.

To keep the `uri` attribute, you need to declare the tag file in a TLD, as shown in Listing 6-17.

186

Listing 6-17. wow.tld for a Tag File

```
<?xml version="1.0" encoding="UTF-8"?>
<taglib xmlns="http://java.sun.com/xml/ns/javaee"
    xmlns:xsi="http://www.w3.org/2001/XMLSchema-instance"
    xsi:schemaLocation="http://java.sun.com/xml/ns/javaee ~CCC
http://java.sun.com/xml/ns/j2ee/web-jsptaglibrary_2_1.xsd"
    version="2.1">
  <description>My library of tag files</description>
  <tlib-version>1.0</tlib-version>
  <short-name>wow</short-name>
  <uri>tagFiles</uri>
  <tag-file>
    <description>Displays the day of the week</description>
    <display-name>weekday</display-name>
    <name>weekday</name>
    <path>/WEB-INF/tags/weekday.tag</path>
    </tag-file>
</taglib>
```

Then, in the `taglib` directive of `weekday_t.jsp`, you can replace `tagdir="/WEB-INF/tags"` with `uri="tagFiles"`.

As an example of the `variable` directive, replace in `weekday.tag` the line

```
out.print(WD[cal.get(Calendar.DAY_OF_WEEK)]);
```

with the following two:

```
%><%@variable name-given="dayw" scope="AT_END"%><%
jspContext.setAttribute("dayw", WD[cal.get(Calendar.DAY_OF_WEEK)]);
```

The action will then save the string with the day of the week into the attribute `dayw` instead of sending it directly to the output. To display the action's result from within `weekday_t.jsp`, insert the following expression element after executing the action:

```
<%=pageContext.getAttribute("dayw")%>
```

As you will see later in this chapter, you can also replace the somewhat cumbersome expression element with the more compact EL expression ${dayw}.

Bodied Tag

Listing 6-18 shows the tag file equivalent to the tag handler WeekdayBodyTag.java, which you saw in Listing 6-12. I wrote it by modifying the tag file weekday.tag that implemented the bodyless tag as shown in Listing 6-15. Listing 6-19 is the tag file equivalent to weekday_b.jsp (see Listing 6-14), which invoked the bodied tag handler. I wrote it by modifying weekday_t.jsp of Listing 6-16, which used the bodyless tag file.

Listing 6-18. weekdayBody.tag

```
<%@tag import="java.util.Date, java.text.SimpleDateFormat"
       import="java.util.Calendar, java.util.GregorianCalendar"%>
<jsp:doBody var="dateAttr"/>
<%
  String date = (String)jspContext.getAttribute("dateAttr");
  final String[] WD = {"","Sun","Mon","Tue","Wed","Thu","Fri","Sat"};
  GregorianCalendar cal = new GregorianCalendar();
  if (date.length() > 0) {
    SimpleDateFormat fmt = new SimpleDateFormat("yyyy-MM-dd");
    fmt.setLenient(true);
    Date d = fmt.parse(date);
    cal.setTime(d);
    }
  out.print(WD[cal.get(Calendar.DAY_OF_WEEK)]);
  %>
```

The standard action element jsp:doBody evaluates the body of the weekdayBody action and stores its output as a string into the page-scoped attribute dateAttr. The first line of the scriptlet then copies the attribute into the JSP variable named date. After that, the bodied tag file is identical to the bodyless one. This was not really necessary, but the subsequent code accesses the date twice, first to check that it isn't empty and then to parse it. I didn't like to invoke the getAttribute method twice. It seemed less tidy.

If you omit the attribute var, doBody sends the body's result to the output; if you replace var with varReader, the result is stored as a java.io.Reader object instead of a java.lang.String; and if you add the attribute scope, you can specify var/varReader to be defined as a request, session, or application attribute, instead of in the page scope.

You should know that jsp:invoke is very similar to jsp:doBody but operates on a JSP fragment instead of the action body. For example, by writing the following two lines in a tag file

```
<%@attribute name="fragName" fragment="true"%>
<jsp:invoke fragment="fragName"/>
```

you pass to it a JSP fragment. Like doBody, invoke admits the attributes var, varReader, and scope. Both standard actions can only be used within tag files.

Listing 6-19. weekday_bt.jsp

```
<%@page language="java" contentType="text/html"%>
<%@taglib tagdir="/WEB-INF/tags" prefix="wow"%>
<html><head><title>weekday bodied tag</title></head><body>
weekdayBody today: <wow:weekdayBody></wow:weekdayBody><br/>
weekdayBody ${param.d}: <wow:weekdayBody>${param.d}</wow:weekdayBody><br/>
</body></html>
```

You can import the project tagtest in Eclipse and test the example by typing in your browser http://localhost:8080/tldtest/weekday.jsp?d=2012-1225.

The tag Directive

In the previous section, you encountered the import attribute of the tag directive. Table 6-2 lists the other attributes that are available. They are all optional.

Table 6-2. *Attributes of the tag Directive*

Attribute	Description
description	The name says it all.
display-name	A short name intended for tools. The default is the name of the tag file without the .tag extension.
body-content	Same as the <body-content> tag in a TLD (see the comments after Listing 6-11).
dynamic-attributes	If the attribute is present, its value identifies a scoped attribute where you store a map with names and values of the dynamic attributes you use when executing the tag.
example	A string with a brief description of an example.
small-icon	Path, relative from the tag file, of a small icon intended for tools.
large-icon	Yes, you guessed correctly!
language	Equivalent to its namesake of the page directive.
pageEncoding	Ditto.
isELIgnored	Ditto.

The attribute Directive

You have already encountered the attributes name and required. Table 6-3 briefly describes the remaining ones (all optional).

Table 6-3. *Attributes of the attribute Directive*

Attribute	Description
description	This attribute is almost universal.
rtexprvalue	Same as the equally-named tag in a TLD (see the comments after Listing 6-11).
type	Ditto.
fragment	If set to true, it means that the attribute is a JSP fragment to be evaluated by the tag file. If false (the default), the attribute is a normal one and is therefore evaluated by Tomcat before being passed to the tag file. Do not specify rtexprvalue or type when you set fragment to true. Tomcat will set them for you, respectively, to true and javax.servlet.jsp.tagext.JspFragment.
example	A string with a brief description of an example.
small-icon	Path, relative from the tag file, of a small icon intended for tools.

There are also two mutually exclusive pairs of attributes that are associated with JavaServer Faces: deferredValue/deferredValueType and deferredMethod/deferredMe thodSignature. Let's not put the cart before the oxen.

The variable Directive

Table 6-4 briefly describes all the attributes.

Table 6-4. *Attributes of the variable Directive*

Attribute	Description
description	No surprises here.
name-given / name-from-attribute	You have seen name-given in the example. One of these two attributes must be present. The value of name-given cannot be the same of the value of the name attribute of an attribute directive or the value of a dynamic-attributes attribute of a tag directive. See after the end of this table for an explanation of how to use name-from-attribute.
alias	It works together with name-from-attribute. Again, see the following details.
scope	Can be AT_BEGIN, AT_END, or NESTED (the default). Once more, too much text to keep it in this table. See the following details.
variable-class	The name of the class of the variable (default is java.lang.String).
declare	Set to false (the default is true) if the variable is *not* declared.

While name-given provides the name of a JSP attribute (which, as you will see in the next section, coincides with the name of an EL variable), name-from-attribute provides the name of another JSP attribute containing the name of the JSP attribute you are interested in. Then, alias provides the name of an EL variable local to the tag file that Tomcat synchronizes with the JSP attribute. For example, if you declare

```
<%@variable alias="ali" name-from-attribute="attrName"%>
```

Tomcat, before continuing execution of the tag file, makes available to it the page-scoped attribute named ali and sets it to the value of the attribute named attrName. This name redirection makes possible for JSP pages that use differently named attributes to use the same tag file. For example, a.jsp might include the line

```
session.setAttribute("greet", "Good morning!");
```

and b.jsp might have

```
application.setAttribute("novel", "Stranger in a Strange Land");
```

If `a.jsp` contains

```
pageContext.setAttribute("attrName", "greet");
```

and `b.jsp`

```
pageContext.setAttribute("attrName", "novel");
```

they can both invoke the tag file that includes the `variable` directive shown earlier. The tag file will then have an `ali` attribute containing `"Good morning!"` in the first case and `"Stranger in a Strange Land"` in the second case.

The attribute `scope` tells when Tomcat creates or updates the attribute in the calling page with the value of the attribute that is local to the tag file (perhaps a name like *synchronization* would have been clearer than `scope`). With `AT_BEGIN`, Tomcat does it before the tag file invokes a segment or immediately before exiting the tag file; with `NESTED`, only before invoking a segment; and with `AT_END`, only before leaving the tag file. Additionally, with `NESTED`, Tomcat saves the value of the calling-page attribute upon entering the tag file and restores it upon leaving it. But this only if an attribute with the given name exists in the calling page before entering the tag file.

JSTL and EL

Many developers have implemented similar custom actions to remove or at least reduce the need for scripting elements. Eventually, a new effective standard known as JavaServer Pages Standard Tag Library (JSTL) was born.

To use this distribution with your web applications, you have to download the following JAR (or the equivalent files for the version that will be current when you will be reading this book) from `https://tomcat.apache.org/taglibs/standard/` and add files to the /WEB-INF/lib directory of your application:

- `taglibs-standard-spec-1.2.5.jar`
- `taglibs-standard-impl-1.2.5.jar`

However, JSTL is of little use without the Expression Language (EL), which lets you access and manipulate objects in a compact and efficient way and can be used within the body of actions. I will first introduce you to EL, so that you'll be well prepared to understand the JSTL examples.

JSP Expression Language

EL was introduced in JSP 2.0 as an alternative to the scripting elements. You can use EL expressions in template text and also in action attributes specified to be capable of accepting runtime expressions.

EL Expressions

EL supports two representations: ${expr} and #{expr}. To explain when you can or should use them, I must first clarify the distinction between lvalues and rvalues.

The *l* stands for *left*, and the *r* stands for *right*. These values refer to the fact that in most computer languages, the assigned value is on the right-hand side of an assignment statement, while the value to be assigned to it is on the left-hand side. For example, the Java statement

```
ka[k] = j*3;
```

means that the result of the evaluation of j*3 (an rvalue) is to be assigned to the value resulting from the evaluation of ka[k] (an lvalue). Clearly, an lvalue must be a reference to something you can assign values to (a variable or some attribute of an object), while there is no such restriction on rvalues.

Suppose that you have a page with a form. Wouldn't it be nice if you could specify *directly in the input elements of the form* the references to where the user's inputs should be stored? For example, it'd be nice to specify something like <input id="firstName" value="*variableName*">, with *variableName* specifying where you want to store the input typed by the user. Then, when the form is submitted, there should be a mechanism to automatically take the user's input and store it where you specified. Perhaps you could also define a new attribute of the input element to provide a validating method. Inside the input element, you would then already have everything you need to accept the user's input, validate it, and store it away.

This sounds great, but if you set the value attribute of the input element to ${formBean.firstName}, this evaluates to an rvalue. The value of the firstName attribute of formBean is assigned to the value attribute of the input element, and that's it. You need a way of *deferring* evaluation of formBean.firstName and use it as an *lvalue* when you really need it, that is, when you handle the form that was submitted.

You achieve that by replacing the $ before the EL braces with a #. The # tells Tomcat to defer evaluation and use its result as an lvalue or an rvalue, depending on the context.

EL expressions with the dollar sign are evaluated like everything else. In any other aspect, parsing and evaluation of the two representations are identical. You will use the # representation when we will talk about JSF. For now, you can learn about EL using the $ representation.

Using EL Expressions

The expr in ${expr} can contain literals, operators, and references to objects and methods. Table 6-5 shows some examples and their results.

Table 6-5. *EL Expressions*

EL Expression	Result
${1 <= (1/2)}	false
${5.0 > 3}	true
${100.0 == 100}	true
${'a' < 'b'}	true
${'fluke' gt 'flute'}	false
${1.5E2 + 1.5}	151.5
${1 div 2}	0.5
${12 mod 5}	2
${empty param.a}	true if the request parameter a is null or an empty string
${sessionScope.cart.nItems}	The value of the nItems property of the session-scoped attribute named cart
${aBean.aProp}	The value of the aProp property of the aBean bean
${aMap[entryName]}	The value of the entry named entryName in the map named aMap

The operators behave in general like in Java, but with one important difference: the equality operator (==) applied to string variables compares their contents, not whether the variables refer to the same instance of a string. That is, it behaves like Java's String. equals() method.

In addition to EL operators identical to Java operators, you also have most of their literal equivalents: not for !, div for /, mod for %, lt for <, gt for >, le for <=, ge for >=, eq for ==, ne for !=, and for &&, and or for ||. You also have the unary operator empty, to be used as shown in one of the examples in Table 6-2.

The EL operators '.' (i.e., the dot) and [] (i.e., indexing) are more powerful and forgiving than the corresponding Java operators.

When applied to a bean, as in ${myBean.prop}, the dot operator is interpreted as an indication that the value of the property should be returned, as if you'd written myBean.getProp() in a scripting element. As a result, for example, the line of code

```
${pageContext.servletContext.servletContextName}
```

is equivalent to this:

```
<%=pageContext.getServletContext().getServletContextName()%>
```

Furthermore, ${first.second.third}, equivalent to <%=first.getSecond().getThird()%>, returns null when first.second evaluates to null, although in the expression, we try to dereference it with .third. The JSP scripting equivalent would throw a NullPointerException. For this to work, all classes must implement the getter methods of properly formed Java beans.

Array indexing allows you to try to access an element that doesn't exist, in which case it simply evaluates to null. For example, if you have an array of ten elements, the EL expression ${myArray[999]} returns null instead of throwing an ArrayIndexOutOfBoundsException, as Java would have done. It is not as bad as in the plain old "C" language, in which an index out of bounds would have returned the value it found in memory. With EL, you can check for null. And in general, you should do so, because you cannot rely on an exception being thrown, as it would be in Java.

You can use both the dot and indexing operator to access maps. For example, the following two EL expressions both return the value associated with the key named myKey:

```
${myMap.myKey}
${myMap["myKey"]}
```

There is a tiny difference, though: you cannot use the dot operator if the name of the key contains a character that confuses EL. For example, ${header["user-agent"]} is OK, but ${header.user-agent} doesn't work, because the dash between user and agent in the second expression is interpreted as a minus sign. Unless you have a variable named agent, both header.user and agent evaluate to null and, according to the EL specification document, ${null - null} evaluates to zero. Therefore, the second expression would return a zero. You would encounter a different, but potentially more serious, problem if you had a map key containing a dot. For example, you could use ${param["my.par"]} without problems, but ${param.my.par} would probably result in a null or, almost certainly, in something other than what you are looking for. This would be bad in any case, because null is a possible valid outcome. I suggest you use the bracketed form in all occasions and simply forget this issue.

Similar to JSP, EL contains implicit objects, which you find listed in Table 6-6.

Table 6-6. *EL's Implicit Objects*

Object	Description
pageContext	The context of the JSP page. In particular, pageContext. servletContext gives you a reference to the same object referenced in JSP by the implicit variable application. Similarly, pageContext. session is equivalent to JSP's session, pageContext.request to JSP's request, and pageContext.response to JSP's response.
Param	Maps a request parameter name to its first value.
paramValues	Maps a request parameter name to an array of its values.
header	Maps a request header name to its first value.
headerValues	Maps a request header name to an array of its values.
Cookie	Maps a cookie name to a single cookie.
initParam	Maps the name of a context initialization parameter to its value.
pageScope	Maps page-scoped variable names to their values.
requestScope	Maps request-scoped variable names to their values.
sessionScope	Maps session-scoped variable names to their values.
${aBean.aProp}	The value of the aProp property of the aBean bean.
applicationScope	Maps application-scoped variable names to their values.

Caution   You *cannot* use JSP scripting variables within EL expressions.

You've probably noticed that EL doesn't include any way of declaring variables. Within EL expressions, you can use variables set with the `c:set` JSTL core action (which I will describe in the next section) or scoped attributes. For example, all of the following definitions let you use the EL expression `${xyz}`:

```
<c:set var="xyz" value="33"/>
<% session.setAttribute("xyz", "44"); %>
<% pageContext.setAttribute("xyz", "22"); %>
```

However, you have to pay attention to scope precedence. The variable set with `c:set` and the attribute in `pageContext` *are the same variable*. That is, `c:set` defines an attribute in the page context. The attribute in `sessionContext` is a different variable, and you cannot access it with `${xyz}` because it is "hidden" behind the attribute with the same name in the page context. To access a session attribute, you have to prefix its name with `sessionScope`, as in `${sessionScope.xyz}`. If you don't specify a scope, EL looks first in the page, then in the request, then in the session, and finally in the application scope.

Caution   You cannot nest EL expressions. Expressions such as `${expr1[${expr2}]}` are illegal.

You can make composite expressions consisting of several EL expressions and additional text, as in the following example:

```
<c:set var="varName" value="Welcome ${firstName} ${lastName}!"/>
```

However, you cannot mix the `${}` and `#{}` forms.

JSP Standard Tag Library

JSTL consists of five tag libraries, as listed in Table 6-7. If you are wondering, i18n stands for *internationalization*, abbreviated by replacing the eighteen letters in the middle with the number 18.

Table 6-7. *JSTL Tag Libraries*

Area	Functionality
core	Variable support, flow control, URL management, and miscellaneous
i18n	Locale, message formatting, and number and date formatting
functions	String manipulation and length of collection objects
SQL	Handling of databases
XML	XML core, flow control, and transformation

Table 6-8 lists all the tags defined in the five libraries.

Table 6-8. *The JSTL Tags*

Core	i18n	Functions	Database	XML
c:catch	fmt:bundle	fn:contains	sql:dateParam	x:choose
c:choose	fmt:formatDate	fn:containsIgnoreCase	sql:param	x:forEach
c:forEach	fmt:formatNumber	fn:endsWith	sql:query	x:if
c:forTokens	fmt:message	fn:escapeXml	sql:setDataSource	x:otherwise
c:if	fmt:param	fn:indexOf	sql:transaction	x:out
c:import	fmt:parseDate	fn:join	sql:update	x:param
c:otherwise	fmt:parseNumber	fn:length		x:parse
c:out	fmt:requestEncoding	fn:replace		x:set
c:param	fmt:setBundle	fn:split		x:transform
c:redirect	fmt:setLocale	fn:startsWith		x:when
c:remove	fmt:setTimeZone	fn:substring		
c:set	fmt:timeZone	fn:substringAfter		
c:url		fn:substringBefore		
c:when		fn:toLowerCase		
		fn:toUpperCase		
		fn:trim		

As you have already seen in a couple of examples, to use the JSTL libraries in JSP pages, you must declare them in `taglib` directives as follows:

```
<%@taglib prefix="c" uri="http://java.sun.com/jsp/jstl/core"%>
<%@taglib prefix="fmt" uri="http://java.sun.com/jsp/jstl/fmt"%>
<%@taglib prefix="fn" uri="http://java.sun.com/jsp/jstl/functions"%>
<%@taglib prefix="sql" uri="http://java.sun.com/jsp/jstl/sql"%>
<%@taglib prefix="x" uri="http://java.sun.com/jsp/jstl/xml"%>
```

I will describe JSTL-XML and JSTL-SQL in the next chapters, while in the following sections of this chapter, I will describe JSTL-core and JSTL-i18n. I will not talk about the functions because they are pretty self-explanatory.

The Core Library

To explain some of the most used actions, I will go back to the example `req_params.jsp` of Chapter 1 (Listing 1-10) and add new scriptlets with JSTL actions in the same Eclipse project "test". You can copy the code in the folder named `jstl` that you will find in the software package for this chapter. Listing 6-20 shows you how you do it.

c:out, c:set, and c:forEach (and fn:length)

Listing 6-20. req_params_jstl.jsp

```
01: <%@page language="java" contentType="text/html"%>
02: <%@taglib prefix="c" uri="http://java.sun.com/jsp/jstl/core"%>
03: <%@taglib prefix="fn" uri="http://java.sun.com/jsp/jstl/functions"%>
04: <html><head><title>Request Parameters with JSTL</title></head><body>
05:   Map size = <c:out value="${fn:length(paramValues)}"/>
06:   <table border="1">
07:     <tr><td>Map element</td><td>Par name</td><td>Par value[s]</td></tr>
08:     <c:set var="k" value="0"/>
09:     <c:forEach var="par" items="${paramValues}"><tr>
10:       <td><c:out value="${k}"/></td>
11:       <td><c:out value="'${par.key}'"/></td>
12:       <td><c:forEach var="val" items="${par.value}">
13:         <c:out value="'${val}'"/>
```

```
14:            </c:forEach></td>
15:        <c:set var="k" value="${k+1}"/>
16:        </tr></c:forEach>
17:      </table>
18: </body></html>
```

Notice that, as there are no scripting elements, I have removed the importing of Java libraries.

Lines 02 and 03 show the `taglib` directives for JSTL core and functions. In line 05, you can see how to use the `fn:length` function to determine the size of the EL implicit object `paramValues` and the `c:out` action to send the value of an EL expression to the output. You could have just written the naked EL expression, but `c:out` automatically converts characters that have special HTML meaning to the corresponding HTTP entities. For example, it writes & instead of &. Therefore, it's better to use `c:out`.

`c:set` initializes an index in line 08 and increments it in line 15. In lines 09 and 12, `c:forEach` lets you go through the elements of maps and arrays.

If you type in your browser

```
http://localhost:8080/test/req_params_jstl.jsp?a=b&c=d&a=zzz&empty=&empty=
```

you'll get the same output shown in Figure 6-2 for `req_params.jsp` (see Figure 1-24).

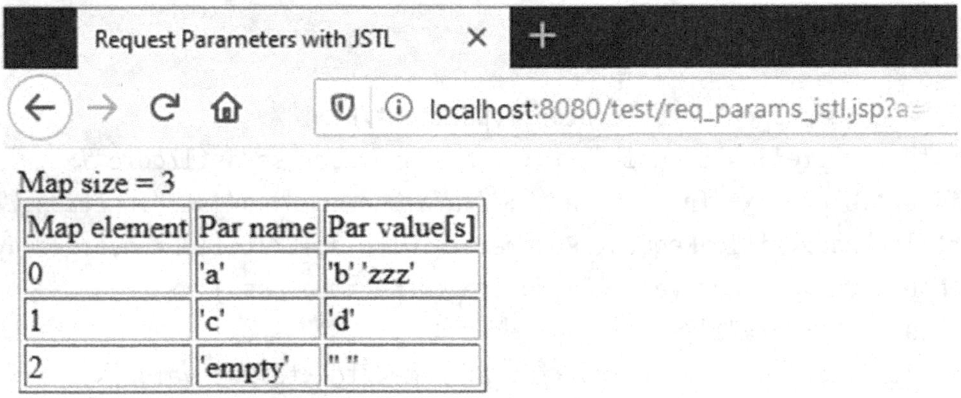

Figure 6-2. *Output of req_params_jstl.jsp*

In essence, `c:out` is for EL expressions what an expression scripting element is for JSP (i.e., Java) expressions. Besides the attribute `value`, it supports `default`, to provide a fallback output, and `escapeXml` that you set to `false` to prevent the escaping of XML characters, which are escaped by default.

With `c:set`, besides defining `var` and `value`, you can also specify the scope of the variable with the attribute `scope`. Finally, in alternative to `var`, you can use the pair of attributes `property` and `target` to specify which property of which object you want to modify.

In the example, you have seen that `c:forEach` lets you loop over a list of objects with the two attributes `var` and `items`. Alternatively, you can go through a list by means of the attributes `begin`, where 0 indicates the first element, `end`, and `step`. Further, if you define the name of a variable by setting the attribute `varStatus`, `c:forEach` will store in it an object of type `javax.servlet.jsp.jstl.core.LoopTagStatus`.

As these attributes are pretty straightforward, the best way for you to become familiar with them is to write a small page and see what happens when you set them to different values.

Before moving on, have a look at Table 6-9. It lists what types of objects you can assign to the attribute `items` and, correspondingly, what type of objects you get in the variable defined through `var`.

Table 6-9. *c:forEach Types*

Items	var
Array of instances of class C	Instance of C
Array of primitive values (e.g., of `int`)	Wrapped element (e.g., in `Integer`)
String of comma-delimited substrings	Substring
`java.util.Collection`	Element obtained by invoking `iterator()`
`java.util.Map`	Instance of `java.util.Map.Entry`
`java.util.Iterator`	An `Iterator` element
`java.util.Enumeration`	An `Enumeration` element
`javax.servlet.jsp.jstl.sql.Result`	SQL rows

c:if, c:choose, c:when, and c:otherwise

The JSTL versions of Java's `if` and `switch` are particularly useful tags. For example, the body of the following action is executed only if the EL expression calculates to `true`:

```
<c:if test="EL-expression"> ... </c:if>
```

Unfortunately, there is no c:else, but the JSTL version of switch (c:choose) is much more powerful than its Java counterpart. In fact, it's more like a chain of if..else:

```
<c:choose>
  <c:when test="EL-expression-1"> ... </c:when>
  <c:when test="EL-expression-2"> ... </c:when>
  ...
  <c:otherwise> ... </c:otherwise>
</c:choose>
```

Besides test, which lets you define the condition you want to test, c:if supports the two attributes var and scope, which c:if uses to store the condition's result.

There is no attribute supported by c:choose and c:otherwise, and c:when only supports test.

c:catch, c:remove, and c:url

With c:catch you can catch the exceptions that occur within its body. It accepts a var attribute, where it stores the result of the exception, of type java.lang.Throwable. For example, the following two lines will insert into the output the string "java.lang. ArithmaticException: / by zero":

```
<c:catch var="e"><% int k = 1/0; %></c:catch>
<c:if test="${e != null}"><c:out value="${e}"/></c:if>
```

c:remove lets you remove the variable defined in its pair of attributes var and scope.

c:url formats a string into a URL, which it then inserts into the output, like in the following example:

```
<a href="<c:url value="/tests/hello.jsp"/>">Hello World</a>
```

Notice the nested double quotes. This is not a problem, because Tomcat processes the action on the server and replaces it with a string representing the URL. The client doesn't see the inner double quotes.

You can also specify a var/scope pair of attributes to store the generated URL into a scoped variable and the attribute context to refer to another application. If you use the bodied form of c:url, you can define with c:param additional parameters that will be appended to the URL.

c:import, c:redirect, and c:param

`c:import` and `c:redirect` are generalized versions of the standard actions `jsp:include` and `jsp:forward`. The main difference is that the JSTL actions are not limited to the scope of the current application. They let you include or forward to any URL via the attribute `url`, which is in both cases the only attribute required.

The general syntax of c:import is as follows:

```
<c:import url="expr1" context="expr2" charEncoding="expr3" var="name"
scope="scope">
  <c:param name="expr4" value="expr5"/>
  ...
  </c:import>
```

By now, everything should be pretty clear to you. The only thing worth mentioning is that the default value for `charEncoding` is `"ISO-8859-1"`. I prefer to use UTF-8 because it is equally supported by all operating systems. Also, UTF-8 can handle non-European languages and has become the de facto standard on the Web. In case you are curious, UTF stands for UCS Transformation Format, where UCS means Universal Character Set.

`c:redirect` is equivalent to invoking `javax.servlet.http.HttpServletResponse.sendRedirect` and only admits the two attributes `url` and `context`. When designing a website, you might find it useful to remember that `c:redirect` changes the page that the user sees, thereby affecting the setting of bookmarks, while with `jsp:forward`, the user remains unaware of the page change.

c:forTokens

In addition to `c:forEach`, the JSTL provides a form of string tokenizer, which lets you easily extract from a string the substrings separated by one or more delimiters.

If you have a comma as a single delimiter, you can use `c:forEach`, but if you have more than one delimiter, or if the only delimiter is not a comma, `c:forTokens` is for you.

The general syntax of c:forTokens is as follows:

```
<c:forTokens var="name" items="expr1" delims="expr2" varStatus="name"
   begin="expr3" end="expr4" step="expr5">
  ...
</c:forTokens>
```

The i18n Library: Writing Multilingual Applications

You can take one of two approaches to internationalizing a web application: you can either provide a different version of the JSP pages for each locale and select them via a servlet when processing each request, or you can save locale-specific data in separate resource bundles and access them via i18n actions. The JSTL internationalization actions support both, but I will concentrate on the second approach, where the work of switching between languages is actually done in JSP.

fmt:setLocale, fmt:setBundle, fmt:setMessage, and fmt:param

Suppose that you want to support English and Italian. The first thing you have to do is identify all the strings that are going to be different in the two languages and define two bundles, one for each language (see Listings 6-21 and 6-22).

Listing 6-21. MyBundle_en.java

```
package myPkg.i18n;
import java.util.*;
public class MyBundle_en extends ListResourceBundle {
  public Object[][] getContents() {return contents;}
  static final Object[][] contents = {
    {"login.loginmess","Please login with ID and password"},
    {"login.submit","Submit"},
    {"login.choose","Choose the language"},
    {"login.english","English"},
    {"login.italian","Italian"}
    };
  }
```

Listing 6-22. MyBundle_it.java

```
package myPkg.i18n;
import java.util.*;
public class MyBundle_it extends ListResourceBundle {
  public Object[][] getContents() {return contents;}
  static final Object[][] contents = {
    {"login.loginmess","Loggati con ID e password"},
```

```
      {"login.submit","Invia"},
      {"login.choose","Scegli la lingua"},
      {"login.english","Inglese"},
      {"login.italian","Italiano"}
      };
   }
```

As you can see, a bundle is nothing other than a Java class that extends the class
`java.util.ListResourceBundle`. In this example, you will only find a simple login
page, but in reality, you'll have to include all the language-specific messages of your
application. I used the prefix `login` to show you that it's possible to group messages
within a bundle.

Listing 6-23 shows the login page that supports two languages. To try it out, copy the
folder named `international` from the software package international for this chapter
and import it in Eclipse. Then type in your browser http://localhost:8080/international.

Listing 6-23. index.jsp of a Multilingual Application

```
01: <%@page language="java" contentType="text/html"%>
02: <%@taglib prefix="c" uri="http://java.sun.com/jsp/jstl/core"%>
03: <%@taglib prefix="fmt" uri="http://java.sun.com/jsp/jstl/fmt"%>
04: <c:set var="langExt" value="en"/>
05: <c:if test="${param.lang!=null}">
06:    <c:set var="langExt" value="${param.lang}"/>
07:    </c:if>
08: <fmt:setLocale value="${langExt}"/>
09: <fmt:setBundle basename="myPkg.i18n.MyBundle"
10:    var="lang" scope="session"/>
11: <html><head><title>i18n</title></head><body>
12: <h1><fmt:message key="login.loginmess" bundle="${lang}"/></h1>
13: <form method="post" action="home.jsp">
14:    <input name=id>
15:    <input name=passwd>
16:    <input type="submit"
17:      value="<fmt:message key="login.submit" bundle="${lang}"/>"
18:      >
19: <h2><fmt:message key="login.choose" bundle="${lang}"/></h2>
```

207

```
20: <a href="index.jsp?lang=en">
21:   <fmt:message key="login.english" bundle="${lang}"/>
22:   </a>
23:  
24: <a href="index.jsp?lang=it">
25:   <fmt:message key="login.italian" bundle="${lang}"/>
26:   </a>
27: </body></html>
```

Lines 04–07 ensure that the page variable langExt is not null by setting it to en when the page is requested the first time. Line 08 sets the locale to the requested language code. The list of valid language codes is defined in the International Organization for Standardization (ISO) 639 standard. They're in lowercase (e.g., it for Italian), so you can't confuse them with the country codes defined in the ISO 3166 standard, which are in uppercase (e.g., IT for Italy).

In line 09, you set the bundle. Notice that it looks like the fully qualified class name of the two bundle classes but without the trailing underscore and language code. This is exactly how it should be done. Otherwise, the JSTL won't find your messages. After executing fmt:setBundle, the session variable lang points to the bundle in the correct language, thanks to the locale and the basename attribute.

After that, an element like the following one will insert in the appropriate language the message identified by the value of the key attribute:

```
<fmt:message key="keyName" bundle="${lang}"/>
```

Notice how the double quotes are nested in line 17 without causing any problem. This is because the actions are processed first. By the time Tomcat arrives to process the HTML, only the outer double quotes remain.

Figure 6-3 shows what the page looks like the first time you view it.

Figure 6-3. *The first time you view index.jsp*

Figure 6-4 shows how the page looks when you choose Italian by clicking the corresponding bottom link.

Figure 6-4. *The Italian version of index.jsp*

If Tomcat cannot find a bundle, it will display the key name preceded and followed by three question marks, as shown in Figure 6-5. This indicates that you must have made a mistake in the directory names.

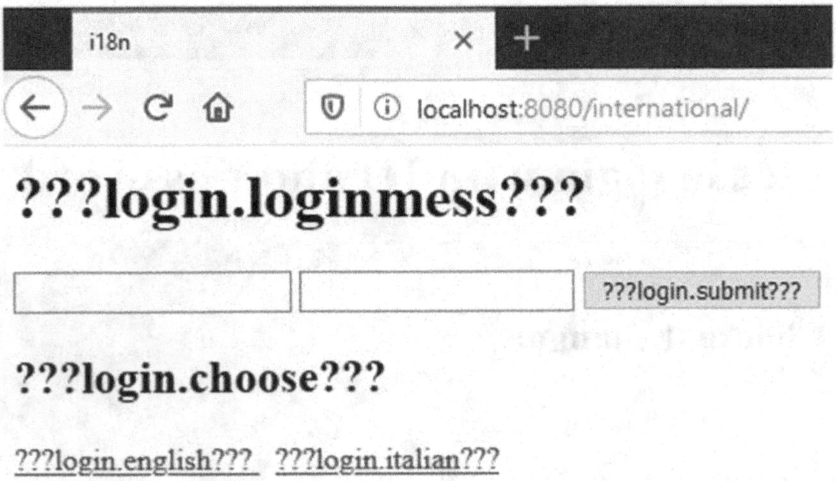

Figure 6-5. *index.jsp cannot find the messages*

Besides value, fmt:setLocale admits two additional attributes. The first one, scope, defines the scope of the locale. In the example, the default (i.e., page) is used, but scope lets you, for example, save the locale as a session attribute. The remaining attribute, variant, lets you specify nonstandardized locales.

fmt:setMessage also supports a var/scope pair of attributes to let you store the generated string into a scoped variable. You can also place the sub-action fmt:param inside the body of fmt:message and set its attribute value to a string that you want to append to the message.

fmt:bundle, fmt:setTimeZone, and fmt:timeZone

Similar to fmt:SetBundle is fmt:bundle, but while you choose the basename the same way you do with fmt:setBundle, you cannot store your choice in a scoped variable. Instead, the basename you choose applies to all elements inside the body of fmt:bundle. Additionally, fmt:bundle also supports the attribute prefix, which extends the basename. For example, if you replace lines 09–10 in Listing 6-23 with

```
<fmt:bundle basename="myPkg.i18n.MyBundle" prefix="login.">
```

and insert </fmt:bundle> immediately above the last line, you then replace the existing line 21

```
<fmt:message key="login.english" bundle="${lang}"/>
```

with

```
<fmt:message key="english"/>
```

`fmt:setTimeZone` sets the current time zone to what specified in the attribute `value`, like in

```
<fmt:setTimeZone value="America/Los_Angeles"/>
```

but it can also store a time zone into a scoped variable specified by the `var/scope` attribute pair.

When you define a time zone with `fmt:timeZone`, on the other hand, it only applies to the elements that appear in the body of the action.

fmt:parseNumber and fmt: formatNumber

`fmt:parseNumber` and `fmt:formatNumber` deal with numbers, percentages, and currencies. Both actions can store their result into a scoped variable through the usual `var/scope` pair of attributes or send it to the output if those attributes are missing.

Note that `fmt:formatNumber` is bodyless and expects to find the number to be formatted in the `value` attribute. `fmt:parseNumber` also supports `value` in its bodyless form, but if the attribute is missing, it takes as input the content of its body.

Both actions support a `type` attribute that can have the values `"number"`, `"currency"`, or `"percent"`.

Both actions also support a `pattern` attribute that lets you specify in detail a custom format. Table 6-10 lists the available symbols.

Table 6-10. *Pattern Symbols for the Number Actions*

Symbol	Meaning
0	A digit
E	Exponential form
#	A digit; 0 when absent
.	Decimal period
,	Group of digits separator
;	Format separator
-	Default negative prefix
%	Displays a percent sign after multiplying the number by 100
?	Displays a per mille sign after multiplying the number by 1000
¤	Place marker for the actual currency sign
X	Place marker for any other character used in the prefix or suffix
'	To quote special characters in the prefix or suffix

Try out `fmt:formatNumber` with different patterns and see what you get. Some symbols are obvious, others, less so.

Additionally, `fmt:parseNumber` supports the attributes `parseLocale`, `integerOnly` (that you must set to `false` when parsing a floating-point number), and `timeZone`.

Yet, on the other hand, `fmt:formatNumber` supports the attributes `currencyCode` (only when `type` is set to `"currency"`), `currencySymbol` (ditto), `groupingUsed` (set to `false` if you don't want a separator between triplets of integer digits), `maxIntegerDigits`, `minIntegerDigits`, `maxFractionDigits`, and `minFractionDigits`. The last four attributes specify the maximum and minimum number of digits you want before and after the decimal point.

fmt:ParseDate, fmt:formatDate, and fmt:requestEncoding

Like `fmt:parseNumber` and `fmt:formatNumber`, `fmt:ParseDate` and `fmt:formatDate` can store their result into a scoped variable or send it to the output. Also, `fmt:formatDate` is bodyless, while `fmt:parseDate` can be either bodyless or bodied. Not surprisingly, both actions support the `timeZone` attribute and the format attributes `dateStyle` (with possible values "full", "long", "medium", "short", or "default") and timeStyle (ditto). The Date Actions also support a pattern attribute. See Table 6-11 for a list of available symbols.

Table 6-11. *Pattern Symbols for the Date Actions*

Symbol	Meaning
G	Era designator (e.g., AD)
y	Year
M	Month
d	Day of the month
h	Hour (12-hour time)
H	Hour (24-hour time)
m	Minute
s	Second
S	Millisecond
E	Day of the week
D	Day of the year
F	Day of the week within the month (e.g., 2 means second Tue of the month)
w	Week of the year
W	Week of the month
a	AM/PM
k	Hour (12-hour time)
K	Hour (24-hour time)
z	Time zone
'	Escape for text
''	Quote

Additionally, fmt:parseDate supports the attribute parseLocale, and fmt:formatDate supports type (with possible values "date", "time", and "both").

With the remaining i18n action, `fmt:requestEncoding`, you specify what character encoding you expect for the text that the user types in forms, for example:

```
<fmt:requestEncoding value="UTF-8"/>
```

This action makes sense because the locale of the user might be different from the locale of the page. Note that if you develop a custom action that uses the method `ServletResponse.setLocale()` to set the locale of the response, it will take precedence over the character encoding set in `fmt:requestEncoding`.

Summary

In this chapter, you have learned everything about JSP standard actions and how to develop custom actions with JSP's tag extension mechanism.

You saw detailed examples that explained how to develop and use custom actions with and without body, both implemented with tag handlers and with tag files.

After explaining the Expression Language, I described in general terms the JSP Standard Tag Library and explained in detail the core and the internationalization tags.

In the next chapter, I will introduce you to XML, an understanding of which is essential for developing professional web applications.

CHAPTER 7

XML and JSP

HTML is probably the first markup language most of us came into contact with. It is a great language, but it's not without its problems.

For example, HTML mixes content data with the way the information is presented, thereby making it difficult to present the same data in different ways and to standardize presentations across multiple sets of data. Cascading Style Sheets (CSS) significantly reduces this problem but doesn't completely eliminate it, and it also forces you to learn yet another language.

Another problem, partly due to the way in which HTML is defined, is that the browsers are very forgiving about inconsistently written pages. In many cases, they're able to render pages with unquoted attribute values and tags that aren't closed properly. This encourages sloppiness in coding and wastes computer resources.

XML (whose standard is available at `www.w3.org/standards/xml/`) lets you organize information into a treelike structure in which each item of information represents a leaf. Its power and flexibility lie in the idea of defining its syntax and a mechanism for defining tags. This makes it possible for you to define your own markup language tailored for the type of information you're dealing with. This also lets you define XHTML, a version of HTML clean of inconsistencies, as a well-formatted XML file.

Also, XML is the perfect vehicle for exchanging structured information. In fact, XML's purpose is precisely to describe information.

I have introduced XML starting from HTML, because you're familiar with HTML and they're both markup languages. However, the usefulness of XML goes well beyond providing a better syntax for HTML. The great advantage of using XML in preference to proprietary formats whenever information needs to be structured is that standardized parsers make the manipulation of XML documents easy. In this chapter, you will also learn how to parse an XML document in JSP with XML custom tags and XPath.

XML represents one of the most used standard methods for the representation of information in many organizations. The other method is JSON (JavaScript Object Notation). JSON is not in the scope of this book, but it is important to introduce it

© Luciano Manelli and Giulio Zambon 2020
L. Manelli and G. Zambon, *Beginning Jakarta EE Web Development*,
https://doi.org/10.1007/978-1-4842-5866-8_7

against XML standard. It is a syntax used for storing and exchanging data adopted by organizations for communication instead of XML documents.

Both JSON and XML are used by a lot of programming languages: on one hand XML supports various data types, it offers the capability to display data being a markup language, and it is more secure; on the other, JSON is easy to retrieve (it can be parsed also by JavaScript functions), and it is faster and shorter because it fetches a JSON string. At last, XML presents attributes that let it a better document descriptor and it is more human readable, so it is used for configuration files. So, the choice of technology depends on the scope of your web application.

Cascading Style Sheets

Style sheets are used to separate presentation from content (whose standard is available at `www.w3.org/Style/CSS/`). The term cascading refers to the fact that you can write a series of style sheets, whereby each one builds upon and refines the styles defined in the more general ones.

You need the following three components to define styles: `selector {property: value}`

The selector is the HTML element you want to define, the property is the name of one of the elements' attributes, and the value is the attribute value. You can define several attributes for the same element by separating them with a semicolon, and you can style several elements with a single definition by separating them with a comma. To define more than one style for the same element, you can associate a class name to each separate style, for example:

```
<style type="text/css">
  p {font-size: 130%}
  p.bold {font-weight: bold}
  p.italic {font-style: italic}
</style>
```

Then, you can use the styles as follows:

```
<p>This is a default paragraph, large size</p>
<p class="bold">This is a large and bold paragraph</p>
<p class="bold italic">This is a large, bold, and italic paragraph</p>
<p class="italic" style="font-size: 100%;">This is an italic normal sized
paragraph</p>
```

You can place `style` elements inside the `head` or `body` HTML elements of your pages or define styles for individual elements by placing style definitions separated by semicolons in their `style` attribute.

The XML Document

To explain XML, I'll start by giving you a simple example that will accompany us throughout this chapter. For this purpose, I'll use the file shown in Listing 7-1. You can import in Eclipse the project "xml-validate" to analyze the following examples.

Listing 7-1. enterprises.xml

```
<?xml version="1.0" encoding="UTF-8"?>
<starfleet>
  <title>The two most famous starships in the fleet</title>
  <starship name="USS Enterprise" sn="NCC-1701">
    <class name="Constitution"/>
    <captain>James Tiberius Kirk</captain>
    </starship>
  <starship name="USS Enterprise" sn="NCC-1701-D">
    <class name="Galaxy"/>
    <captain>Jean-Luc Picard</captain>
    </starship>
  </starfleet>
```

The first line defines the standard and the character set used in the document. The tags are always closed, either with an end tag when they have a body (e.g., `<title>...</title>`) or with a slash if they're empty (e.g., `<class .../>`). There can be repeated tags (e.g., `starship`), and the attribute names are not unique (e.g., `name`).

As you can see, the tags reflect the logical structure of the data, although there are certainly many ways of structuring the same information. Each tag identifies an *element node* labeled with a name (e.g., `starfleet`, `title`, and `class`, also called an *element type*), often characterized by *attributes* that consist of a *name* and a *value* (e.g., `sn="NCC-1701"`), and possibly containing *child nodes* (e.g., `captain` inside `starship`), also called *sub-elements*.

XML documents can also contain processing instructions for the applications that handle them (enclosed between `<?` and `?>`), comments (enclosed between `<!--` and `-->`), and document-type declarations (more about that later). Notice that `enterprises.xml` doesn't provide any information concerning how the data it contains might be presented.

XML relies on the less-than sign to identify the tags. Therefore, if you want to use it for other purposes, you have to escape it by writing the four characters `<` instead. To escape larger blocks of text, you can use the CDATA section, as in the following example:

```
<![CDATA[<aTag>The tag's body</aTag>]]>
```

Looking at `enterprises.xml`, you might ask yourself why `sn` is an attribute of `starship`, while `captain` is a child element. Couldn't you make `captain` an attribute, as in the following example?

```
<starship name="USS Enterprise" sn="NCC-1701" captain="Jean-Luc Picard">
```

Yes, you could. It all depends on what you think you might like to do with the element in the future. With `captain` defined as an element, you can define attributes for it, such as its birth date. This wouldn't be possible if you had defined `captain` as an attribute. And the same applies to the `class` element. You could also replace the `starship` attributes `name` and `sn` with two children elements, but how much sense would it make?

We have to make one last consideration about empty vs. bodied elements. By defining the captain's name as the body of the element, as in

```
<captain>Jean-Luc Picard</captain>
```

you make it impossible for it to have children elements. Alternatively, you could have defined this:

```
<captain name="Jean-Luc Picard"></captain>
```

perhaps shortened, as in

```
<captain name="Jean-Luc Picard"/>
```

Defining Your Own XML Documents

The usefulness of being able to use XML tags tailored to your needs is greatly expanded by the possibility of formally specifying them in a separate document. This enables you to verify the validity of the XML documents and also to communicate their structure to others. Without a specification in a standardized format, you would have to describe your document structure in plain language or via examples. It wouldn't be the most efficient way, and it certainly wouldn't be good enough for automatic validation. The two most widely used methods to specify document structures are XML DTDs and XML schemas. You will see later on in this chapter that you can select which method your XML document uses for validation by adding an appropriate element to it.

XML DTDs

DTDs are better known than XML schemas, which have been developed more recently. They are also easier to understand. DTDs were originally developed for the XML predecessor, Standard Generalized Markup Language (SGML), and they have a very compact syntax. Listing 7-2 shows how a DTD for `enterprises.xml` would look.

Listing 7-2. starfleet.dtd

```
01: <!ELEMENT starfleet (title,starship*)>
02: <!ELEMENT title (#PCDATA)>
03: <!ELEMENT starship (class,captain)>
04: <!ATTLIST
05:     starship name CDATA #REQUIRED
06:     sn CDATA #REQUIRED>
07: <!ELEMENT class EMPTY>
08: <!ATTLIST class name CDATA #REQUIRED>
09: <!ELEMENT captain (#PCDATA)>
```

Line 01 defines the `starfleet` element as consisting of one `title` element and an undefined number of `starship` elements. Replacing the asterisk with a plus sign would require `starship` to occur at least once, and a question mark would mean zero or one starships. If you replaced `starship` with (`starship|shuttle`), it would mean that you could have a mix of `starship` and `shuttle` elements following the `title` (just as an example, because you haven't defined `shuttle`).

Line 02 specifies `title` to be a string of characters (the PC of PCDATA stands for *parsed character*). Line 07 shows how to specify that an element not be allowed to have a body. To complete the description of how to define elements, I only need to add that if you replaced `EMPTY` with `ANY`, it would mean that the element could contain any type of data.

Lines 04–06 specify the attributes for `starship`. The general format of an attribute list declaration is as follows:

`<!ATTLIST elementName attributeName attributeType defaultValue>`

Where *attributeType* can have a dozen of possible values, including `CDATA` (to indicate character data), an enumeration of all strings allowed (enclosed in parentheses and with bars as separators, as in `(left|right|center)`), `ID` (to indicate a unique identifier), and `IDREF` (the ID of another element). The *defaultValue* can be a quoted value (e.g., "0" or "a string"), the keyword `#REQUIRED` (to indicate that it's mandatory), the keyword `#IMPLIED` (to indicate that it can be omitted), or the keyword `#FIXED` followed by a value (to force the attribute to have that value).

XML Schemas

The most significant difference from DTDs is that the schemas are in XML syntax themselves (whose standard is available at `www.w3.org/standards/xml/schema`). This makes the schemas more extensible and flexible than DTDs. Furthermore, schemas can perform a more sophisticated validation thanks to their support data types. Let's see the XML schema for `enterprises.xml` (see Listing 7-3).

Listing 7-3. starfleet.xsd

```
01: <?xml version="1.0" encoding="UTF-8"?>
02: <xs:schema xmlns:xs="http://www.w3.org/2001/XMLSchema"
03:     xmlns="http://localhost:8080/xml-validate/xsd"
04:     targetNamespace="http://localhost:8080/xml-validate/xsd"
05:     elementFormDefault="qualified"
06:     attributeFormDefault="unqualified"
07:     >
08:   <xs:annotation>
09:     <xs:documentation xml:lang="en">
10:       Schema for Starfleet
```

```
11:        </xs:documentation>
12:      </xs:annotation>
13:    <xs:element name="starfleet">
14:      <xs:complexType>
15:        <xs:sequence>
16:          <xs:element name="title" type="xs:string" maxOccurs="1"/>
17:          <xs:element name="starship" type="ShipType"
                  maxOccurs="unbounded"/>
18:          </xs:sequence>
19:        </xs:complexType>
20:      </xs:element>
21:    <xs:complexType name="ShipType">
22:      <xs:all>
23:        <xs:element name="class" type="ClassType" minOccurs="1"/>
24:        <xs:element name="captain" type="xs:string" minOccurs="1"/>
25:        </xs:all>
26:      <xs:attribute name="name" type="xs:string" use="required"/>
27:      <xs:attribute name="sn" type="xs:string" use="required"/>
28:      </xs:complexType>
29:    <xs:complexType name="ClassType">
30:      <xs:attribute name="name" type="xs:string" use="required"/>
31:      </xs:complexType>
32:    </xs:schema>
```

Lines 02–07 establish that this schema conforms to the standard XML schema and define the schema's namespace and how XML files are supposed to refer to elements and attributes. To understand it all, you need to learn quite a bit about namespaces and schemas.

Lines 08–12 are essentially a comment.

Lines 13–20 specify the starfleet element, which is of a complex type, as defined in Line 14. This means that starfleet can have attributes and/or can contain other elements. Line 15 tells you in which way starfleet is complex: it contains a sequence of elements. Elements in xs:sequence must appear in the order in which they are specified (in this case, title followed by starship).

Line 16 specifies that `title` is of type `xs:string`, which is a primitive type hard-coded in the standard XML Schema. Line 16 also tells you that there can be maximum one `title` per `starfleet`. It is also possible to define `minOccurs`, and the default for both `minOccurs` and `maxOccurs` is 1. This means that by omitting `minOccurs`, you make `title` mandatory.

Line 17 declares that the `starship` element is of type `ShipType`, which is defined somewhere else in `starfleet.xsd`. This is an alternative to defining the type of an element inside its body, as we did with the `starfleet` element. Naming a type lets you use it for several element definitions and as a base for more complex types. However, I have only extracted the type specification from the body of `starship` to make the code more readable. `maxOccurs="unbounded"` states that there can be as many `starship` elements in `starfleet` as you need.

Lines 21–28 define the type of the `starship` element. It's a complex type, but it's different from that of `starfleet`. The `xs:all` group means that there can only be up to one element each of all those listed, in any order. This would normally mean that each `starship` could be empty or contain a `class`, a `captain`, or both as children. However, we want to make ship `class` and `captain` mandatory. To achieve this result, we specified the attribute `minOccurs="1"` for both elements.

Lines 26–27 define the two attributes of `starship`. The `use` attribute lets you specify that they are mandatory.

If you now look again at `enterprises.xml`, you'll notice that the `class` element has an attribute (`name`). Because of this attribute, you must define its type as complex, although `class` has no body. This is done in lines 29–31. As you can see, you specify an empty body by creating a complex type without sub-elements.

Occurrence Constraints

In `starfleet.xsd`, we used three attributes to limit the number of occurrences: `minOccurs` and `maxOccurs` when declaring elements and `use` when declaring attributes. While the constraints for elements accept non-negative integers as values (with 1 as the default), `use` can only have one of the following values: `required`, `optional` (the default), and `prohibited`. You can use two additional attributes when declaring either elements or attributes: `default` and `fixed`.

When applied to an attribute, `default` supplies the value of an optional attribute in case it is omitted when you define its element in the XML document (it is an error to provide a default for attributes that are `required`). Note that when you define elements in an XML document, they're always created with all their attributes, whether you explicitly define them in the XML document or not, because their existence is determined by their presence in the schema. When applied to an element, `default` refers to the element content, but it never results in the creation of elements. It only provides content for empty elements, for example, `<xs:attribute name="country" type="xs:string" default="USA"/>`.

The `fixed` constraint forces an attribute value or an element content to have a particular value. You can still define a value in the XML document, but it must match the fixed value assigned in the schema.

Data Types

There are four Data types:

- String Data types are used for values containing character strings.

- Date Data types are used for values containing date and time.

- Numeric Data types are used for values containing numeric elements.

- Miscellaneous Data types are used for other specific values.

Those types are all primitive unless String and Numeric that present also derived types. Table 7-1 summarizes the full list of primitive types.

Table 7-1. *XML Primitive Types*

Type	Example/Description
String Data types String	It contains characters, line feeds, and tab character, for example, "This is a string".
Numeric Data types Decimal	It contains numeric values, for example, `123.456`.
Date Data types Date	Like the date portion of `dateTime`, but with the addition of the time zone.
dateTime	For example, `2007-12-05T15:00:00.345-05:00` means 345 milliseconds after 3 PM Eastern Standard Time (EST) of December 5, 2007; fractional seconds can be omitted.

(continued)

Table 7-1. (*continued*)

Type	Example/Description
Duration	For example, P*a*Y*b*M*c*DT*d*H*e*M*f*S means *a* years, *b* months, *c* days, *d* hours, *e* minutes, and *f* seconds; a minus at the beginning, when present, indicates "in the past".
gDay	For example, 25.
gMonth	For example, 12.
gMonthDay	For example, 12–25.
gYear	For example, 2007.
gYearMonth	For example, 2007–12; g stands for Gregorian calendar, which is the calendar we use.
Time	Like the time portion of dateTime.
Miscellaneous Data types	
base64Binary	MIME encoding consisting of A–Z, a–z, 0–9, +, and /, with A = 0 and / = 63.
Boolean	For example, true and false.
Double	Formatted like float, but uses 64 bits.
Float	32-bit floating point, for example, 1.2e-4.
hexBinary	Hexadecimal encoding, for example, 1F represents the number 31 and corresponds to a byte containing the bit sequence 01111111.
NOTATION	Externally defined formats.
QName	Qualified XML name, for example, xs:string.
anyURI	Either an absolute or a relative URI.

The XML Schema standard also defines additional types called *derived,* among which are those listed in Table 7-2.

Table 7-2. XML Derived Types

Type	Example/Description
Data types derive from the String data type	
language	A natural language code as specified in the ISO 639 standard (e.g., FR for French and EN-US for American English)
normalizedString	A string that doesn't contain any carriage return, line feed, or tab characters
token	A string that doesn't contain any carriage return, line feed, tab characters, leading or trailing spaces, or sequences of two or more consecutive spaces
Name	A string that contains a valid XML name
Data types derive from the Numeric data type	
Byte	An integer number between -2^7 (-128) and 2^7-1 (127)
Int	An integer number between -2^{31} ($-2,147,483,648$) and $2^{31}-1$ (2,147,483,647)
Integer	An integer number
Long	An integer number between -2^{63} ($-9,223,372,036,854,775,808$) and $2^{63}-1$ (9,223,372,036,854,775,807)
negativeInteger	An integer number < 0
nonNegativeInteger	An integer number >= 0
nonPositiveInteger	An integer number <= 0
positiveInteger	An integer number > 0
short	An integer number between -2^{15} ($-32,768$) and $2^{15}-1$ (32,767)
unsignedByte	An integer number between 0 and 2^8-1 (255)
unsignedInt	An integer number between 0 and $2^{32}-1$ (4,294,967,295)
unsignedLong	An integer number between 0 and $2^{64}-1$ (18,446,744,073,709,551,615)
unsignedShort	An integer number between 0 and $2^{16}-1$ (65,535)

Simple Types

If you need to modify an already defined type without adding attributes or other elements, you can define a so-called *simple type* instead of recurring to a complex one. For example, the following code defines a string that can only contain up to 32 characters:

```
<xs:simpleType name="myString">
  <xs:restriction base="xs:string">
    <xs:maxLength value="32"/>
    </xs:restriction>
  </xsLsimpleType>
```

Besides `maxLength`, you can also apply the `length` and `minLength` attributes to listlike types. Additionally, you can use the `whiteSpace` and `pattern` attributes.

The possible values for `whiteSpace` are `preserve` (the default), `replace`, and `collapse`. With `replace`, all carriage return, line feed, and tab characters are replaced with simple spaces. With `collapse`, leading and trailing spaces are removed, and sequences of multiple spaces are collapsed into single spaces.

With `pattern`, you define a regular expression that must be matched. For example, the following code specifies that only strings consisting of at least one letter of the alphabet are valid:

```
<xs:pattern value="[A-Za-z]+"
```

For non-list types, you can also use the attributes `minExclusive`, `minInclusive`, `maxExclusive`, `maxInclusive`, `totalDigits`, `fractionDigits`, and `enumeration`. For example, this code defines a number with three decimal figures >= 10 and < 20:

```
<xs:simpleType name="xxyyyType">
  <xs:restriction base="xs:decimal">
    <xs:totalDigits value="6"/>
    <xs:fractionDigits value="3"/>
    <xs:minInclusive value="10.000"/>
    <xs:maxExclusive value="20.000"/>
    </xs:restriction>
  </xs:simpleType>
```

And here's an example of enumeration:

```
<xs:simpleType name="directionType">
  <xs:restriction base="xs:string">
    <xs:enumeration value="left"/>
    <xs:enumeration value="right"/>
    <xs:enumeration value="straight"/>
  </xs:restriction>
</xs:simpleType>
```

REGULAR EXPRESSIONS

A regular expression is a string that matches a set of strings according to certain rules. The basic component of a regular expression is called an *atom*. It consists of a single character (specified either individually or as a *class* of characters enclosed between square brackets) indicating that any of the characters in the class are a match. For example, both "a" and "[a]" are regular expressions matching the lowercase character 'a', while "[a-zA-Z]" matches all letters of the English alphabet.

Things can get complicated, because you can also subtract a class from a group or create a *negative group* by sticking a ^ character at the beginning of it. For example, "[(^abc) - [ABC]]" matches any character with the exclusion of the characters 'a', 'b', and 'c' in uppercase or lowercase. This is because the group ^abc matches everything with the exclusion of the three letters in lowercase, and the subtraction of [ABC] removes the same three letters in uppercase. Obviously, you could have obtained the same effect with the regular expression "[^aAbBcC]".

The characters \|.-^?*+{}()[] are special and must be escaped with a backslash. You can also use \n for newlines, \r for returns, and \t for tabs.

With atoms, you can build *pieces* by appending to it a *quantifier*. Possible quantifiers are ? (the question mark), + (the plus sign), * (the asterisk), and {n,m}, with n <= m indicating non-negative integers. The question mark indicates that the atom can be missing; the plus sign means any concatenation of one or more atoms; the asterisk means any concatenation of atoms (including none at all); and {n,m} means any concatenation of length >= n and <= m (e.g., "[a-z]{2,7}" means all strings containing between two and seven lowercase alphabetic characters). If you omit m but leave the comma in place, you leave the upper limit unbounded. If, on the other hand, you also omit the comma, you define a string of fixed length (e.g., "[0-9]{3}" means a string of exactly three numeric characters). You can concatenate pieces simply by writing them one after the other. For example, to define an identifier consisting of alphanumeric characters and underscores but beginning with a letter, you could write the expression "[a-zA-Z]{1}[a-zA-Z0-9_]*". The general term *branch* is used to indicate a single piece or a concatenation of pieces when the distinction is not relevant.

To specify partial patterns, you can insert at the beginning and/or at the end of each atom a sequence formed with a period and an asterisk. For example, ".*ABC.*" identifies all strings containing in any position the substring ABC. Without dot-asterisk wildcarding, "ABC" only matches a string of exactly three characters of length.

Several branches can be further composed by means of vertical bars to form a more general regular expression. For example, "[a-zA-Z]* | [0-9]*" matches all strings composed entirely of letters or of digits but not a mix of the two.

Instead of defining a new simple type by imposing a restriction, you can also specify that it consists of a list of items of an existing simple type. For example, the following code defines a type consisting of a series of directions:

```
<xs:simpleType name="pathType">
  <xs:list itemType="directionType"/>
</xs:simpleType>
```

Finally, besides xs:restriction and xs:list, you can define a new simple type by means of xs:union, which lets you combine two different preexisting types. For example, the following code defines a type that can be either a number between 1 and 10 or one of the strings "< 1" and "> 10":

```
<xs:simpleType name="myNumber">
  <xs:union>
    <xs:simpleType>
      <xs:restriction base="xs:positiveInteger">
        <xs:maxInclusive value="10"/>
      </xs:restriction>
    </xs:simpleType>
```

```
<xs:simpleType>
  <xs:restriction base="xs:string">
    <xs:enumeration value="< 1"/>
    <xs:enumeration value="> 10"/>
  </xs:restriction>
</xs:simpleType>
  </xs:union>
</xs:simpleType>
```

Complex Types

You've already seen some examples of complex types in `starfleet.xsd`. There are three models that you can use to group the elements contained in a complex type: `sequence` (in which the elements must appear in the specified sequence), `all` (in which there can only be up to one element each of all those listed, but they can appear in any order), and `choice` (in which the contained elements are mutually exclusive). Note that while `all` can only contain individual elements, `sequence` and `choice` can contain other groups. For example, the fragment

```
<xs:sequence>
  <xs:choice>
    <xs:element name="no" ... />
    <xs:all>
      <xs:element name="yes1" ... />
      <xs:element name="yes2" ... />
    </xs:all>
  </xs:choice>
  <xs:element name="whatever" ... />
</xs:sequence>
```

defines an element that contains one of the following combinations of elements:

- `whatever`
- `no`, `whatever`
- `yes1`, `whatever`

- yes2, whatever

- yes1, yes2, whatever

- yes2, yes1, whatever

Complex type definitions provide many additional options, but are not always easy to handle. One might even argue that they've been overengineered. Therefore, to describe them in detail would exceed the scope of this manual. Nevertheless, the information I have provided on primitive and simple types, together with the description of the three model groups, is already enough to cover most cases.

Validation

An XML document is said to be *valid* if it passes the checks done by a validating parser against the document's DTD or XML schema. For the parser to be able to operate, the XML document must be *well formed*, which means that all tags are closed, the attributes are quoted, the nesting is done correctly, and so on. A validating parser, besides checking for well formedness, also checks for validity.

You actually have to validate two documents: the XML file and the DTD or XML Schema. In the example, those are `enterprises.xml` and `starfleet.dtd/starfleet.xsd`, respectively. The simplest way to do the validation is to use a development environment like Eclipse, which validates the documents as you type. An alternative is to use online services. For example, the tool available at `http://xmlvalidation.com` can check XML files, DTD files, and XML schemas.

In general, you need to go through three steps to validate an XML document:

1. Associate the document to the DTD/schema against which it is to be validated.

2. Define an exception handler to specify what happens when a validation error is detected.

3. Parse the document with a validating parser, which validates your XML document against the DTD/schema.

PARSERS

A parser is a piece of software that breaks down a document into tokens, analyzes the syntax of the tokens to form valid expressions, and finally interprets the expressions and performs corresponding actions.

DOM parsers build a tree of nodes after loading the whole document in memory. Therefore, they require quite a bit of memory. SAX, on the other hand, parses the documents from streams and therefore has a smaller memory footprint. The flexibility of the DOM also costs in terms of performance, and DOM implementations tend to be slower than SAX implementations, although they might overall be more efficient with small XML files that don't stretch memory usage. The two most widely used packages implementing DOM and SAX are Xerces and Java API for XML Processing (JAXP). I have used JAXP in all the examples of this chapter: it is present in the JDK package.

However, you could also use the Xerces package. Xerces are the developer of SAX, and the version of SAX included in JAXP is not identical to the original one. You can install the Xerces version downloaded from `http://xerces.apache.org/`. All you need to do is click "`Xerces-J-bin.2.12.1.zip`" (the binary distribution) under the heading `Xerces2 Java` (there might be a newer version when you go there), expand `Xerces-J-bin.2.12.1.zip`, and copy `xercesimpl.jar` in the project's `lib` folder of the software package of this chapter. The latest version release of xercesImpl.jar (2.12.1) contains DOM level 3, SAX 2.0.2, and the JAXP 1.4 APIs as well as of the XNI API (the Xerces Native Interface). I have included `starfleet_validate_sax_schema_xerces.jsp` in the software package (xml-validate) of this chapter as an example.

Using JSP to Validate XML Against a DTD

To validate an XML file against a DTD, you must first associate the XML document with the DTD by adding a DOCTYPE declaration to the XML file. The declaration, which you should insert immediately after the `<?xml...?>` line, is as follows:

```
<!DOCTYPE starfleet SYSTEM "http://localhost:8080/xml-validate/dtd/
starfleet.dtd">
```

Notice that the file `starfleet.dtd` doesn't need to be in the WEB-INF\dtd\ folder. We had to place the DTDs there because Tomcat expected them there, but if you do the validation yourself, Tomcat is out of the loop. You can therefore place your DTDs wherever you like.

The next step is the definition of an exception handler. This is a Java object of a class that extends `org.xml.sax.helpers.DefaultHandler` and replaces three of its methods: `warning`, `error`, and `fatalError`. Once the handler is registered with the parser, the parser executes the appropriate method upon encountering a validation problem. The default behavior of `DefaultHandler` is to do nothing. Therefore, you need to overwrite the methods in order to report the errors. Listing 7-4 shows you the code of a possible handler into the `WEB-INF\classes\myPkg` folder of your application directory (in `src\myPkg` folder in `Eclipse environment`). It's really up to you to decide what level of reporting you'd like to have, but I have decided to report all validation problems and interrupt the parsing.

Listing 7-4. ParsingExceptionHandler.java

```java
package myPkg;
import org.xml.sax.helpers.DefaultHandler;
import org.xml.sax.SAXParseException;
public class ParsingExceptionHandler extends DefaultHandler {
  public SAXParseException parsingException = null;
  public String errorLevel = null;
  public void warning(SAXParseException e) {
    errorLevel = "Warning";
    parsingException = e;
    }
  public void error(SAXParseException e) {
    errorLevel = "Error";
    parsingException = e;
    }
  public void fatalError(SAXParseException e) {
    errorLevel = "Fatal error";
    parsingException = e;
    }
  }
```

As you can see, it's pretty simple. You define two public attributes: one to save the exception generated by the parser and one to save the error level. You then update the two attributes in each one of the three methods. After each parsing, you can check one of the attributes for `null` in order to determine whether the parsing succeeded or not.

You are now ready to perform the validation. Listing 7-5 shows you a JSP page that implements a SAX parser.

Listing 7-5. starfleet_validate_sax.jsp (first cut)

```
<%@page language="java" contentType="text/html"%>
<%@page import="javax.xml.parsers.SAXParserFactory"%>
<%@page import="javax.xml.parsers.SAXParser"%>
<%@page import="org.xml.sax.InputSource"%>
<%@page import="myPkg.ParsingExceptionHandler"%>
<html><head><title>Starfleet validation (SAX - DTD)</title></head><body>
<%
  SAXParserFactory factory = SAXParserFactory.newInstance();
  factory.setValidating(true);
  SAXParser parser = factory.newSAXParser();
  InputSource inputSource = new InputSource("webapps/xml-validate/xml/
  enterprises.xml");
  ParsingExceptionHandler handler = new ParsingExceptionHandler();
  parser.parse(inputSource, handler);
%>
</body></html>
```

After instantiating the parser factory and setting its `validating` property to `true`, you direct the factory to create a SAX parser. Then you instantiate the `InputSource` class to access the XML document and the exception handler. After that, all you need to do is execute the parser.

This implementation is not very nice, though, because it causes the dumping of a stack trace whenever the validation fails. It is better to wrap the parsing inside a `try/catch` as shown in Listing 7-6, so that you can display validation errors without stack trace.

Note that before you can execute the improved version of `starfleet_validate_sax.jsp`, you need to download the `StringEscapeUtils` from Apache Commons. Their purpose is to convert special characters to their corresponding HTML entities, so that they display correctly in your web page. Go to http://commons.apache.org/proper/ commons-text/download_text.cgi and click the link commons-text-1.8-bin.zip.

To install it, unzip the file and copy commons-text-1.8.jar to WEB-INF\lib folder of the application. In that way, you will not run the risk of later needing a different version of the same library for another application and introducing a conflict when both versions are copied in Tomcat's lib folder.

Listing 7-6. starfleet_validate_sax.jsp

```
<%@page language="java" contentType="text/html"%>
<%@page import="javax.xml.parsers.SAXParserFactory"%>
<%@page import="javax.xml.parsers.SAXParser"%>
<%@page import="org.xml.sax.InputSource"%>
<%@page import="org.apache.commons.text.StringEscapeUtils"%>
<%@page import="myPkg.ParsingExceptionHandler"%>
<html><head><title>Starfleet validation (SAX - DTD)</title></head><body>
<%
  SAXParserFactory factory = SAXParserFactory.newInstance();
  factory.setValidating(true);
  SAXParser parser = factory.newSAXParser();
  InputSource inputSource = new InputSource("webapps/xml-validate/xml/
  enterprises.xml");
  ParsingExceptionHandler handler = new ParsingExceptionHandler();
  try { parser.parse(inputSource, handler); }
  catch (Exception e) { }
  if (handler.errorLevel == null) {
    out.println("The document is valid.");
    }
  else {
    out.println(
        "*** Validation " + handler.errorLevel + ": "
      + StringEscapeUtils.escapeHtml4(handler.parsingException.toString())
      );
    }
  %>
</body></html>
```

Now, if you type `http://localhost:8080/xml-validate/with-dtd/starfleet_ validate_sax.jsp` in a browser, you should get a one-liner confirming that `enterprises.xml` is correct.

To use a DOM parser instead of SAX, make a copy of `starfleet_validate_sax.jsp`, name it `starfleet_validate_dom.jsp`, and replace six lines with seven new lines, as shown in Listing 7-7.

Listing 7-7. starfleet_validate_dom.jsp

```
<%@page language="java" contentType="text/html"%>
<%@page import="javax.xml.parsers.DocumentBuilderFactory"%>
<%@page import="javax.xml.parsers.DocumentBuilder"%>
<%@page import="org.xml.sax.InputSource"%>
<%@page import="org.apache.commons.text.StringEscapeUtils"%>
<%@page import="myPkg.ParsingExceptionHandler"%>
<html><head><title>Starfleet validation (DOM - DTD)</title></head><body>
<%
  DocumentBuilderFactory factory = DocumentBuilderFactory.newInstance();
  factory.setValidating(true);
  DocumentBuilder parser = factory.newDocumentBuilder();
  InputSource inputSource = new InputSource("webapps/xml-validate/xml/
  enterprises.xml");
  ParsingExceptionHandler handler = new ParsingExceptionHandler();
  parser.setErrorHandler(handler);
  try { parser.parse(inputSource); }
  catch (Exception e) { }
  if (handler.errorLevel == null) {
    out.println("The document is valid.");
  }
  else {
    out.println(
        "*** Validation " + handler.errorLevel + ": "
      + StringEscapeUtils.escapeHtml4(handler.parsingException.toString())
      );
  }
%>
</body></html>
```

Using JSP to Validate XML Against a Schema

The procedure used to validate an XML file against a schema is almost identical to the procedure explained in the previous section for validating against a DTD.

To avoid confusion, I made copies of enterprises.xml and starfleet_validate_ sax.jsp and renamed them, respectively, enterprises_schema.xml and starfleet_ validate_sax_schema.jsp.

In enterprises_schema.xml, to change from DTD to schema, you only need to remove the DOCTYPE declaration and add to the starfleet tag some attributes:

```
<starfleet
    xmlns="http://localhost:8080/xml-validate/xsd"
    xmlns:xsi="http://www.w3.org/2001/XMLSchema-instance"
    xsi:schemaLocation="http://localhost:8080/xml-validate/xsd
        http://localhost:8080/xml-validate/xsd/starfleet.xsd"
    >
```

Listing 7-8 shows starfleet_validate_sax_schema.jsp with the differences from starfleet_validate_sax.jsp highlighted in bold.

Listing 7-8. starfleet_validate_sax_schema.jsp

```
<%@page language="java" contentType="text/html"%>
<%@page import="javax.xml.parsers.SAXParserFactory"%>
<%@page import="javax.xml.parsers.SAXParser"%>
<%@page import="org.xml.sax.InputSource"%>
<%@page import="org.apache.commons.text.StringEscapeUtils"%>
<%@page import="myPkg.ParsingExceptionHandler"%>
<html><head><title>Starfleet validation (SAX - schema)</title></head><body>
<%
  SAXParserFactory factory = SAXParserFactory.newInstance();
  factory.setValidating(true);
  factory.setNamespaceAware(true);
  factory.setFeature("http://apache.org/xml/features/validation/schema",
  true);
  SAXParser parser = factory.newSAXParser();
  InputSource inputSource =
```

```
  new InputSource("webapps/xml-validate/xml/enterprises_schema.xml");
ParsingExceptionHandler handler = new ParsingExceptionHandler();
try { parser.parse(inputSource, handler); }
catch (Exception e) { }
if (handler.errorLevel == null) {
  out.println("The document is valid.");
  }
else {
  out.println(
      "*** Validation " + handler.errorLevel + ": "
    + StringEscapeUtils.escapeHtml4(handler.parsingException.toString())
    );
  }
%>
</body></html>
```

As you can see, apart from updating the page title and the name of the XML file, you only need to switch on two features of the parser that tell it to use a schema instead of a DTD.

What I said about changing SAX to DOM in starfleet_validate_sax.jsp also applies to starfleet_validate_sax_schema.jsp. You will find starfleet_validate_dom_schema.jsp in the software package for this chapter.

JSTL-XML and XSL

The XML actions specified in JSTL are meant to address the basic XML needs that a JSP programmer is likely to encounter.

To make XML file contents easier to access, the W3C specified the XML Path Language (XPath). The name XPath was chosen to indicate that it identifies paths within XML documents (see www.w3.org/TR/xpath). The JSTL-XML actions rely on that language to identify XML components.

To avoid confusion between EL expressions and XPath expressions, the actions that require an XPath expression always use the select attribute. In this way, you can be sure that all expressions outside select are EL expressions. Several XML actions are the XPath counterparts of equivalent core actions, with the attribute select replacing the attribute value (when present). They are x:choose, x:forEach, x:if, x:out, x:otherwise, x:set, and x:when.

The remaining three actions are x:parse and the pair x:transform and x:param. But before you can learn about them, we have to talk about the Extensible Stylesheet Language (XSL).

XSL is a language for expressing style sheets that describe how to display and transform XML documents. The specification documents are available from www.w3.org/Style/XSL/.

While CSS only needs to define how to represent the predefined HTML tags, XSL has to cope with the fact that there are no predefined tags in XML! How do you know whether a <table> element in an XML file represents a table of data as you know it from HTML or an object around which you can sit for dinner? That's why XSL is more than a style-sheet language. It actually uses XPath (the language to navigate in XML documents), XQuery (the language for querying XML documents), and XSLT (a language to transform XML documents that can completely change their structure).

XPath

XPath expressions identify a set of XML nodes through patterns. Extensible Stylesheet Language Transformations (XSLT) templates (see later in this chapter for XSLT examples) then use those patterns when they apply transformations. Possible XPath nodes can be any of these: document/root, comment, element, attribute, text, processing instruction, and namespace.

Take a look at the following XML document:

```
<?xml version="1.0" encoding="UTF-8"?>
<whatever xmlns:zzz="http://myWeb.com/whatever">
  <!-- bla bla -->   <?myAppl "xyz"?>
  <item name="anything">
    <subitem>The quick brown fox</subitem>
    </item>
</whatever>
```

The document (or root) node is <whatever>, <!-- bla bla --> is a comment node, <subitem>...</subitem> is an element node, name="anything" is an attribute node, the string The quick brown fox is a text node, <?myAppl "xyz"?> is a processing-instruction node, and xmlns:zzz="http://myWeb.com/whatever" is a namespace node.

As with URLs, XPath uses a slash as a separator. Absolute paths start with a slash, while all other paths are relative. Similar to file directories, a period indicates the current node, while a double period indicates the parent node.

Several nodes with the same name are distinguished by indexing them, as Java does with array elements. For example, let's say you have the following XML code:

```
<a> <b>whatever</b> <b>never</b> </a>
<c> <non_b>no</non_b> <b>verywell</b> </c>
<a> <b attr="zz">nice</b> <b attr="xxx">ok</b> </a>
```

The pattern /a/b selects the four <b> elements, which contain whatever, never, nice, and ok. The <b> element with verywell isn't selected, because it's inside <c> instead of <a>. The pattern /a[1]/b[0] selects the <b> element with nice. Attribute names are prefixed by an @. For example, /a[1]/b[1]/@attr refers to the attribute that has the value xxx in the example.

A clever thing in XPath: you can use conditions as indexes. For example, /a/b[@attr="zz"] selects the same <b> element selected by /a[1]/b[0], while /a[b] selects all <a> elements that have <b> as a child (in the example, both), and /a[b="never"] selects the first <a> element. A final example: /a/b[@attr][0] selects the first <b> element that is contained in an <a> and has the attribute attr (i.e., it selects once again the element /a[1]/b[0]).

XPath defines several operators and functions related to node sets, positions, or namespaces, and it defines string, numeric, boolean, and conversion operations.

A *node set* is a group of nodes considered collectively. A node set resulting from the execution of an XPath expression doesn't necessarily contain several nodes. It can consist of a single node or even none. Keep in mind that the nodes belonging to a node set can be organized in a tree, but not necessarily. For example, the expression $myDoc//C identifies all C elements in a document that was parsed into the variable myDoc. It is unlikely that they form a tree.

Within XPath, you have access to the implicit JSP objects you're familiar with. Table 7-3 lists the mappings.

Table 7-3. *XPath Mappings of Implicit JSP Objects*

JSP	XPath
`pageContext.findAttribute("attrName")`	`$attrName`
`request.getParameter("parName")`	`$param:paramName`
`request.getHeader("headerName")`	`$header:headerName`
`cookie's value for name foo`	`$cookie:foo`
`application.getInitParameter("initParName")`	`$initParam:initParName`
`pageContext.getAttribute("attrName", PageContext.PAGE_SCOPE)`	`$pageScope:attrName`
`pageContext.getAttribute("attrName", PageContext.REQUEST_SCOPE)`	`$requestScope:attrName`
`pageContext.getAttribute("attrName", PageContext.SESSION_SCOPE)`	`$sessionScope:attrName`
`pageContext.getAttribute("attrName", PageContext.APPLICATION_SCOPE)`	`$applicationScope:attrName`

Before we look at an XPath example, I would like to give you a more rigorous reference of its syntax and explain some terms that you are likely to encounter "out there."

To identify a node or a set of nodes, you need to navigate through the tree structure of an XML document from your current position within the tree (the *context node*) to the target. The path description consists of a series of steps separated by slashes, whereby each step includes the navigation direction (the *axis specifier*), an expression identifying the node[s] (the *node test*), and a condition to be satisfied (the *predicate*) enclosed between square brackets.

A slash at the beginning indicates that the path begins at the root node, while paths relative to the context node begin without a slash. Two consecutive colons separate the axis specifier and the node test. For example, this code identifies the second attribute of all B elements immediately below the root element A:

```
/child::A/child::B/attribute::*[position()=2]
```

You can express the same path with an abbreviated syntax, as follows:

```
/A/B/@*[2]
```

where `child`, `::`, and `position()=` are simply omitted and `attribute` is represented by @.
Table 7-4 shows the possible axis specifiers and their abbreviated syntax.

Table 7-4. *Axis Specifiers*

Specifier	Abbreviated Syntax
Ancestor	Not available (n/a)
ancestor-or-self	n/a
Attribute	@
Child	Default; do not specify it
Descendant	//
descendant-or-self	n/a
Following	n/a
following-sibling	n/a
Namespace	n/a
Parent	(i.e., two dots)
Preceding	n/a
preceding-sibling	n/a
Self	(i.e., a single dot)

As node tests, you can use node names with or without a namespace prefix, or you can use an asterisk to indicate all names. With abbreviated syntax, an asterisk on its own indicates all element nodes, and @* indicates all attributes.

You can also use `node()` as a node test to indicate all possible nodes of any type. Similarly, `comment()` indicates all comment nodes, `text()` indicates all text nodes, and `processing-instruction()` indicates all processing-instruction nodes.

For example, the following code selects all elements B descendant of A that have the attribute xx set to `'z'`:

```
A//B[@xx='z']
```

while to select all elements C anywhere in the tree that have the attribute yy, you can do this:

```
//C[@yy]
```

To form expressions, besides the operators you have already seen (i.e., slash, double slash, and square brackets), you have available all standard arithmetic and comparison operators (i.e., +, -, *, div, mod, =, !=, <, <=, >, and >=). Additionally, you have and and or for boolean operations and the union operator | (i.e., the vertical bar) to merge two node sets.

References to variables are indicated by sticking a dollar sign before them, as shown in the following example:

```
<x:parse doc="${sf}" varDom="dom"/>
<x:forEach var="tag" select="$dom//starship">
```

where I parse an XML document into the variable dom and then use $dom when I refer to it in an XPath expression.

An XPath Example

So far, everything has been pretty dry and abstract. To spice things up a bit, we are going to write a JSP page that parses an XML file, selects its elements and attributes, and displays them in an HTML table. Listing 7-9 shows the XML file we'll play with, starfleet.xml. It is an expanded version of the file enterprises.xml (Listing 7-1) you have already encountered in the validation section of this chapter. Import in Eclipse the project "testxPath" to analyze the following example. Before you proceed with the example, you will need also to download from http://xalan.apache.org/xalan-j/downloads.html and copy the *XPath* related library **xalan.jar** into your *lib* project folder.

Listing 7-9. starfleet.xml

```
<?xml version="1.0" encoding="UTF-8"?>
<starfleet>
  <starship name="Enterprise" sn="NX-01">
    <class commissioned="2151">NX</class>
    <captain>Jonathan Archer</captain>
    </starship>
  <starship name="USS Enterprise" sn="NCC-1701">
```

```
    <class commissioned="2245">Constitution</class>
    <captain>James Tiberius Kirk</captain>
  </starship>
  <starship name="USS Enterprise" sn="NCC-1701-A">
    <class commissioned="2286">Constitution</class>
    <captain>James T. Kirk</captain>
  </starship>
  <starship name="USS Enterprise" sn="NCC-1701-B">
    <class commissioned="2293">Excelsior</class>
    <captain>John Harriman</captain>
  </starship>
  <starship name="USS Enterprise" sn="NCC-1701-C">
    <class commissioned="2332">Ambassador</class>
    <captain>Rachel Garrett</captain>
  </starship>
  <starship name="USS Enterprise" sn="NCC-1701-D">
    <class commissioned="2363">Galaxy</class>
    <captain>Jean-Luc Picard</captain>
  </starship>
  <starship name="USS Enterprise" sn="NCC-1701-E">
    <class commissioned="2372">Sovereign</class>
    <captain>Jean-Luc Picard</captain>
  </starship>
</starfleet>
```

Notice that it doesn't include the DOCTYPE element necessary for DTD validation or the namespace declarations necessary for schema validation. This is because in this example we are not going to do any validation. Listing 7-10 shows the JSP page that does the conversion to HTML, and Figure 7-1 shows its output as it appears in a web browser when you type http://localhost:8080/testxPath/xpath/starfleet.jsp in your browser.

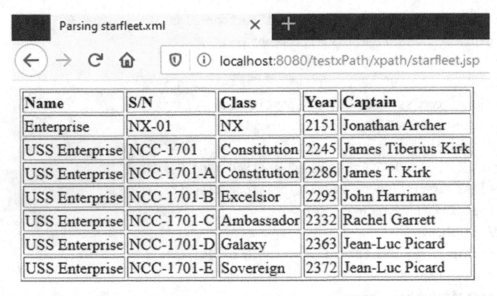

Figure 7-1. *Starfleet information parsing XML file*

Listing 7-10. starfleet.jsp

```
01: <%@page language="java" contentType="text/html"%>
02: <%@taglib uri="http://java.sun.com/jsp/jstl/core" prefix="c"%>
03: <%@taglib uri="http://java.sun.com/jsp/jstl/xml" prefix="x"%>
04: <c:import url="starfleet.xml" var="sf"/>
05: <x:parse doc="${sf}" varDom="dom"/>
06: <html><head>
07:   <title>Parsing starfleet.xml</title>
08:   <style>th {text-align:left}</style>
09:   </head>
10: <body>
11: <table border="1">
12:   <tr><th>Name</th><th>S/N</th><th>Class</th><th>Year</th><th>Captain
      </th></tr>
13:   <x:forEach var="tag" select="$dom//starship">
14:     <tr>
15:       <td><x:out select="$tag/@name"/></td>
16:       <td><x:out select="$tag/@sn"/></td>
17:       <td><x:out select="$tag/class"/></td>
18:       <td><x:out select="$tag/class/@commissioned"/></td>
```

244

```
19:        <td><x:out select="$tag/captain"/></td>
20:        </tr>
21:      </x:forEach>
22:    </table>
23: </body>
24: </html>
```

In line 04, you load the XML file in memory, and in line 05, you parse it into an object of type `org.apache.xerces.dom.DeferredDocumentImpl`, which implements the standard interface `org.w3c.dom.Document` of a Document Object Model (DOM). In lines 13–21, you loop through all the `starship` tags of the DOM, regardless of how "deep" they are in the structure. You can achieve this with the double slash. Inside the `x:forEach` loop, the variable `tag` refers in turn to each `starship`, and you can display the information contained in attributes and sub-elements. Notice that the `select` paths inside the loop always start with the slash. This is because the root element in each loop iteration is a `starship` tag, not `starfleet`, which is the root element of the document.

x:parse

With `starfleet.jsp`, you have just seen an example of how to use `x:parse` and XPath to convert XML into HTML. Table 7-5 summarizes all attributes that `x:parse` supports.

Table 7-5. *x:parse Attributes*

Attribute	Description
doc	Source XML document to be parsed.
varDom	Name of the EL variable to store the parsed XML data as an object of type `org.w3c.dom.Document`.
scopeDom	Scope for `varDom`.
filter	Filter of type `org.xml.sax.XMLFilter` to be applied to the source XML.
systemId	System identifier for parsing the XML source. It is a URI that identify the origin of the XML data, potentially useful to some parsers.
var	Name of the variable to store the parse XML data (of implementation-dependent type).
scope	Scope for `var`.
xml	Text of the document to parse.

Instead of storing the XML source code in the attribute doc, you can also make x:parse a bodied action and store the source XML in its body.

What About JSON?

Now can we represent Starfleet in another way and convert it in HTML with another technology? The answer is JSON. JSON is a free and independent data format derived from JavaScript. It is regularly used for reading data from a web server, and for displaying them the data in a web page, simply because its format is only text. Now, it is useful to introduce at first JavaScript basics.

JavaScript

JavaScript is the most widely used client-side scripting language on the Web. By adding it to your web pages, you can make your pages do things, such as prevalidate forms or immediately react to a user's actions. The syntax of JavaScript was modeled on that of Java. Therefore, if you know Java, you should find JavaScript easy to learn.

One noteworthy difference from Java is that you can omit variable declarations in the top-level code. Moreover, JavaScript lacks Java's static typing and strong type checking. This gives you more freedom, but it comes with the risk of messing things up in a big way. JavaScript relies on built-in objects, but it does not support classes or inheritance. It is an interpreted language, and object binding is done at runtime.

JavaScript is also the most popular implementation of ES.ECMAScript (abbreviated to ES) standard upon which it is based. This standard, its implementations and its evolution in time, represents the importance of this technology. Moreover, ESNext is the name that indicates the future version of JavaScript and of its new features than will be added to different engines implemented in projects widely used in web application (e.g., node.js, angular.js, etc.). Similarly JavaScript is also the base of TypeScript, an open source programming language used for developing JavaScript applications.

Parsing JSON

Now, I will introduce a simple example that uses the JSON.parse function of JavaScript for parsing a JSON file in an html script. You can import in Eclipse the project "jsonexample" to analyze it. JSON.parse is a function that converts a string (written in JSON) into a JavaScript object. Its simplicity shows why it is used in many sectors as

NoSQL database management or social media websites. It is characterized by a comma-separated list of properties and delimited by braces. It is also can be validated to ensure that required properties are met.

JSON supports six types shown in Table 7-6.

Table 7-6. *JSON Types*

Attribute	Description
Number	Signed decimal number
String	Sequence of characters
Boolean	Values true or false
Array	Ordered list of zero or more values
Object	Collection of properties where the keys are strings
Null	Empty value

Now I create a JavaScript file containing JSON syntax, and then I parse it with the parse command of JavaScript. First, we create a Starfleet JSON object (similar to XML object). It is an array of starship written inside square brackets like JavaScript as shown in Listing 7-11.

Listing 7-11. JSON Starfleet Example File

```
"starship":
    [
        {
            "Name": "Enterprise",
            "SN": "NX-01",
            "Class": "NX",
            "Year": "2151",
            "Captain": "Jonathan Archer"
        },
        {
            "Name": "USS Enterprise",
            "SN": "NCC-1701",
```

```
                              "Class": "Constitution",
                              "Year": "2245",
                              "Captain": "James Tiberius Kirk"
                    },
                    {

                              "Name": "USS Enterprise",
                              "SN": "NCC-1701-B",
                              "Class": "Excelsior",
                              "Year": "2293",
                              "Captain": "John Harriman"
                    },
                    {

                              "Name": "USS Enterprise",
                              "SN": "NCC-1701-C",
                              "Class": "Ambassador",
                              "Year": "2332",
                              "Captain": "Rachel Garrett"
                    },
                    {

                              "Name": "USS Enterprise",
                              "SN": "NCC-1701-D",
                              "Class": "Galaxy",
                              "Year": "2363",
                              "Captain": "Jean-Luc Picard"
                    },
                    {

                              "Name": "USS Enterprise",
                              "SN": "NCC-1701-E",
                              "Class": "Sovereign",
                              "Year": "2372",
                              "Captain": "Jean-Luc Picard"
                    }
          ]
```

In this example, the starship is a type array within five objects with the following keys: Name, SN, Class, Year, and Captain.

Now, create the JavaScript string containing JSON syntax in the external file shown in Listing 7-12.

Listing 7-12. starfleet.js

```javascript
var starfleet ='{          "starship":          ['+
'{          "Name": "Enterprise",     "SN": "NX-01",      "Class": "NX","Year":
"2151","Captain": "Jonathan Archer"},'+
'{  "Name": "USS Enterprise","SN": "NCC-1701", "Class":
"Constitution","Year": "2245","Captain": "James Tiberius Kirk"},'+
'{          "Name": "USS Enterprise","SN": "NCC-1701-B","Class":
"Excelsior","Year": "2293","Captain": "John Harriman"},'+
'{          "Name": "USS Enterprise","SN": "NCC-1701-C","Class":
"Ambassador","Year": "2332","Captain": "Rachel Garrett"},'+
'{          "Name": "USS Enterprise","SN": "NCC-1701-D","Class":
"Galaxy","Year": "2363","Captain": "Jean-Luc Picard"},'+
'{          "Name": "USS Enterprise","SN": "NCC-1701-E","Class":
"Sovereign","Year": "2372","Captain": "Jean-Luc Picard" } ]}';
```

Then, use the JavaScript following built-in function in the HTML file to parse the JSON file:

```javascript
var obj = JSON.parse(starfleet);
```

Finally, use the just created object in the html page as shown in Listing 7-13.

Listing 7-13. jsontest.html

```html
<html>
<head>
<script type="text/javascript" src="js/starfleet.js"></script>
<title>Example JSON</title>
</head>
<body>

        <table border="1" id="jsonTable">
            <tr>
                    <th>Name</th>
                    <th>S/N</th>
```

```
                <th>Class</th>
                <th>Year</th>
                <th>Captain</th>
        </tr>
    </table>

    <script type="text/javascript">
            var obj = JSON.parse(starfleet);
            for (i = 0; i < obj.starship.length; i++) {
                    var table = document.getElementById("jsonTable");
                    var row = table.insertRow(i + 1);
                    var cell1 = row.insertCell(0);
                    var cell2 = row.insertCell(1);
                    var cell3 = row.insertCell(2);
                    var cell4 = row.insertCell(3);
                    var cell5 = row.insertCell(4);
                    cell1.innerHTML = obj.starship[i].Name;
                    cell2.innerHTML = obj.starship[i].SN;
                    cell3.innerHTML = obj.starship[i].Class;
                    cell4.innerHTML = obj.starship[i].Year;
                    cell5.innerHTML = obj.starship[i].Captain;
            }
    </script>
</body>
</html>
```

I have highlighted in bold the following JavaScript methods:

- **JSON.parse** used to convert the string into a JavaScript object

- **insertRow** used to dynamically insert a new row in an html table

- **insertCell** used to dynamically insert a new cell in a row

- **innerHTML** property used to insert an element in the HTML content

Figure 7-2 represents the html file in the browser.

Name	S/N	Class	Year	Captain
Enterprise	NX-01	NX	2151	Jonathan Archer
USS Enterprise	NCC-1701	Constitution	2245	James Tiberius Kirk
USS Enterprise	NCC-1701-B	Excelsior	2293	John Harriman
USS Enterprise	NCC-1701-C	Ambassador	2332	Rachel Garrett
USS Enterprise	NCC-1701-D	Galaxy	2363	Jean-Luc Picard
USS Enterprise	NCC-1701-E	Sovereign	2372	Jean-Luc Picard

Figure 7-2. *Starfleet information parsing JSON file*

As you can see, it is the same of Figure 7-1. Very simple, isn't it?

There are a lot of websites and books that analyze JSON in detail: the validation, the standardization, the grammar, the features, the fields of application, and its Java third-party APIs (e.g., mJson.Gson) available for parsing and creating JSON objects. This is only a simple introduction for everyone who is interested to this technology and to a smart comparison with XML.

XSLT: Transformation from One XML Format to Another

At the beginning of this chapter, I showed you the file enterprises.xml (Listing 7-1), and, later on, to explain XPath, I expanded it to starfleet.xml (Listing 7-9).

But the information contained in enterprises.xml is not just a sub-set of the larger starfleet.xml, because also the encoding is different. In particular, the differences from starfleet.xml are

- The presence of a title element

- The removal in the class element of the commissioned attribute

- The replacement of the class body with an attribute named name

Listing 7-14 shows you an XSL style sheet that lets you extract enterprises.xml from starfleet.xml. You will find the following examples in the software package "xml-style" for this chapter that you can import in Eclipse.

Listing 7-14. enterprises.xsl

```
01: <?xml version="1.0" encoding="UTF-8"?>
02: <xsl:stylesheet version="1.0" xmlns:xsl="http://www.w3.org/1999/XSL/
Transform">
03: <xsl:output method="xml" version="1.0" encoding="UTF-8" indent="yes"/>
04: <xsl:template match="/">
05:   <starfleet>
06:     <title>The two most famous starships in the fleet</title>
07:     <xsl:for-each select="starfleet/starship">
08:       <xsl:if test="@sn='NCC-1701' or @sn='NCC-1701-D'">
09:         <xsl:element name="starship">
10:           <xsl:attribute name="name">
11:             <xsl:value-of select="@name"/>
12:           </xsl:attribute>
13:           <xsl:attribute name="sn">
14:             <xsl:value-of select="@sn"/>
15:           </xsl:attribute>
16:           <xsl:element name="class">
17:             <xsl:attribute name="name">
18:               <xsl:value-of select="class"/>
19:             </xsl:attribute>
20:           </xsl:element>
21:           <xsl:copy-of select="captain"/>
22:         </xsl:element>
23:       </xsl:if>
24:     </xsl:for-each>
25:   </starfleet>
26: </xsl:template>
27: </xsl:stylesheet>
```

Lines 01 and 02 state that the file is in XML format and specify its namespace. In line 02, you could replace xsl:stylesheet with xsl:transform, because the two keywords are considered synonyms.

Line 03 specifies that the output is also an XML document. XML is the default output format, but by writing it explicitly, you can also request that the output be indented. Otherwise, by default, the generated code would be written on a single very long line. The element also lets you specify an encoding other than ISO-8859-1.

The xsl:template element associates a template to an element, and in line 04, you write match="/" to specify the whole source document. In lines 05–06 and 25, you write the enterprise and title elements to the output.

The loop between lines 07 and 24 is where you scan all the starship elements. Immediately inside the loop, you select the two starships you're interested in with an xsl:if. In XSL, you could have also used the choose/when/otherwise construct that you encountered in Chapter 6 when I described JSTL-core, but in this case, it would not be appropriate, because you do not need an else.

The actual work is done in lines 09–22. The xsl:element and xsl:attribute elements create a new element and a new attribute, respectively, while xsl:value-of copies data from the source XML file to the output. Notice that the XPath expressions in the select attributes are relative to the current element selected by xsl:for-each. Also, notice that the only difference between the source and the output is handled in lines 17–19, where you assign to the name attribute of the class element what was originally in the element's body. The class attribute commissioned is simply ignored, so that it doesn't appear in the output.

The xsl:copy-of element copies the whole element to the output, including attributes and children elements. If you only want to copy the element tag, you can use xsl:copy.

XSL includes more than 30 elements, but the dozen or so that I have just described cover the vast majority of what you are likely to need. You will find the official documentation about XSLT at www.w3.org/TR/xslt.

XSLT: Transformation from XML to HTML

As you have seen, you can use XPath in a JSP page to navigate through an XML document and display it in HTML format. In this section, I'm going to show you how you can use XSLT to transform the same starfleet.xml directly into HTML. The two strategies are subtly different: with JSP, you pick up the nodes one by one and display them in HTML; with XSLT, you specify how the nodes of the XML files are to be mapped into HTML elements.

Let's cut to the chase and go directly to the XSLT file, shown in Listing 7-15.

Listing 7-15. starfleet.xsl

```
<?xml version="1.0" encoding="UTF-8"?>
<xsl:stylesheet version="1.0" xmlns:xsl="http://www.w3.org/1999/XSL/
Transform">
<xsl:output method="html" version="4.0" encoding="UTF-8" indent="yes"/>
<xsl:template match="/">
<html><head>
  <title>Styling starfleet.xml</title>
  <style>th {text-align:left}</style>
  </head>
<body>
<h2>The Most Famous Starships in the Fleet</h2>
<table border="1">
  <tr><th>Name</th><th>S/N</th><th>Class</th><th>Commissioned</
th><th>Captain</th></tr>
  <xsl:for-each select="starfleet/starship">
    <xsl:sort select="class/@commissioned"/>
    <tr>
      <td><xsl:value-of select="@name"/></td>
      <td><xsl:value-of select="@sn"/></td>
      <td><xsl:value-of select="class"/></td>
      <td><xsl:value-of select="class/@commissioned"/></td>
      <td><xsl:value-of select="captain"/></td>
    </tr>
  </xsl:for-each>
  </table>
</body>
</html>
</xsl:template>
</xsl:stylesheet>
```

After the first example (Listing 7-14), it should be clear how this works. There is just one point I would like to clarify: if you wanted to, you could omit the third line because, although the default output format is XML, XSL automatically recognizes that you're generating HTML if the first tag it encounters is `<html>`. Nevertheless, I recommend that you define the output format explicitly so that you can set HTML version, encoding, and indentation.

XSL Transformation: Browser Side vs. Server Side

I still haven't told you how to apply an XSL style sheet to an XML file to perform the transformation. This is because I first have to clarify the distinction between browser-side vs. server-side transformation.

Browser-Side XSL Transformation

All browsers can process XML and XSL. For example, let's type http://localhost:8080/ xml-style/xsl/starfleet.xml in most browsers; you see the file with little markers on the left of each element, as shown in Figure 7-3. By clicking the markers, you can collapse or expand the elements as if they were folders.

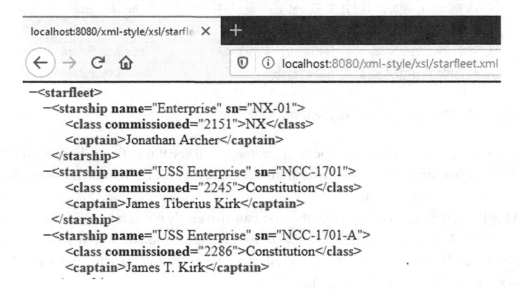

Figure 7-3. *Browsing an XML file without XSL*

The browsers can provide this feature because they "know" how to display XML. You probably will see a message at the top of the page indicates that the browser displays the file as a node tree in a generic way because the file doesn't refer to any XSL style sheet. But all browsers color-code the different components.

255

Making the association is simple; write at the top of the xml file the line

```
<?xml-stylesheet type="text/xsl" href="starfleet.xsl"?>
```

Now, if you ask the browser to display http://localhost:8080/xml-style/xsl/starfleet.xml, now it will know what style sheet to use. Figure 7-4 shows the result.

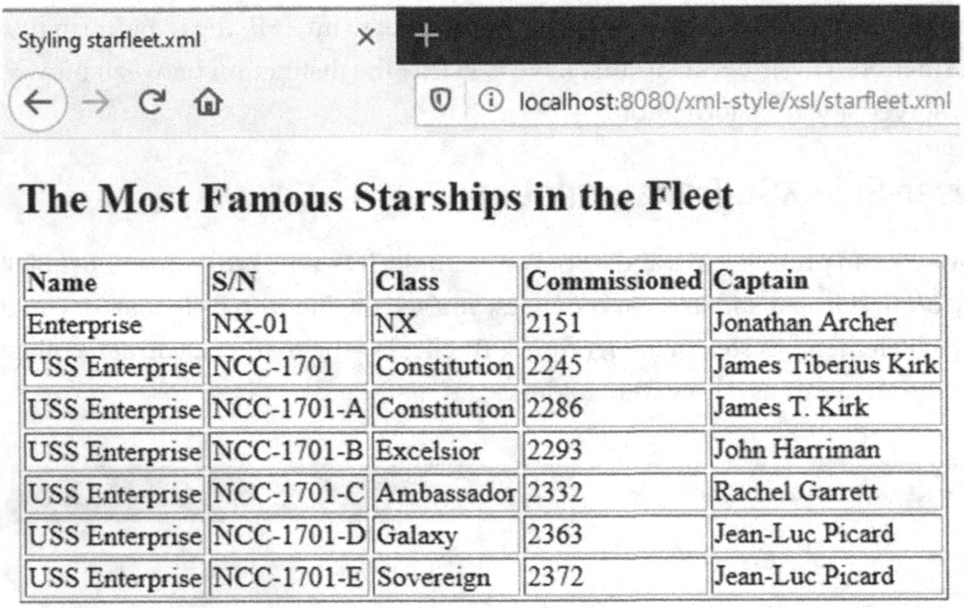

Name	S/N	Class	Commissioned	Captain
Enterprise	NX-01	NX	2151	Jonathan Archer
USS Enterprise	NCC-1701	Constitution	2245	James Tiberius Kirk
USS Enterprise	NCC-1701-A	Constitution	2286	James T. Kirk
USS Enterprise	NCC-1701-B	Excelsior	2293	John Harriman
USS Enterprise	NCC-1701-C	Ambassador	2332	Rachel Garrett
USS Enterprise	NCC-1701-D	Galaxy	2363	Jean-Luc Picard
USS Enterprise	NCC-1701-E	Sovereign	2372	Jean-Luc Picard

Figure 7-4. *Browsing an XML file with XSL*

With any browser, if you view the page source, you'll see the XML file, because it is the browser that does the transformation from XML to HTML. Therefore, the source file is in fact the XML document.

One thing to keep in mind is that the user can also easily obtain your XSL file, because its URL is shown in the XML source. You can display its source and discover the relative URL of the style sheet. Then, you only need to type http://localhost:8080/xml-style/xsl/starfleet.xsl to see the XSL file.

Server-Side XSL Transformation

You can do the transformation on the server and make its output available, rather than making the XML and XSL files visible to the user. In that way, you can keep XML and XSL in private folders. Listing 7-16 shows you how to do the XSL server-side transformation with a JSP page.

Listing 7-16. enterprises_transform.jsp

```
01: <%@page language="java" contentType="text/html"%>
02: <%@page import="java.io.File"%>
03: <%@page import="java.io.FileOutputStream"%>
04: <%@page import="javax.xml.transform.TransformerFactory"%>
05: <%@page import="javax.xml.transform.Transformer"%>
06: <%@page import="javax.xml.transform.Source"%>
07: <%@page import="javax.xml.transform.SourceLocator"%>
08: <%@page import="javax.xml.transform.TransformerException"%>
09: <%@page import="javax.xml.transform.Result"%>
10: <%@page import="javax.xml.transform.stream.StreamSource"%>
11: <%@page import="javax.xml.transform.stream.StreamResult"%>
12: <%@page import="myPkg.TransformerExceptionHandler"%>
13: <%
14:   File inFile = new File("webapps/xml-style/xsl/starfleet.xml");
15:   File xslFile = new File("webapps/xml-style/xsl/enterprises.xsl");
16:   String outFilename = "webapps/xml-style/out/enterprises_out.xml";
17:   TransformerExceptionHandler handler = new
      TransformerExceptionHandler();
18:   try {
19:     TransformerFactory factory = TransformerFactory.newInstance();
20:     Transformer transformer = factory.newTransformer(new
        StreamSource(xslFile));
21:     transformer.setErrorListener(handler);
22:     Source source = new StreamSource(inFile);
23:     Result result = new StreamResult(new FileOutputStream(outFilename));
24:     transformer.transform(source, result);
25:   }
26:   catch (TransformerException e) {
27:   }
28:   if (handler.errorLevel == null) {
29:     out.println("Transformation completed.");
30:   }
```

```
31:    else {
32:      out.println(
33:          "*** Transformation " + handler.errorLevel + ": "
34:        + handler.transformationException
35:        );
36:    }
37:  %>
```

It looks more complicated than it actually is. Moreover, I have hard-coded the file names for simplicity, but you can add to the JSP page a simple input form to set inFile and xslFile, and you'll have a small utility you can use to transform all XML files. Following the MVC architecture, you should place the application logic in a servlet (i.e., the Controller), not in a JSP page. But I just wanted to show you in the simplest possible way how this is done in JSP/Java.

enterprises_transform.jsp performs the XML transformation on the server side as follows:

1. It instantiates a generic TransformerFactory and uses it to create a Transformer that implements the XSL (lines 19 and 20).

2. In line 21, it registers with the transformer the exception handler that was instantiated in line 17. This is similar to what you did to handle validation exceptions.

3. It opens an input stream to read the XML file and an output stream to write the document that will result from the transformation (lines 22 and 23).

4. It finally does the transformation (line 24).

The exception reporting is almost a carbon copy of the method I described when talking about validation (Listings 7-5 to 7-7), and the exception handler for transformations (Listing 7-17) is compiled and used exactly like the handler for validations shown in Listing 7-4.

Listing 7-17. TransformerExceptionHandler.java

```java
package myPkg;
import javax.xml.transform.TransformerException;
public class TransformerExceptionHandler
    implements javax.xml.transform.ErrorListener {
  public TransformerException transformationException = null;
  public String errorLevel = null;
  public void warning(TransformerException e) {
    errorLevel = "Warning";
    transformationException = e;
    }
  public void error(TransformerException e) {
    errorLevel = "Error";
    transformationException = e;
    }
  public void fatalError(TransformerException e) {
    errorLevel = "Fatal error";
    transformationException = e;
    }
}
```

The JSP page enterprises_transform.jsp applies the style sheet enterprises. xsl to starfleet.xml to produce enterprises_out.xml. If you change the file names in lines 15–16 to starfleet.xsl and starfleet_out.html, the same page will generate a file that, when viewed in a browser, will appear identical to what you see in Figure 7-4.

My apologies if you find all these variations of XML files somewhat confusing. My purpose is to show you most of the possibilities you have for validating and converting XML files. In real life, you will pick the solution that suits your needs best and stick to it. In any case, I'm not done yet, because there is still one way of implementing server-side transformations that I want to show you.

x:transform and x:param

x:transform applies an XSL style sheet to an XML document. Table 7-7 summarizes its attributes.

Table 7-7. *x:transform Attributes*

Attribute	Description
Doc	The well-formed source XML document to be transformed. It can be an object of type `java.lang.String`, `java.io.Reader`, `javax.xml.transform.Source`, `org.w3c.dom.Document`, or an object resulting from x:parse or x:set.
Xslt	The transformation style sheet of type `java.lang.String`, `java.io.Reader`, or `javax.xml.transform.Source`.
var	Name of the EL variable to store the transformed XML document as an object of type `org.w3c.dom.Document`.
scope	Scope for var.
docSystemId	System identifier for parsing the XML source. It is a URI that identifies the origin of the XML data, potentially useful to some parsers.
xsltSystemId	Like docSystemId but for the XSL style sheet.
result	Result object to accept the transformation's result.

Listing 7-18 shows the JSP page starfleet_tag_transform.jsp, which performs on the server the same transformation done by the browser when displaying what is shown in Figure 7-4. You will see the familiar table typing http://localhost:8080/xml-style/starfleet_tag_transform.jsp in your browser.

Listing 7-18. starfleet_tag_transform.jsp

```
<%@page language="java" contentType="text/html"%>
<%@taglib prefix="c" uri="http://java.sun.com/jsp/jstl/core"%>
<%@taglib prefix="x" uri="http://java.sun.com/jsp/jstl/xml"%>
<c:import url="/xsl/starfleet.xml" var="xml"/>
<c:import url="/xsl/starfleet.xsl" var="xsl"/>
<x:transform doc="${xml}" xslt="${xsl}"/>
```

At this point, you might ask: why on earth did we go through the complex implementation of `enterprise_transform.jsp` and `TransformerExceptionHandler.java` (Listings 5-13 and 5-14) when we can achieve an equivalent result with six lines of code?

There are two reasons: the first one is that you might in the future encounter a situation in which you need to do it the "hard way"; the second reason is that I like to "peek under the hood" every now and then, and I thought you might like to do the same.

JSP in XML Syntax

JSP pages with scripting elements aren't XML files. This implies that you cannot use XML tools when developing JSP pages. However, it is possible to write JSP in a way to make it correct XML. The trick is to use standard JSP actions, JSTL with EL, and possibly non-JSTL custom actions. Actually, there are some "special standard" JSP actions defined to support the XML syntax (`jsp:root`, `jsp:output`, and `jsp:directive`). In any case, such XML modules are called *JSP documents*, as opposed to the *JSP pages* written in the traditional non-XML-compliant way.

As a first example, let's convert the `hello.jsp` page shown in Listing 1-7 to a `hello.jspx` document. Listing 7-19 shows hello.jspx. You will find the folder "jspx" in the software package "testxPath" for this chapter.

Listing 7-19. Partial hello.jspx

```
01: <?xml version="1.0" encoding="UTF-8"?>
02: <jsp:root
03:    xmlns:jsp="http://java.sun.com/JSP/Page"
04:    xmlns:c="http://java.sun.com/jsp/jstl/core"
05:    xmlns:fn="http://java.sun.com/jsp/jstl/functions"
06:    version="2.1"
07:    >
08: <jsp:directive.page
09:    language="java"
10:    contentType="application/xhtml+xml;charset=UTF-8"
11:    />
12: <html>
13: <head><title>Hello World in XHTML</title></head>
```

```
14: <body>
15:   <jsp:text>Hello World!</jsp:text>
16: </body>
17: </html>
18: </jsp:root>
```

Line 01 states that the file is XML-compliant. The `root` element in lines 02–07 has several purposes. For example, it lets you use the `jsp` extension instead of the recommended `jspx`. It's also a convenient place where you can group namespace declarations (`xmlns`). The namespace declaration for the JSTL core tag library is the XML equivalent of the `taglib` directive in JSP pages. You don't need to specify the JSP namespace in JSP pages, but you cannot omit it in a JSP document; otherwise, the `jsp:` tags won't be recognized.

Lines 08–11 are the XML equivalent of the `page` directive of JSP pages. Also the `include` directive has its XML equivalent with the element `<jsp:directive.include file="`*relativeURL*`"/>`.

Notice that the string "Hello World!" in line 15 is enclosed within the `jsp:text` element. This is necessary, because in XML you cannot have "untagged" text.

To be consistent and make possible the full validation of the generated HTML, you should also include the proper `DOCTYPE`. The best way to do this is to use the attributes of the `jsp:output` action, which was specifically designed for this purpose. You only need to replace the `<html>` tag in line 12 with the following three elements:

```
<jsp:output omit-xml-declaration="false"/>
<jsp:output
  doctype-root-element="html"
  doctype-public="-//W3C//DTD XHTML 1.0 Strict//EN"
  doctype-system="http://www.w3.org/TR/xhtml1/DTD/xhtml1-strict.dtd"
  />
<html xmlns="http://www.w3.org/1999/xhtml">
```

Yes, it's quite a bit of work just to write "Hello World!", but this overhead is going to stay the same for JSP documents of any size. The first line causes the `<?xml ... ?>` elements to be written at the beginning of the generated HTML page, while the second element generates the `DOCTYPE`.

Now you're finally ready to tackle the conversion of the scriptlet in `hello.jsp` to XML syntax. Listing 7-20 shows the complete `hello.jspx`.

Listing 7-20. hello.jspx

```
<?xml version="1.0" encoding="UTF-8"?>
<jsp:root
  xmlns:jsp="http://java.sun.com/JSP/Page"
  xmlns:c="http://java.sun.com/jsp/jstl/core"
  xmlns:fn="http://java.sun.com/jsp/jstl/functions"
  version="2.1"
  >
<jsp:directive.page
  language="java"
  contentType="application/xhtml+xml;charset=UTF-8"
  />
<jsp:output omit-xml-declaration="false"/>
<jsp:output
  doctype-root-element="html"
  doctype-public="-//W3C//DTD XHTML 1.0 Strict//EN"
  doctype-system="http://www.w3.org/TR/xhtml1/DTD/xhtml1-strict.dtd"
  />
<html xmlns="http://www.w3.org/1999/xhtml">
<head><title>Hello World in XHTML</title></head>
<body>
  <jsp:text>Hello World!</jsp:text>
  <br/>
  <jsp:text> User-agent: </jsp:text>
  <c:set var="usAg" value="${header['user-agent']}"/>
  <c:out value="${usAg}" />
</body>
</html>
</jsp:root>
```

As a second example of converting a JSP page to a JSP document, you can compare starfleet.jspx (Listing 7-21) with the original starfleet.jsp (Listing 7-10).

Listing 7-21. starfleet.jspx

```
<?xml version="1.0" encoding="UTF-8"?>
<jsp:root
  xmlns:jsp="http://java.sun.com/JSP/Page"
  xmlns:c="http://java.sun.com/jsp/jstl/core"
  xmlns:x="http://java.sun.com/jsp/jstl/xml"
  version="2.1"
  >
<jsp:directive.page
  language="java"
  contentType="application/xhtml+xml;charset=UTF-8"
  />
<jsp:output omit-xml-declaration="false"/>
<jsp:output
  doctype-root-element="html"
  doctype-public="-//W3C//DTD XHTML 1.0 Strict//EN"
  doctype-system="http://www.w3.org/TR/xhtml1/DTD/xhtml1-strict.dtd"
  />
<c:import url="starfleet.xml" var="sf"/>
<x:parse doc="${sf}" varDom="dom"/>
<html xmlns="http://www.w3.org/1999/xhtml">
<head>
  <title>Parsing starfleet.xml</title>
  <style>th {text-align:left}</style>
  </head>
<body>
<table border="1">
  <tr><th>Name</th><th>S/N</th><th>Class</th><th>Year</th><th>Captain
  </th></tr>
  <x:forEach var="tag" select="$dom//starship">
    <tr>
      <td><x:out select="$tag/@name"/></td>
      <td><x:out select="$tag/@sn"/></td>
      <td><x:out select="$tag/class"/></td>
      <td><x:out select="$tag/class/@commissioned"/></td>
```

```
    <td><x:out select="$tag/captain"/></td>
    </tr>
  </x:forEach>
 </table>
</body>
</html>
</jsp:root>
```

The first 17 lines are identical to the corresponding lines of hello.jspx, while the rest of the document is identical to the corresponding lines of starfleet.jsp, with the only addition of the closing tag for jsp:root. This is because starfleet.jsp didn't include any scripting element or untagged text.

What About Eshop and the XML Syntax?

You have just learned about writing JSP documents instead of JPS pages. What impact does that have on what I just said in Chapter 5 about database access? None! This is a consequence of the MVC model: JSP is the view, while only the model has to do with databases.

However, the switch from traditional to XML syntax has an impact on how you execute the data manager methods. For example, you can write the JSP page OrderConfirmation.jsp to save an order in the database with a couple of scriptlets, as shown in Listing 7-22.

Listing 7-22. OrderConfirmation.jsp

```
01: <%@page language="java" contentType="text/html"%>
02: <%@page import="java.util.Hashtable"%>
03: <jsp:useBean id="dataManager" scope="application"
04:   class="eshop.model.DataManager"/>
05: <html>
06: <head>
07:   <meta http-equiv="Content-Type" content="text/html; charset=UTF-8"/>
08:   <title>Order</title>
09:   <link rel="stylesheet" href="/eshop/css/eshop.css" type="text/css"/>
10:   </head>
```

```
11: <body>
12: <jsp:include page="TopMenu.jsp" flush="true"/>
13: <jsp:include page="LeftMenu.jsp" flush="true"/>
14: <div class="content">
15:    <h2>Order</h2>
16:    <jsp:useBean id="customer" class="eshop.beans.Customer"/>
17:    <jsp:setProperty property="*" name="customer"/>
18: <%
19:       long orderId = dataManager.insertOrder(
20:                      customer,
21:                      (Hashtable)session.getAttribute("shoppingCart")
22:                      );
23:    if (orderId > 0L) {
24:       session.invalidate();
25:    %>
26:       <p class="info">
27:          Thank you for your purchase.<br/>
28:          Your Order Number is: <%=orderId%>
29:          </p>
30: <%
31:       }
32:    else {
33:       %><p class="error">Unexpected error processing the order!</p><%
34:       }
35:    %>
36:    </div>
37: </body>
38: </html>
```

Or you can write the JSP document OrderConfirmation.jspx, as shown in Listing 7-23. I have included the whole E-shop project converted to XML format in the software package for this chapter. You will find it both in WAR format and already expanded in the folder named eshopx. To launch it, similarly to eshop, type http://localhost:8080/eshopx/shop.

Listing 7-23. OrderConfirmation.jspx

```
01: <?xml version="1.0" encoding="UTF-8"?>
02: <jsp:root
03:    xmlns:jsp="http://java.sun.com/JSP/Page"
04:    xmlns:c="http://java.sun.com/jsp/jstl/core"
05:    xmlns:eshop="urn:jsptld:/WEB-INF/tlds/eshop.tld"
06:    version="2.1"
07:    >
08: <jsp:directive.page
09:    language="java"
10:    contentType="application/xhtml+xml;charset=UTF-8"
11:    />
12: <jsp:output omit-xml-declaration="false"/>
13: <jsp:output
14:    doctype-root-element="html"
15:    doctype-public="-//W3C//DTD XHTML 1.0 Strict//EN"
16:    doctype-system="http://www.w3.org/TR/xhtml1/DTD/xhtml1-strict.dtd"
17:    />
18: <c:url var="cssUrl" value="/css/eshop.jspx"/>
19: <html xmlns="http://www.w3.org/1999/xhtml">
20: <head>
21:    <title>Order</title>
22:    <link rel="stylesheet" href="${cssUrl}" type="text/css"/>
23:    </head>
24: <body>
25: <jsp:include page="TopMenu.jspx" flush="true"/>
26: <jsp:include page="LeftMenu.jspx" flush="true"/>
27: <div class="content">
28:    <h2>Order</h2>
29:    <jsp:useBean id="customer" class="eshop.beans.Customer"/>
30:    <jsp:setProperty property="*" name="customer"/>
31:    <eshop:insertOrder var="orderID" customer="${customer}"/>
32:    <c:choose>
33:      <c:when test="${orderID > 0}">
34:        <p class="info">
```

```
35:          Thank you for your purchase.<br/>
36:          Your Order Number is: <c:out value="${orderID}"/>
37:          </p>
38:        </c:when>
39:      <c:otherwise>
40:        <p class="error">Unexpected error processing the order!</p>
41:        </c:otherwise>
42:        </c:choose>
43:    </div>
44:  </body>
45:  </html>
46: </jsp:root>
```

Let's concentrate on the highlighted code, where the actual work is done. The saving of the order information in the database, which you do in the JSP page (Listing 7-21) by executing a data manager's method (lines 19–22), you do in the JSP document (Listing 7-22) by executing a custom action (line 31). The same custom action also invalidates the session (which was done in line 24 of the JSP page).

The if/else Java construct in lines 23, 31–32, and 34 of the JSP page becomes in the JSP document the JSTL core construct choose/when/otherwise in lines 32–33, 38–39, and 41–42.

Informing the user of the order acceptance is in HTML and remains basically the same (JSP lines 26–29 become JSPX in lines 34–37). In fact, you could have replaced the scripting expression of the JSP page with the EL expression of the JSP document, making the code identical.

The introduction of the custom action insertOrder is necessary because scriptlets, being Java code, can make assignments and execute methods, while EL expressions cannot. Therefore, when you remove scriptlets because they're not valid XML code, you have to move the computation to Java beans or custom actions.

In line 05 of OrderConfirmation.jspx, you declare eshop.tld, which contains the definition of the insertOrder action (see Listing 7-24).

Listing 7-24. InsertOrderTag Definition in eshop.tld

```
<tag>
  <description>Insert an order into storage</description>
  <display-name>insertOrder</display-name>
```

```
<name>insertOrder</name>
<tag-class>eshop.tags.InsertOrderTag</tag-class>
<body-content>empty</body-content>
<attribute>
  <name>var</name>
  <required>true</required>
  <rtexprvalue>true</rtexprvalue>
  </attribute>
<attribute>
  <name>customer</name>
  <required>true</required>
  <rtexprvalue>true</rtexprvalue>
  </attribute>
</tag>
```

As you can see, you pass two parameters to the custom action: the name of the variable where the order ID is to be returned and an object containing the customer data (name, address, and credit-card information). You don't absolutely need the second parameter, because the action code could have retrieved the customer data from the page context as follows:

```
(Customer)pageContext.getAttribute("customer")
```

On the other hand, you could have passed to the action a third parameter referencing the shopping cart, but I decided to let the action retrieve it from the session as follows:

```
(Hashtable)pageContext.getSession().getAttribute("shoppingCart")
```

It's not always obvious what constitutes a better design. I felt that the shopping cart, being a session attribute, was obviously shared across JSP documents. Therefore, it was OK for the action to retrieve it directly from the session. The customer data, however, was a page attribute, normally not shared with other modules. Passing it "behind the scenes" to a Java class didn't seem appropriate. Listing 7-25 shows you the action code in its entirety.

Listing 7-25. InsertOrderTag.java

```java
package eshop.tags;

import java.util.Hashtable;
import javax.servlet.http.HttpSession;
import javax.servlet.jsp.tagext.TagSupport;
import javax.servlet.ServletContext;

import eshop.beans.CartItem;
import eshop.beans.Customer;
import eshop.model.DataManager;

public class InsertOrderTag extends TagSupport {
  static final long serialVersionUID = 1L;
  private String var;
  private Customer customer;

  public void setVar(String var) {
    this.var = var;
    }
  public void setCustomer(Customer customer) {
    this.customer = customer;
    }
  public int doEndTag() {
    ServletContext context = pageContext.getServletContext();
    DataManager dataManager =(DataManager)context.
    getAttribute("dataManager");
    HttpSession session = pageContext.getSession();
    @SuppressWarnings("unchecked")
    Hashtable<String, CartItem> cart =
        (Hashtable<String, CartItem>)session.getAttribute("shoppingCart");
    long orderID = dataManager.insertOrder(customer, cart);
    if (orderID > 0L) session.invalidate();
    pageContext.setAttribute(var, new Long(orderID).toString());
    return EVAL_PAGE;
    }
  }
```

Notice how you obtain the servlet context (corresponding to the JSP implicit object `application`) from `pageContext`, and from it the data manager, so that you can then execute the same `insertOrder` method you invoked directly from within the JSP page.

Summary

In this chapter, you learned about the structure and the syntax of XML documents, DTDs, and XML schemas.

You then saw several ways of how to validate XML documents against DTDs and schemas. Next, I introduced you to XSL and explained examples of XPath use and of transformation from XML to XML and from XML to HTML. For the last case, I also introduced a comparison with JSON.

Moreover, I showed how you can convert JSP pages with directives and scripting elements into JSP documents that are fully XML-compliant. To conclude, I showed you an implementation of E-shop application with the XML syntax.

Brace yourself, because in the next chapter I will finally talk about JSF!

CHAPTER 8

JavaServer Faces 2.3

In this chapter, I'll introduce you to JSF and show you how to use it to create user interfaces for web-based applications. Within the MVC application architecture I described in Chapter 3 (refer to Figure 3-2), JSF takes the place of the controller, thereby mediating every interaction between JSP (the View) and the Model, which encapsulates the application data. JSF makes the development of web applications easier by

- Letting you create user interfaces from a set of standard UI components wired to server-side objects

- Making available four custom-tag libraries to handle those UI components

- Providing a mechanism for extending the standard UI components

JSF transparently saves state information of the UI components and repopulates forms when they redisplay. This is possible because the states of the components live beyond the lifespan of HTTP requests. JSF operates by providing a controller servlet and a component model that includes event handling, server-side validation, data conversion, and component rendering. Not surprisingly, JSF doesn't change the basic page life cycle that you already know from JSP: the client makes an HTTP request, and the server replies with a dynamically generated HTML page.

Be warned that JSF isn't very easy to use, and it requires a non-negligible initial effort to get it going. However, the reward comes once you've familiarized yourself with JSF and can then develop user interfaces more quickly and efficiently.

You can download the latest JSF specification (JSR 372—JSF 2.3) by going to `www.jcp.org/en/jsr/detail?id=372` and clicking the download page link.

JavaServer Faces may be built-in or not depending on the used server: Tomcat needs to manually install the JSF components. So, you have to download the latest version of JSF that is currently developed in two implementations of the specification: Mojarra and MyFaces. I chose the second one: you will find the latest version of Apache MyFaces

© Luciano Manelli and Giulio Zambon 2020

L. Manelli and G. Zambon, *Beginning Jakarta EE Web Development*,

https://doi.org/10.1007/978-1-4842-5866-8_8

JSF at `http://myfaces.apache.org/download.html`. In the zip file, you can find the following jar:

- myfaces-impl-2.3.6.jar

- myfaces-api-2.3.6.jar

- commons-beanutils-1.9.4.jar

- commons-collections-3.2.2.jar

- commons-digester-1.8.jar

- commons-logging-1.1.1.jar

To be able to use JSF, you will need to copy these `jars` (or a newer version) into the lib folder of your project or to Tomcat's `lib` folder.

You also need JAXB libraries that give an efficient and standard way of mapping between XML and Java code. Go to `https://eclipse-ee4j.github.io/jaxb-ri/`, download the library jakarta.xml.bind-api.jar, and copy it into your *lib* project folder or Tomcat server.

Let's begin with a simple JSF application, so that you can see how JSF works in practice.

The simplef Application

You should start by importing in Eclipse the project named `simplef` you will find in the software package for this chapter. You can try it out by typing `http://localhost:8080/ simplef/` in your web browser. Figure 8-1 is an example of what you'll see.

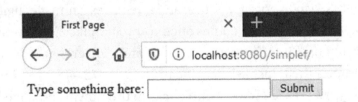

Figure 8-1. *The first page of simplef*

As you can see, there isn't much to it. If you type, say, "qwerty" and click `Submit`, you will see the page shown in Figure 8-2.

274

Figure 8-2. *The second page of simplef*

Apart from the URL, which is not what you might expect, everything is pretty boring. If you click Another, you go back to the first page, as shown in Figure 8-3.

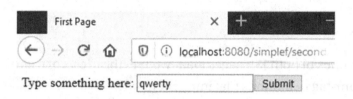

Figure 8-3. *Back to the first page of simplef*

Again, nothing to get excited about. But notice that the string you typed in the first page appeared in the second one and again in the first one as the default for the input field. What is exciting in this example is how easily this was accomplished with JSF. Listings 8-1 and 8-2 show the two JSP pages of the example.

Listing 8-1. first.jsp

```
<%@taglib uri="http://java.sun.com/jsf/html" prefix="h"%>
<%@taglib uri="http://java.sun.com/jsf/core" prefix="f"%>
<html><head><title>First Page</title></head><body>
<f:view>
  <h:form>
    <h:outputText value="Type something here: "/>
    <h:inputText value="#{aStringBean.str}" />
    <h:commandButton action="goOn" value="Submit" />
    </h:form>
  </f:view>
</body></html>
```

Listing 8-2. second.jsp

```
<%@taglib uri="http://java.sun.com/jsf/html" prefix="h"%>
<%@taglib uri="http://java.sun.com/jsf/core" prefix="f"%>
<html><head><title>Second page</title></head><body>
<f:view>
  <h:form>
    <h:outputText value="&quot;#{aStringBean.str}&quot; "/>
    <h:commandButton action="goBack" value="Another" />
    </h:form>
</f:view>
</body></html>
```

The first two lines of both JSP pages load two JSF libraries, core and html, that contain all custom-tag definitions that implement JSF.

The first JSF element you encounter in both pages is f:view, which is a container for all JSF actions. The next one is h:form, the JSF element that generates the pair <form>..</form> of HTML tags. The three JSF elements h:outputText, h:inputText, and h:commandButton generate, respectively, the three HTML elements .., <input type="text"../>, and <input type="submit"../>. If you had used h:commandLink instead of h:commandButton, JSF would have generated a hyperlink with the HTML-tag a and the attribute href instead of a submit button.

Notice that the value attributes of h:inputText in first.jsp and h:outputText in second.jsp contain the EL expression #{aStringBean.str}. This is the first time you encounter a practical example of an EL expression representing an lvalue (see the Expression Language section in Chapter 6).

The expression ${aStringBean.str} would have been evaluated by Tomcat immediately. Tomcat would have replaced it with the value obtained by executing the method aStringBean.getStr().

But, with the # replacing the $, the only thing that happens is that JSF assigns an identifier to the attribute str of the object aStringBean.

Listing 8-3 shows the HTML page that first.jsp generates (reformatted by me for easy reading).

Listing 8-3. HTML Generated by first.jsp

```
<html><head><title>First Page</title></head><body>
<form id="j_id_jsp_445772234_1" name="j_id_jsp_445772234_1" method="post"
action="/simplef/first.jsf;jsessionid=5A9800A3233E5F9410006529CEDD234F"
enctype="application/x-www-form-urlencoded">

Type something here: <input id="j_id_jsp_445772234_1:j_id_jsp_445772234_3"
name="j_id_jsp_445772234_1:j_id_jsp_445772234_3" type="text" value="" />
<input id="j_id_jsp_445772234_1:j_id_jsp_445772234_4" name="j_id_
jsp_445772234_1:j_id_jsp_445772234_4" type="submit" value="Submit" />
<input type="hidden" name="j_id_jsp_445772234_1_SUBMIT" value="1" />
<input type="hidden" name="javax.faces.ViewState" id="j_id__v_0:javax.
faces.ViewState:1" value="RDgzRTFGQzg4MkVCQTQONTAwMDAwMDAx"
autocomplete="off" />
</form>
</body></html>
```

Whenever you see id, the generated code actually contained j_id_jsp_445772234. The two lines in bold are the result of the three JSF elements h:outputText, h:inputText, and h:commandButton.

JSF assigned to #{aStringBean.str} the identifier j_id_jsp_445772234_1:j_id_jsp_445772234_3. When processing on the server the request your browser sends when you click Submit, JSF will assign the value you have typed (e.g., the string "qwerty") to the str attribute of the object aStringBean. By saving the string in this way, JSF will have it available for the value of h:outputText in second.jsp and as the default value for h:inputText in first.jsp when it will need to render that page again.

To continue the explanation of how JSF works, I would like to direct your attention to the fact that the URLs that appear in the browser do not match the names of the JSP pages. For example, you start the application by typing in your browser http://localhost:8080/simplef/. What trick then takes you to first.jsp? If you open the default JSP page index.jsp that you find inside the simplef folder, you will see the one-liner shown in Listing 8-4.

Listing 8-4. index.jsp

```
<html><body><jsp:forward page="/first.jsf"/></body></html>
```

But in the same folder, there is no file named `first.jsf`! To begin understanding what happens, you have to look at the `web.xml` file (see Listing 8-5).

Listing 8-5. web.xml

```xml
<?xml version="1.0" encoding="UTF-8"?>
<web-app xmlns:xsi="http://www.w3.org/2001/XMLSchema-instance"
        xmlns="http://xmlns.jcp.org/xml/ns/javaee"
        xsi:schemaLocation="http://xmlns.jcp.org/xml/ns/javaee http://
        xmlns.jcp.org/xml/ns/javaee/web-app_4_0.xsd" version="4.0">
 <servlet>
  <servlet-name>Faces Servlet</servlet-name>
  <servlet-class>javax.faces.webapp.FacesServlet</servlet-class>
  <load-on-startup>1</load-on-startup>
  </servlet>
<servlet-mapping>
  <servlet-name>Faces Servlet</servlet-name>
  <url-pattern>*.jsf</url-pattern>
  </servlet-mapping>
</web-app>
```

It defines a servlet of type `javax.faces.webapp.FacesServlet`. It is the JSF servlet, which I have informally called "JSF". It is that servlet that assigns IDs to attributes and transfers data between pages. `web.xml` also maps the extension `jsf` to the servlet, thereby forcing all requests for pages with extension `jsf` to be sent to it.

This reveals part of the mystery: when you type `http://localhost:8080/simplef/` in your browser, Tomcat executes `index.jsp`, which forwards the request to `first.jsf` (which actually doesn't exist). But, because of the servlet mapping in `web.xml`, Tomcat diverts your request to the JSF servlet.

The rest of the mystery is easily explained: JSF replaces the extension `jsf` with `jsp`, which means that the request can finally reach `first.jsp`. The extension `jsp` is the default, but you can replace it by inserting in the `web-app` element of `web.xml` an element like that shown in Listing 8-6.

Listing 8-6. Defining the JSF Default Suffix in web.xml

```
<context-param>
  <param-name>javax.faces.DEFAULT_SUFFIX</param-name>
  <param-value>.jspx</param-value>
</context-param>
```

The next mystery that we have to solve is how the request generated by the form in first.jsp reaches second.jsp. In other words, how does the action "goOn" cause a request to reach second.jsp?

To solve this second mystery, you have to look at another file you find in WEB-INF: faces-config.xml (see Listing 8-7).

Listing 8-7. faces-config.xml

```
<?xml version="1.0" encoding="UTF-8"?>
<faces-config xmlns="http://xmlns.jcp.org/xml/ns/javaee"
         xmlns:xsi="http://www.w3.org/2001/XMLSchema-instance"
         xsi:schemaLocation="http://xmlns.jcp.org/xml/ns/javaee http://
         xmlns.jcp.org/xml/ns/javaee/web-facesconfig_2_3.xsd"
         version="2.3" >
  <managed-bean>
    <managed-bean-name>aStringBean</managed-bean-name>
    <managed-bean-class>AString</managed-bean-class>
    <managed-bean-scope>session</managed-bean-scope>
    <managed-property>
      <property-name>str</property-name>
      <property-class>java.lang.String</property-class>
      <null-value></null-value>
      </managed-property>
    </managed-bean>
  <navigation-rule>
    <from-view-id>/first.jsp</from-view-id>
    <navigation-case>
      <from-outcome>goOn</from-outcome>
      <to-view-id>/second.jsp</to-view-id>
      </navigation-case>
    </navigation-rule>
```

```
<navigation-rule>
  <from-view-id>/second.jsp</from-view-id>
  <navigation-case>
    <from-outcome>goBack</from-outcome>
    <to-view-id>/first.jsp</to-view-id>
    </navigation-case>
  </navigation-rule>
</faces-config>
```

Concentrate for the time being on the part I have highlighted. It tells JSF that when the page `first.jsp` ends with outcome goOn (i.e., executes h:commandButton with action goOn), control should go to `second.jsp`. In a more complex application, `first.jsp` would include different actions, which would correspond to different navigation-case elements. Then, the JSF servlet would have a function analogous to that of a Java switch statement.

We are almost there. The next thing that needs some explanation is the managed-bean element that you see in `faces-config.xml` immediately above the first navigation rule. It tells JSF to manage a session-scoped object named aStringBean of type AString, and to manage its attribute named str, which should be initialized to null. This also means that the JSF servlet will instantiate the object automatically.

This is where the name aStringBean you saw in the EL expressions of both `first.jsp` and `second.jsp` comes from. I could have chosen any name, but it is good practice to end the names of such managed beans with Bean.

Also, the default scope is request. But by specifying session, I ensured that the aStringBean is not destroyed after the first request. In the example, it would have meant that the input element in the second execution of `first.jsp` would have been without default. The request scope would have been sufficient to "remember" the default if `first.jsp` had executed itself instead of `second.jsp`. Note that you should be careful not to go overboard with storing information in the session, because you could affect the performance of your application. Remember that every new user causes a new session to be created.

The last piece that you need in order to complete the resolution of the JSF puzzle is the definition of the class AString. For this, see Listing 8-8.

Listing 8-8. AString.java

```
import java.io.Serializable;
public class AString implements Serializable {
  String str;
  public String getStr() { return str; }
  public void setStr(String s) { str = s; }
  }
```

For `simplef` to work, `AString.class` should be in the `classes` subdirectory of `WEB-INF`.

`AString` is the simplest possible bean that you need for JSF. The implementation of `Serializable` is there because it makes possible for Tomcat to save the object to disk and to retrieve it from disk. The server possibly uses a hard disk to park session data when it is under a heavy load or when it is restarted. This is one more reason for keeping the session's size as contained as possible. Note that Tomcat can only save objects that it is able to convert to output streams of data, and that requires the objects to be serializable.

The simplefx Application

In the previous section, I showed you how to build a simple JSF application with JSP pages. To use JSF with JSP documents (i.e., in XML format), you only have to make minimal changes. To convert `first.jsp` (Listing 8-1) to `first.jspx`, you only need to make the standard changes described in the last section of Chapter 7 and replace the two JSF `taglib` actions with the corresponding namespace declarations, as shown in Listing 8-9. You can find in the software package for this chapter the project simplefx.

Listing 8-9. first.jspx

```
<?xml version="1.0" encoding="UTF-8"?>
<jsp:root
  xmlns:jsp="http://xmlns.jcp.org/JSP/Page"
  xmlns:f="http://xmlns.jcp.org/jsf/core"
  xmlns:h="http://xmlns.jcp.org/jsf/html"
  version="2.1"
  >
```

```
<jsp:directive.page
  language="java"
  contentType="application/xhtml+xml;charset=UTF-8"
  />
<jsp:output omit-xml-declaration="false"/>
<jsp:output
  doctype-root-element="html"
  doctype-public="-//W3C//DTD XHTML 1.0 Strict//EN"
  doctype-system="http://www.w3.org/TR/xhtml1/DTD/xhtml1-strict.dtd"
  />
<html xmlns="http://www.w3.org/1999/xhtml">
<head><title>First Page</title></head>
<body>
<f:view>
  <h:form>
    <h:outputText value="Type something here: "/>
    <h:inputText value="#{aStringBean.str}"/>
    <h:commandButton action="goOn" value="Submit"/>
    </h:form>
  </f:view>
</body>
</html>
</jsp:root>
```

After converting second.jsp to second.jspx in the same way, you also need to insert into web.xml the context-param element shown in Listing 8-6; otherwise, JSF will keep looking for files with extension jsp. Finally, to complete the conversion to XML, you will need to make a global replace from jsp to jspx in faces-config.xml, so that the navigation rules will keep working.

Notice that we didn't need to do any conversion inside the body elements of the JSP pages. This is because there were no scripting elements to convert. With JSTL, JSF, and other custom actions that you acquire or develop yourself, you can write JSP in XML format without much effort.

You saw that in faces-config.xml you need to specify to which document you want the control to move when you request a particular action from within a particular document. The navigation elements for the simplexf applications are those shown in Listing 8-10.

Listing 8-10. Navigation Rules for simplexf

```
<navigation-rule>
  <from-view-id>/first.jspx</from-view-id>
  <navigation-case>
    <from-outcome>goOn</from-outcome>
    <to-view-id>/second.jspx</to-view-id>
    </navigation-case>
  </navigation-rule>
<navigation-rule>
  <from-view-id>/second.jspx</from-view-id>
  <navigation-case>
    <from-outcome>goBack</from-outcome>
    <to-view-id>/first.jspx</to-view-id>
    </navigation-case>
  </navigation-rule>
```

In particular, the first navigation rule tells JSF that when it executes the element
`<h:commandButton action="goOn" value="Submit"/>` in `first.jspx`, it should transfer
control to `second.jspx` (which JSF renames `second.jsf` so that a subsequent request
from the user goes back to the JSF servlet).

The JSF Life Cycle

Now that you have seen an example of JSF, let's have a closer look at how JSF does its job.
For that, refer to Figure 8-4. Note that the figure only shows what JSF does when the user
types valid values into the input fields of the page that sends the request. Read on for
more details.

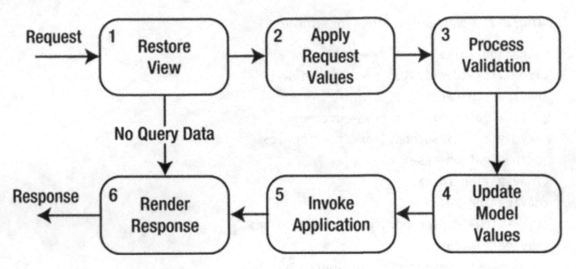

Figure 8-4. *The JSF life cycle*

1. **Restore View**: The JSF servlet builds the view of the requested page as a component tree that contains the information associated with all components of the page. If the page is requested for the first time, JSF creates an empty view, wires event handlers and validators (if any) to its components, and saves it in a FacesContext object, before jumping directly to Render Response. By saving the view, JSF makes it possible to repopulate the page if necessary, for example, when the user doesn't fill out a form as required. If the same page was displayed before and component states were saved, JSF uses that information to restore the page to its current state.

2. **Apply Request Values**: JSF goes through the component tree and executes each component's decode method, which extracts values from the request parameters, or possibly from cookies or headers. It also automatically converts the parameters that are associated with object properties of nonstring types. Conversion errors cause error messages to be queued to the FacesContext object. In some cases, typically when the user clicks controls, the servlet also generates request events and queues them to FacesContext. For components that have the immediate event-handling property set to true, JSF also validates them and saves them in their component instances within FacesContext.

3. **Process Validation**: The servlet invokes the `validate` methods for all components of the validators that had been registered during Restore View. The validation rules are those you define or, by default, those predefined by JSF. For each `validate` method that returns `false`, the servlet marks the component as invalid and queues an error message to the `FacesContext`. At the end of this phase, if there are validation errors, JSF jumps directly to Render Response, so that error messages can be displayed to the user.

4. **Update Model Values**: During this phase, the values of the components are copied to the corresponding properties of the managed beans that are wired to them. JSF does it by executing the component method `updateModel`, which also performs type conversions when necessary. Conversion errors cause error messages to be queued to `FacesContext`.

5. **Invoke Application**: During this phase, the servlet processes the application-level events by executing the corresponding handlers. When the user submits a form or clicks a link of a JSF application, the JSF servlet generates a corresponding application-level event. One of the tasks you have to do when developing a JSF application is to assign a handler to each one of the possible application events. This is where you also specify what should happen next, by returning outcomes that you have linked to possible next pages, either with a navigation case or implicitly, as I showed you in the previous section.

6. **Render Response**: The servlet creates a response component tree and delegates the rendering of the page to Tomcat. Each component renders itself as Tomcat goes through the corresponding JSF tags. At the end of this phase, the state of the response is saved so that the servlet can access it during the Restore View phase of subsequent requests to the same page.

Event Handling

Before looking at an application, I need to spend a few words on the JSF mechanism to handle events, because you cannot really understand how JSF works unless you know a thing or two about event handling.

As an example, let's see what role the event handling plays when a user clicks a Submit button. The JSF UI components used to represent button HTML elements are objects of type `javax.faces.component.html.HtmlCommandButton`, which is a class extending the more general `javax.faces.component.UICommand`. As with any other HTML page, by clicking the Submit button in a JSF application, the user triggers the sending to the server of an HTTP request that contains the ID of the button as a parameter name.

As I've already mentioned, during the Apply Request Values phase, JSF executes the `decode` method of each component of the page. First, the `decode` method scans the parameter names to see whether one matches the ID of the component the method belongs to. In our example, the `decode` method of the `UICommand` object associated with the button clicked by the user finds the component ID among the request parameters, precisely because the user clicked the button. As a result of finding its own ID, the component instantiates an event object of type `javax.faces.event.ActionEvent` and queues it up.

At this point, you have to distinguish between situations in which all the input fields of a form need to be validated and those in which only a partial validation is appropriate. For example, in an online shop such as the `eshop` application, the shopper must be able to add further books to the shopping cart even after reaching the checkout page, where the shopper is asked to provide payment information. To make that possible, you must ensure that the validation of the payment data is skipped if the user selects a book category or searches for new titles. If you allowed the validation of empty or partially filled payment fields to proceed, the application would report one or more errors and prevent the shopper from going back to look for new books.

You solve this issue by specifying that the handling of both the book search and the category selection be done during Apply Request Values while leaving the handling of the payment data to follow the normal life cycle. If it turns out that the user wants to shop for new books rather than complete the checkout, control then jumps directly to the Render Response phase, thereby skipping the intermediate phases where payment data would have been validated and processed.

In the next chapter, you will see in detail how this is done in the JSF version of `eshop`.

The JSF Tag Libraries

The first two sections of this chapter showed you examples of simple JSF applications that used a handful of elements: f:view, h:form, h:outputText, h:inputText, and h:commandButton. You will recall that the prefix h was associated with the HTML component library and the prefix f with the JSF core library. Besides those two libraries, JSF consists of two additional custom-tag libraries: facelets, normally associated with the prefix ui, and composite, with prefix composite.

In the rest of this chapter, I will briefly describe the four libraries and show you more examples. In the next chapter, I will describe how to use more of the tags by referring to a JSF version of the eshop application.

The html Library

As its name suggests, JSF's HTML library collects the tags associated with rendering HTML components. As you have already seen in the examples (e.g., with h:inputText), you associate objects of your data model to the corresponding components by assigning value expressions that refer to the objects to specific attributes of the component tags (e.g., <h:inputText value="#{aStringBean.str}"/>).

Although in most cases the names of the tags should already tell you their purpose, I have summarized the correspondence between tags and HTML elements in Table 8-1.

Table 8-1. *html Tags and HTML Elements*

Tag Name	HTML Element
h:body	body
h:button	input type="button"
h:column	--
h:commandButton	input type="submit"
h:commandLink	a
h:dataTable	table
h:doctype	<!DOCTYPE> declaration
h:form	form

(continued)

Table 8-1. (*continued*)

Tag Name	HTML Element
h:graphicImage	img
h:head	head
h:inputHidden	input type="hidden"
h:inputSecret	input type="password"
h:inputText	input type="text"
h:inputTextarea	input type="textarea"
h:link	a
h:message	span or text
h:messages	span or text
h:outputFormat	span or text
h:outputLabel	label
h:outputLink	a
h:outputScript	script
h:outputStylesheet	link
h:outputText	span or text
h:panelGrid	table
h:panelGroup	div or span
h:selectBooleanCheckbox	input type="checkbox"
h:selectManyCheckbox	multiple input type="checkbox"
h:selectManyListbox	select and multiple option
h:selectManyMenu	select and multiple option
h:selectOneListbox	select and multiple option
h:selectOneMenu	select and multiple option
h:selectOneRadio	multiple input type="radio"

The h:select* Elements

There are seven JSF HTML tags to render selections. To show how they differ from each other, I created in Eclipse the small project testf. You will find it in the testf project subfolder of the software package for this chapter. If you import testf.war in Eclipse, you will be able to try it out by typing http://localhost:8080/testf/ in your web browser. Figure 8-5 shows you what you will see in your browser after selecting values in the controls (and hitting the Submit button, although it is not necessary to do so).

Figure 8-5. *The output of testf*

Listing 8-11 shows the JSP document.

Listing 8-11. index.jspx for the testf Project

```
<?xml version="1.0" encoding="UTF-8"?>
<jsp:root
  xmlns:jsp="http://xmlns.jcp.org/JSP/Page"
  xmlns:f="http://xmlns.jcp.org/jsf/core"
  xmlns:h="http://xmlns.jcp.org/jsf/html"
  version="2.1"
  >
<jsp:directive.page
  language="java"
  contentType="application/xhtml+xml;charset=UTF-8"
  />
<jsp:output omit-xml-declaration="false"/>
<jsp:output
  doctype-root-element="html"
  doctype-public="-//W3C//DTD XHTML 1.0 Strict//EN"
  doctype-system="http://www.w3.org/TR/xhtml1/DTD/xhtml1-strict.dtd"
  />
<html xmlns="http://www.w3.org/1999/xhtml">
<head><title>Test</title></head>
<body><f:view><h:form id="form">
  <h:panelGrid columns="2" border="1" cellpadding="5">

    <h:outputText value="h:selectBooleanCheckbox"/>
    <h:panelGroup>
      <h:selectBooleanCheckbox id="checkbox" value="#{myBean.oneValue}"/>
      <h:outputText value=" just a checkbox"/>
      </h:panelGroup>

    <h:outputText value="h:selectManyCheckbox"/>
    <h:selectManyCheckbox id="checkboxes" value="#{myBean.choices1}">
      <f:selectItems value="#{myBean.selects}"/>
      <f:selectItem itemLabel="everything" itemValue="42"/>
      </h:selectManyCheckbox>
```

```
<h:outputText value="h:selectManyListbox"/>
<h:selectManyListbox id="listboxes" value="#{myBean.choices2}">
  <f:selectItems value="#{myBean.selects}"/>
  <f:selectItem itemLabel="too much" itemValue="999"/>
  </h:selectManyListbox>

<h:outputText value="h:selectManyMenu"/>
<h:selectManyMenu id="menus" value="#{myBean.choices3}"
    style="min-height:48px">
  <f:selectItems value="#{myBean.selects}"/>
  <f:selectItem itemLabel="ninety-nine" itemValue="99"/>
  </h:selectManyMenu>

<h:outputText value="h:selectOneListbox"/>
<h:selectOneListbox id="listbox" value="#{myBean.choice1}">
  <f:selectItems value="#{myBean.selects}"/>
  <f:selectItem itemLabel="nine" itemValue="9"/>
  </h:selectOneListbox>

<h:outputText value="h:selectOneMenu"/>
<h:selectOneMenu id="menu" value="#{myBean.choice2}">
  <f:selectItem itemLabel="zero" itemValue="0"/>
  <f:selectItems value="#{myBean.selects}"/>
  </h:selectOneMenu>

<h:outputText value="h:selectOneRadio"/>
<h:selectOneRadio id="radio" value="#{myBean.choice3}">
  <f:selectItem itemLabel="nothing" itemValue="-1"/>
  <f:selectItems value="#{myBean.selects}"/>
  </h:selectOneRadio>

</h:panelGrid>
<h:commandButton value="Submit"/>
</h:form></f:view></body>
</html>
</jsp:root>
```

I have highlighted in bold the selection components. h:selectBooleanCheckbox renders a single checkbox; h:selectManyCheckbox, h:selectManyListbox, and h:selectManyMenu render multiple selections; and h:selectOneListbox, h:selectOneMenu, and h:selectOneRadio render single selections.

In all cases in which you can select one or more of several items, I have included a hard-coded item in addition to a list of items provided by the managed bean through an attribute I chose to name selects:

```
<f:selectItems value="#{myBean.selects}"/>
```

The tags wire to each HTML control a different property of the managed bean. Notice the use of the core JSF tags f:selectItem and f:selectItems to provide the information needed for the options of the HTML select elements.

From this example, you can also see how to use h:panelGrid and h:panelGroup to render an HTML table. Differently from HTML, where you need to identify rows with tr elements and cells within rows with td elements, with h:panelGrid you specify at the beginning the number of columns, and all the components between its begin and end tags "flow" from left to right into the table. If you need more than one component within the same cell, you group them together with h:panelGroup.

Listing 8-12 shows the managed bean used to hold the items you select in the browser.

Listing 8-12. myPkg.MyBean.java for the testf Project

```java
package myPkg;
import java.util.ArrayList;
import javax.faces.model.SelectItem;

public class MyBean {
  @SuppressWarnings("unchecked")
  private ArrayList<String>[] choices = new ArrayList[3];
  private String choice1, choice2, choice3;
  private Object oneValue;
  private SelectItem[] selects;

  public MyBean()  {
    selects = new SelectItem[3];
    selects[0] = new SelectItem("1", "one");
    selects[1] = new SelectItem("2", "two");
```

```
  selects[2] = new SelectItem("3", "three");
  for (int kC = 0; kC < choices.length; kC++) {
    choices[kC] = new ArrayList<String>();
    }
  }

// ---------- Getters
public Object[] getChoices1() { return choices[0].toArray(); }
public Object[] getChoices2() { return choices[1].toArray(); }
public Object[] getChoices3() { return choices[2].toArray(); }
public String getChoice1() { return choice1; }
public String getChoice2() { return choice2; }
public String getChoice3() { return choice3; }
public Object getOneValue() { return oneValue; }
public SelectItem[] getSelects() { return selects; }

// ---------- Setters
public void setChoices(Object[] cc, int kC) {
        int len=0;
        if (cc != null) len = cc.length;
        if (len != 0) {
          choices[kC].clear();
          choices[kC] = new ArrayList<String>(len);
          for (int k = 0; k < len; k++) {
            choices[kC].add((String)cc[k]);
            }
          }
        }
public void setChoices1(Object[] cc) { setChoices(cc, 0); }
public void setChoices2(Object[] cc) { setChoices(cc, 1); }
public void setChoices3(Object[] cc) { setChoices(cc, 2); }
public void setChoice1(String c) { choice1 = c; }
public void setChoice2(String c) { choice2 = c; }
public void setChoice3(String c) { choice3 = c; }
public void setOneValue(Object v) { oneValue = v; }
}
```

There isn't really much to explain. JSF takes care of executing the initialization method of the bean, which initializes three values to be provided for selection through the `select` attribute and sets up the arrays needed to save the user's choices.

The `core` Library

JSF's core library gives you access to APIs that are independent of a particular render kit:

- **Converters**: Converters let you convert between the data types of the components and those of your application objects.

- **Listeners**: You register a listener with a component to handle events that the component generates.

- **Events**: After the listener is registered with a component, the `FacesServlet` fires the events by invoking an event notification method of the corresponding listener.

- **Validators**: Validators examine the value of a component and ensure that it conforms to a set of predefined rules.

In the previous examples, you have already encountered `f:view`, `f:selectItem`, and `f:selectItems`. Most of the core tags perform operations on components. Table 8-2 provides the list of all core tags and the corresponding operations. In the table, I have highlighted in italics the few operations that do not apply to individual components.

Table 8-2. *core Tags*

Tag Name	Operation
f:actionListener	Adds an action listener
f:ajax	*Registers an Ajax behavior for one or more components*
f:attribute	Sets an attribute
f:convertDateTime	Adds a date-time converter
f:converter	Adds a converter
f:convertNumber	Adds a number converter
f:event	Adds a system-event listener
f:facet	Adds a facet
f:loadBundle	*Loads a resource bundle into a Map*
f:metadata	*Declares the metadata facet for a view*
f:param	Adds a parameter
f:phaseListener	*Adds a phase listener to a view*
f:selectItem	Specifies an item for :selectMany* and h:selectOne*
f:selectItems	Specifies items for :selectMany* and h:selectOne*
f:setPropertyAction Listener	Adds an action listener that sets a property
f:subview	*Container for all JSF actions on pages included via jsp:include or c:import*
f:validateBean	Adds a bean validator
f:validateDoubleRange	Adds a double-range validator
f:validateLength	Adds a length validator
f:validateLongRange	Adds a long-range validator
f:validateRegex	Adds a validator against a regular expression
f:validateRequired	Adds a check that a value is present
f:validator	Adds a validator
f:valueChangeListener	Adds a value change listener
f:view	*Container for all JSF actions of a page*
f:viewAction	*Specifies an application-specific action*
f:viewParam	*Adds a parameter to the metadata facet of a view*

I expect that you will find many of the tags listed in Table 8-2 obscure. You will be able to understand most of them after the next sections and chapters, but the use of some of them definitely falls outside the scope of this book.

If you are curious about what a facet is, I can tell you that it is a named subcomponent specific to a particular component. For example, `h:gridPanel` (which renders an HTML table) supports the two facets `header` and `footer`. If you include `<f:facet "header"><h:outputText value="Whatever"/></f:facet>` anywhere within the body of `h:gridPanel`, the rendered table will have the header "Whatever".

I will talk about converters and validators in the next chapter, where I will describe a JSF version of the `eshopx` project I introduced in Chapter 7. In this chapter, as an interesting example of core tags, I will describe how to use `f:ajax`. In order to do that, I will first tell you about Ajax in general and show you how it was used before the introduction of `f:ajax`.

Ajax

I introduced JavaScript in the previous chapter: Asynchronous JavaScript and XML (Ajax) is a mechanism for letting JavaScript communicate with the server *asynchronously*, that is, without reloading the page. This is possible by means of the JavaScript built in object `XMLHttpRequest`.

In practical terms, it works like this: you create an `XMLHttpRequest` object within JavaScript, use it to send a request to the server, get the response, and have fresh data for your web page without having to reload it. Well, it sounds easy, but it's not obvious how to do it, and it's even more tricky to maintain. To explain how to use Ajax, I'll show you a simple example of a page that displays the server time. First, you need to write a JSP page to return the time (see Listing 8-13).

Listing 8-13. time.jsp

```
<%@page language="java" contentType="text/html"
  %><%@page import="java.util.*"
  %><% out.print(new GregorianCalendar().getTime()); %>
```

If you type the URL of this script in a browser, you'll get something like this:

```
Sun May 03 12:57:53 CEST 2020
```

You'll perhaps see some other time zone, but the format will be identical. A good place to check out the abbreviation for your time zone is www.timeanddate.com/time/zones/.

Now that you have a way of getting the server time, you can write the page to display it with Ajax, as shown in Listing 8-14.

Listing 8-14. ajax.xhtml

```
<?xml version="1.0" encoding="UTF-8"?>
<!DOCTYPE html PUBLIC "-//W3C//DTD XHTML 1.0 Transitional//EN"
    "http://www.w3.org/TR/xhtml1/DTD/xhtml1-transitional.dtd"
    >
<html xmlns="http://www.w3.org/1999/xhtml">
<head>
  <title>Example of Ajax</title>
  <script type="text/javascript" src="ajax.js"></script>
  </head>
<body>
  <form name="tForm" action="">
    <span>The time on the server is:</span>
    <input type="text" name="tElement" readonly="readonly" size="30"/>
    <input type="button" value="Update"
        onclick="ajaxFun('tForm', 'tElement');"
        />
  </form>
  </body>
</html>
```

As you can see, I've highlighted two lines. The first is where you load the file ajax.js, which contains the JavaScript code to support the Ajax operation. The second line is where you execute the ajaxFun JavaScript function whenever you click the Update button. Notice that you pass to ajaxFun the names of the form and of the input element to be updated. You could have hard-coded the string "tForm.tElement" within JavaScript, but it would have been bad programming practice to use within ajax.js identifiers defined elsewhere. Global variables invariably lead to code that's a nightmare to maintain and should be avoided whenever possible.

To complete this brief introduction to Ajax, I still need to show you the JavaScript code. However, before I do that, check out Figure 8-6 to see how the browser renders the page. To test the application, import the `ajax` project from the software package for this chapter into Eclipse. Then, type in your browser `http://localhost:8080/ajax/`.

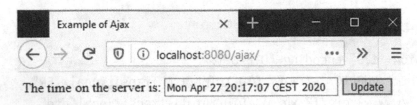

Figure 8-6. *Server time with Ajax*

Listing 8-15 shows the JavaScript code.

Listing 8-15. ajax.js

```
function ajaxFun(tf, te){
  var tElem = eval("document." + tf + "." + te)
  var ajaxReq;
  try { // Firefox, Opera, IE 9, Chrome
    ajaxReq = new XMLHttpRequest();
    }
  catch (e) { // older IEs
    try{
      ajaxReq = new ActiveXObject("Msxml2.XMLHTTP");
      }
    catch (e) {
      try{ // still older IEs
        ajaxReq = new ActiveXObject("Microsoft.XMLHTTP");
        }
      catch (e) {
        alert("Your browser does not support Ajax!");
        return false;
        }
      }
    }
```

```
ajaxReq.open("GET", "time.jsp");
ajaxReq.send(null);
ajaxReq.onreadystatechange = function() {
  if(ajaxReq.readyState == 4) {
    tElem.value = ajaxReq.responseText;
    }
  }
}
```

First, you instantiate an object of type XMLHttpRequest.

When ajaxReq "holds" an object of the correct type, you set up the HTML request method (e.g., GET) and the target URL (in this case, the JSP module time.jsp). At this point, you can send off the request.

The control comes immediately back to JavaScript (the first letter of Ajax stands for *asynchronous*). In general, you don't want the browser to wait for the response, and you want your page to be able to do other things. This asynchronicity makes Ajax more useful than if its operations had to be done in sequence. When the state of the request changes, the browser executes the function ajaxReq.onreadystatechange. In that function, you need to check that the request has been completed: in which case, you can then display the content of the response in the time field. Cool! In case you are curious to know the possible status codes, check out Table 8-3.

Table 8-3. *List of ajaxReq.readyState Codes*

Code	Meaning
0	Uninitiated
1	Loading
2	Loaded
3	Processing
4	Complete

I've taken a minimalist approach for this example. The idea is for your server to send back an XML document, which you can then parse on the client side.

One last thing: Listing 8-16 shows the deployment descriptor for this application.

Listing 8-16. web.xml

```
<?xml version="1.0" encoding="UTF-8"?>
<web-app xmlns:xsi="http://www.w3.org/2001/XMLSchema-instance"
xmlns="http://xmlns.jcp.org/xml/ns/javaee" xsi:schemaLocation="http://
xmlns.jcp.org/xml/ns/javaee http://xmlns.jcp.org/xml/ns/javaee/web-app_4_0.
xsd" version="4.0">
  <display-name>Ajax example</display-name>
  <welcome-file-list>
    <welcome-file>index.xhtml</welcome-file>
    <welcome-file>index.html</welcome-file>
  </welcome-file-list>
</web-app>
```

As you can see, it is almost empty. I have only added a couple of welcome-file elements so that Tomcat tries `index.html` (which is the default) only if `index.xhtml` is not there.

Now that you know how Ajax works without JSF, let's see how to use `f:ajax` to achieve the same result.

f:ajax

Using `f:ajax` instead of the mechanism I described in the previous section has several advantages, the most important of which, in my opinion, is that you no longer need to write code in JavaScript, which adds another flavor of Java to the mix. Further, `f:ajax` is fully integrated with the other JSF libraries.

Figure 8-4 showed the six phases of the JSF life cycle. With `f:ajax` you can selectively *execute* components on the server by processing them through the first five phases or *render* them by passing them through the last phase. You *ajaxify* a component by enclosing it within the body of `f:ajax` or by passing to `f:ajax` the component id.

To convert the Ajax example of the previous section to JSF's Ajax, let's start from `ajaxf.xhtml`, shown in Listing 8-17. The interesting bits are those highlighted in bold.

To test the application, import the `ajaxf project` from the software package for this chapter into Eclipse. After deploying, type `http://localhost:8080/ajaxf` in your web browser.

Listing 8-17. ajaxf.xhtml

```
<?xml version="1.0" encoding="UTF-8"?>
<!DOCTYPE html PUBLIC "-//W3C//DTD XHTML 1.0 Transitional//EN"
    "http://www.w3.org/TR/xhtml1/DTD/xhtml1-transitional.dtd"
    >
<html xmlns="http://www.w3.org/1999/xhtml"
      xmlns:f="http://xmlns.jcp.org/jsf/core"
      xmlns:h="http://xmlns.jcp.org/jsf/html"
      >
<h:head><title>Example of Ajax with JSF</title></h:head>
<h:body>
  <h:form>
    <h:outputText value="The time on the server is: "/>
    <h:outputText id="timeField" value="#{serverTimeBean.when}"/>
    <h:outputText value=" "/>
    <h:commandButton value="Update">
      <f:ajax render="timeField"/>
      </h:commandButton>
    </h:form>
  </h:body>
</html>
```

The first highlighted line simply displays the value of the property when of the managed bean serverTimeBean. It is almost identical to the line

```
<h:outputText value="&quot;#{aStringBean.str}&quot; "/>
```

of second.jsp (Listing 8-2) that you encountered at the very beginning of this chapter.

But this time, I have added to h:outputText the setting of the id attribute. This is because we need to pass it to f:ajax, in the second group of highlighted lines.

The h:commandButton element, contrary to what you saw in previous examples, doesn't transfer control to another page. Its purpose is only to create an event that triggers f:ajax. Accordingly, the action attribute is not there, and if you look at the WEB-INF folder of the application, you will see that no faces-config.xml to handle navigation is present.

Every time the user clicks the Update button, f:ajax sends a request to the server to obtain the value of serverTimeBean.when, which then the h:outputText element with id timeField displays. You don't need to write JavaScript because JSF automatically generates the little script that sends the Ajax request.

But you do need a Java bean like that shown in Listing 8-18.

Listing 8-18. ServerTime.java

```
import javax.faces.bean.ManagedBean;
import javax.faces.bean.SessionScoped;
import javax.faces.bean.ManagedProperty;
import java.util.GregorianCalendar;
public class ServerTime implements Serializable {
  String when;
  public ServerTime() { when = new GregorianCalendar().getTime().toString(); }
  public String getWhen() { return new GregorianCalendar().getTime().toString(); }
  public void setWhen(String w) { when = w; }
  }
```

The code is almost identical to that of AString.java (Listing 8-8), the major differences being that it has an initialization method and, obviously, generates a string with the current server time. In the software package, you will also find the files that complete the application, index.jsp and web.xml, but they are very similar to the equivalent files you already encountered with other applications.

You will obtain the same result if you replace in ajaxf.html the content of the h:body with the code shown in Listing 8-19.

Listing 8-19. Alternate h:body for ajaxf.xhtml

```
<h:form>
  <f:ajax render="@form" event="click"/>
  <h:outputText value="The time on the server is: "/>
  <h:outputText value="#{serverTimeBean.when} "/>
  <h:commandButton value="Update"/>
  </h:form>
```

With this setting, you ajaxify all components of the form. As a result, when you click the Update button, JSF sends an Ajax request, as it did before, and because the render attribute is set to @form, serverTimeBean.when is updated, as before. Events applicable to whole forms are click, dblclick, keydown, keypress, keyup, mousedown, mousemove, mouseout, mouseover, and mouseup.

With input elements in the form, when the user changes the content in any of them, that also triggers an Ajax request. To test it, replace h:commandButton with an h:inputText element as shown in Listing 8-20.

Listing 8-20. Yet Another h:body for ajaxf.xhtml

```
<h:form>
  <h:outputText value="The time on the server is: "/>
  <h:outputText id="timeField" value="#{serverTimeBean.when} "/>
  <h:inputText value="#{serverTimeBean.when}" size="30">
    <f:ajax render="@this timeField" event="blur"/>
    </h:inputText>
</h:form>
```

The resulting page is shown in Figure 8-7.

Figure 8-7. *A modified ajaxf.xhtml*

As long as you remain within the input field, nothing happens. When you hit enter or click outside it, Ajax sends a request to the server to update the property specified in h:inputText. In the example, it sends a request to set serverTimeBean.when to "Tue Apr 28 020". JSF does it in the Update Model Value phase. Then, during Render Response, Tomcat prepares the Javax response with two values obtained from serverTimeBean.when, one for h:outputText and one for h:inputText. As ServerTime.java always produces a fresh time string, that's what is returned to the browser, and what you typed in the input field remains unused in the bean's variable when.

Possible events for input fields are blur, change, click, dblclick, focus, keydown, keypress, keyup, mousedown, mousemove, mouseout, mouseover, mouseup, select, and valueChange. The default is valueChange.

The value of the render attribute can be a single identifier, a space-delimited list of identifiers, or one of the special strings @all, @this, @form, and @none.

The facelet Library

What makes JSF's facelet library interesting is that it supports templating. That is, a mechanism that allows you to minimize duplication of code when developing pages with the same layout or common content.

While JSP with jsp:include provides an easy mechanism to reuse content, it doesn't provide any easy way to define the same layout for different pages. It is up to you to ensure that the pages look identical when viewed in a browser.

The JSF facelet library lets you form a page by defining a layout in an XHTML file and then filling it up with content defined in one or more other XHTMLs. I will show you an example shortly, but first, have a look at Table 8-4, which lists all tags of the facelet library. To help you make sense of the tags, I have flagged those that are part of the templating mechanism.

Table 8-4. facelet Tags

Tag Name	Description	Templating
ui:component	Creates a component	N
ui:composition	Creates a composition	Y
ui:debug	Creates a component to help you debug the page	N
ui:decorate	Defines a fragment containing a composition	Y
ui:define	Defines content to be inserted into a template	Y
ui:fragment	Defines a fragment containing a component	N
ui:include	Includes content from an XHTML file	N
ui:insert	Inserts content into a template	Y
ui:param	Defines a parameter for an included file or a template	Y
ui:repeat	An alternative to h:dataTable and c:forEach	N
ui:remove	Removes what is in its body	N

The templ Application

In this section, I will describe templ, an application that uses facelet templating.

To create it, I started from the example simplefx I explained in this chapter. You will recall that it essentially consisted of two JSP documents that invoked each other: first. jspx asked you to type something into a text field, and second.jspx displayed what you had typed.

To make an example of templating, I added a third page almost identical to the second one, so that I could show you how to define a template for them. To get started, let's look at how the first two pages appear in a web browser (Figures 8-8 and 8-9).

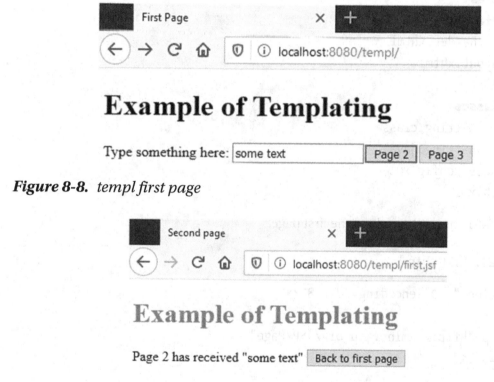

Figure 8-8. *templ first page*

Figure 8-9. *templ second page*

Notice that the header of the second page is gray instead of black. The third page is identical to the second one, but its title is "Third page" and the text before the button starts with "Page 3". To try it out, import in Eclipse the project templ from the software package for this chapter, and then type in a browser http://localhost:8080/templ/.

The application consists of the following folders and files (the folders are in bold for easy reading):

templ
    first.xhtml
    index.jsp
    page2.xhtml
    page3.xhtml
    resources
        css
            styles.css
    templates
        defaults
            header.xhtml
        layout.xhtml
    WEB-INF
        classes
            AString.class
            AString.java
        faces-config.xml
        web.xml

Listing 8-21 shows the code of the first page.

Listing 8-21. first.xhtml

```
<?xml version="1.0" encoding="UTF-8"?>
<jsp:root
  xmlns:jsp="http://xmlns.jcp.org/JSP/Page"
  version="2.1"
  >
<jsp:directive.page
  language="java"
  contentType="application/xhtml+xml;charset=UTF-8"
  />
<jsp:output omit-xml-declaration="false"/>
<jsp:output
```

```
  doctype-root-element="html"
  doctype-public="-//W3C//DTD XHTML 1.0 Strict//EN"
  doctype-system="http://www.w3.org/TR/xhtml1/DTD/xhtml1-strict.dtd"
  />
<html xmlns="http://www.w3.org/1999/xhtml"
      xmlns:f="http://xmlns.jcp.org/jsf/core"
      xmlns:h="http://xmlns.jcp.org/jsf/html"
      xmlns:ui="http://xmlns.jcp.org/jsf/facelets"
      >
<h:head><title>First Page</title></h:head>
<h:body>
<f:view>
  <ui:include src="/templates/defaults/header.xhtml"/>
  <h:form>
    <h:outputText value="Type something here: "/>
    <h:inputText value="#{aStringBean.str}"/>
    <h:commandButton action="go2" value="Page 2"/>
    <h:commandButton action="go3" value="Page 3"/>
    </h:form>
  </f:view>
</h:body>
</html>
</jsp:root>
```

First of all, notice that I renamed the file first.xhtml. This is because facelet elements (i.e., those with prefix ui) only work inside h:body. This means that you can no longer use the HTML body tag. As h:body requires the extension of the document to be xhtml, I had to ditch the extension jspx. The same applies to first.xhtml, which remains a valid JSP document despite the change of name.

Another difference from first.jspx is that I moved the namespace declarations for the core and HTML JSF libraries from jsp:root to the html tag and then added to them the declaration for the JSF facelet library. As none of the JSF tags are used outside the html element, it makes sense to keep them there, which is where they normally are in XHTML documents.

Finally, notice that first.xhtml includes a standard header with ui:include.

So far so good. Nothing too exciting. You could have done the same with jsp:include, without need for facelets. But now let's look at page2.xhtml (Listing 8-22) and in particular to its h:body element.

Listing 8-22. page2.xhtml

```
<?xml version="1.0" encoding="UTF-8"?>
<jsp:root
  xmlns:jsp="http://xmlns.jcp.org/JSP/Page"
  version="2.1"
  >
<jsp:directive.page
  language="java"
  contentType="application/xhtml+xml;charset=UTF-8"
  />
<jsp:output omit-xml-declaration="false"/>
<jsp:output
  doctype-root-element="html"
  doctype-public="-//W3C//DTD XHTML 1.0 Strict//EN"
  doctype-system="http://www.w3.org/TR/xhtml1/DTD/xhtml1-strict.dtd"
  />
<html xmlns="http://www.w3.org/1999/xhtml"
      xmlns:f="http://xmlns.jcp.org/jsf/core"
      xmlns:h="http://xmlns.jcp.org/jsf/html"
      xmlns:ui="http://xmlns.jcp.org/jsf/facelets"
      >
<h:body>
  <ui:composition template="/templates/layout.xhtml">
    <ui:define name="title">Second page</ui:define>
    <ui:define name="pageNum">2</ui:define>
  </ui:composition>
</h:body>
</html>
</jsp:root>
```

Notice that there is no h:head element in page2.xhtml. This is because JSF, when it encounters a ui:composition element, it ignores everything other than the content of h:body. You got it right: JSF only looks at the lines I have highlighted in Listing 8-22.

But then, you might ask, why do we bother with all the stuff that precedes the h:body tag? The reason is that the file must be a valid XML document. But it is true that we can simplify it. That's why I dropped the h:head element (which JSF ignores anyway), without which the code remains valid XML. With a page that doesn't use JSP tags inside h:body, you can also get rid of the JSP elements. This is what I did with page3.xhtml, which you can see in Listing 8-23.

Listing 8-23. page3.xhtml

```
<?xml version="1.0" encoding="UTF-8"?>
<!DOCTYPE html PUBLIC "-//W3C//DTD XHTML 1.0 Transitional//EN"
    "http://www.w3.org/TR/xhtml1/DTD/xhtml1-transitional.dtd"
    >
<html xmlns="http://www.w3.org/1999/xhtml"
    xmlns:f="http://xmlns.jcp.org/jsf/core"
    xmlns:h="http://xmlns.jcp.org/jsf/html"
    xmlns:ui="http://xmlns.jcp.org/jsf/facelets"
    >
<h:body>
  <ui:composition template="/templates/layout.xhtml">
    <ui:define name="title">Third page</ui:define>
    <ui:define name="pageNum">3</ui:define>
  </ui:composition>
</h:body>
</html>
```

Obviously, you cannot remove the JSP header elements and jsp:root when you use JSP code inside h:body. But you can use JSTL and your own custom-tag libraries without declaring the jsp namespace, as long as you declare the appropriate namespaces in the html tag. What you certainly cannot use in any case, with or without JSP declaration, are JSP scripting and directive elements, because anything enclosed between <% and %> is not valid XML.

Let's go back to describing how JSF handles the pages that make use of templates.

The presence of the ui:composition element with a defined template attribute means that it is the template document that generates the page to be sent back to the user as a response, not the page that contains the ui:composition element.

Listing 8-24 shows the template for page*.xhtml.

Listing 8-24. layout.xhtml

```
<?xml version="1.0" encoding="UTF-8"?>
<!DOCTYPE html PUBLIC "-//W3C//DTD XHTML 1.0 Transitional//EN"
"http://www.w3.org/TR/xhtml1/DTD/xhtml1-transitional.dtd">
<html xmlns="http://www.w3.org/1999/xhtml"
      xmlns:f="http://xmlns.jcp.org/jsf/core"
      xmlns:h="http://xmlns.jcp.org/jsf/html"
      xmlns:ui="http://xmlns.jcp.org/jsf/facelets"
      >

<h:head>
  <title>
    <ui:insert name="title">Default Title</ui:insert>
    </title>
  <h:outputStylesheet name="styles.css" library="css"/>
</h:head>

<h:body>
<f:view>
  <ui:insert name="header">
    <ui:include src="/templates/defaults/header.xhtml"/>
    </ui:insert>
  <h:form>
    <h:outputText value="Page "/>
    <ui:insert name="pageNum"/>
    <h:outputText value=" has received &quot;#{aStringBean.str}&quot; "/>
    <h:commandButton action="goBack" value="Back to first page"/>
    </h:form>
</f:view>
</h:body>
</html>
```

310

The two highlighted lines identify two places where the template expects the "client" pages to insert content. If you go back to page2.xhtml and page3.xhtml (Listings 8-22 and 8-23), you will see that the two ui:defines inside ui:composition have the same name attributes as the two ui:inserts of the template.

When layout.xhtml is used to generate the response to a request sent to page2. xhtml, the element <ui:insert name="title">Default Title</ui:insert> is replaced with the string "Second page" and the element <ui:insert name="pageNum"/> is replaced with "2". For page3.xhtml, the string is "Third page" and the page number is "3". Notice that the body of ui:insert is the default value for that insert, to be used when the "client" page doesn't define any value.

Notice that both layout.xhtml and first.xhtml include a default header (shown in Listing 8-25).

Listing 8-25. header.xhtml

```
<?xml version="1.0" encoding="UTF-8"?>
<!DOCTYPE html PUBLIC "-//W3C//DTD XHTML 1.0 Transitional//EN"
    "http://www.w3.org/TR/xhtml1/DTD/xhtml1-transitional.dtd"
    >
<html xmlns="http://www.w3.org/1999/xhtml"
    xmlns:h="http://xmlns.jcp.org/jsf/html"
    xmlns:ui="http://xmlns.jcp.org/jsf/facelets"
    >
<h:body>
  <ui:composition>
    <h1>Example of Templating</h1>
    </ui:composition>
</h:body>
</html>
```

In header.xhtml, the element ui:composition doesn't define a template attribute. Its presence ensures that the rest of the page is ignored when header.xhtml is included with ui:include. Actually, the only line needed in header.xhtml is the one I have highlighted. But the advantage of having a well-formed XHTML page is that you can view it in a browser. With more complex pages, it is sometimes useful to be able to do so.

There is still something I need to clarify. Have you noticed that the header shown in the first page (see Figure 8-8) is black, while the header of the second page (see Figure 8-9) is gray?

This is because the template, with the element

```
<h:outputStylesheet name="styles.css" library="css"/>
```

loads a style sheet that defines the color of headers to be gray.

As `first.xhtml` doesn't use the template, the color of the headers remains the default black. Obviously, nothing prevents you from using the style sheet in `first.xhtml` by placing in its `h:head` the same element used in the template. Alternatively, you can also use the HTML element

```
<link rel="stylesheet" type="text/css" href="/templ/resources/css/styles.css"/>
```

Still on the subject of linking to the style sheet with `h:outputStylesheet`: notice that the name of the `resources` folder doesn't appear anywhere. This means that it is hard-coded within the component and that you are stuck with it. But the folder names `templates` and `defaults` are entirely my choice. Therefore, you can choose the names you like.

To complete the description of the `templ` application, I still need to show you web. xml (Listing 8-26), which is pretty obvious, and `faces-config.xml` (Listing 8-27), which is also self-explanatory.

Listing 8-26. web.xml

```
<?xml version="1.0" encoding="UTF-8"?>
<web-app xmlns:xsi="http://www.w3.org/2001/XMLSchema-instance"
xmlns="http://xmlns.jcp.org/xml/ns/javaee" xsi:schemaLocation="http://
xmlns.jcp.org/xml/ns/javaee http://xmlns.jcp.org/xml/ns/javaee/web-app_4_0.
xsd" version="4.0">
<servlet>
  <servlet-name>Faces Servlet</servlet-name>
  <servlet-class>javax.faces.webapp.FacesServlet</servlet-class>
  <load-on-startup>1</load-on-startup>
  </servlet>
<servlet-mapping>
  <servlet-name>Faces Servlet</servlet-name>
```

```
    <url-pattern>*.jsf</url-pattern>
    </servlet-mapping>
<context-param>
    <param-name>javax.faces.DEFAULT_SUFFIX</param-name>
    <param-value>.xhtml</param-value>
    </context-param>
</web-app>
```

Listing 8-27. faces-config.xml

```xml
<?xml version="1.0" encoding="UTF-8"?>
<faces-config xmlns="http://xmlns.jcp.org/xml/ns/javaee"
        xmlns:xsi="http://www.w3.org/2001/XMLSchema-instance"
        xsi:schemaLocation="http://xmlns.jcp.org/xml/ns/javaee http://
        xmlns.jcp.org/xml/ns/javaee/web-facesconfig_2_3.xsd"
        version="2.3" >
  <managed-bean>
                <managed-bean-name>aStringBean</managed-bean-name>
                <managed-bean-class>AString</managed-bean-class>
                <managed-bean-scope>session</managed-bean-scope>
                <managed-property>
                        <property-name>str</property-name>
                        <property-class>java.lang.String</property-class>
                        <null-value></null-value>
                </managed-property>
        </managed-bean>

  <navigation-rule>
    <from-view-id>/first.xhtml</from-view-id>
    <navigation-case>
      <from-outcome>go2</from-outcome>
      <to-view-id>/page2.xhtml</to-view-id>
      </navigation-case>
    <navigation-case>
      <from-outcome>go3</from-outcome>
      <to-view-id>/page3.xhtml</to-view-id>
      </navigation-case>
```

```
      </navigation-rule>
    <navigation-rule>
      <from-view-id>/page2.xhtml</from-view-id>
      <navigation-case>
        <from-outcome>goBack</from-outcome>
        <to-view-id>/first.xhtml</to-view-id>
        </navigation-case>
      </navigation-rule>
    <navigation-rule>
      <from-view-id>/page3.xhtml</from-view-id>
      <navigation-case>
        <from-outcome>goBack</from-outcome>
        <to-view-id>/first.xhtml</to-view-id>
        </navigation-case>
      </navigation-rule>
    </faces-config>
```

The composite Library

JSF is based on user-interface components, but for a long time, it was difficult to create new components or combine existing components into a new one. JSF introduced the composite library with release 2.0 to make those tasks easier.

Table 8-5 lists all the tags of the composite library. The two tags interface and implementation are special, in that they are containers for other tags.

Table 8-5. *composite Tags*

Tag Name	Description	Valid In
composite:implementation	Container of the XHTML code that implements the component	
composite:interface	Container of interface components	
composite:actionSource	Exposes components that generate action events	interface
composite:attribute	Declares attributes of components	interface
composite:editable ValueHolder	Exposes components with editable values	interface
composite:extension	Inserts XML code in interface components	interface components
composite:facet	Declares a component's facet	interface
composite:insertChildren	Inserts XHTML code into component	implementation
composite:insertFacet	Inserts a facet	implementation
composite:renderFacet	Renders a facet	implementation
composite:valueHolder	Exposes components with non-editable values interface	

Conceptually, to define a new component, you need to go through the following steps:

- Define its namespace (i.e., where it is).
- Specify its functionality (i.e., what it does).
- Define how you use it (i.e., its interface).
- Design how you code it (i.e., its implementation).

Some Examples

To write the first example, let's go through the four points I listed at the end of the previous section:

- Define a namespace. I have chosen gz.

- Specify its functionality. The component should compose a greeting message with a parameterized addressee.

- Define how you use it. Just call it with an attribute to pass to it the addressee.

- Design how you code it. Simple. An h:outputText will do.

The code for the new component is shown in Listing 8-28. To test it, import the project composite from the software package for this chapter into Eclipse, and then type in the browser http://localhost:8080/composite.

Listing 8-28. hello.xhtml

```
<?xml version="1.0" encoding="UTF-8"?>
<!DOCTYPE html PUBLIC "-//W3C//DTD XHTML 1.0 Transitional//EN"
    "http://www.w3.org/TR/xhtml1/DTD/xhtml1-transitional.dtd"
    >
<html xmlns="http://www.w3.org/1999/xhtml"
    xmlns:h="http://xmlns.jcp.org/jsf/html"
    xmlns:composite="http://xmlns.jcp.org/jsf/composite"
    >
<h:head><title>Example of a composite component</title></h:head>
<h:body>
  <composite:interface>
    <composite:attribute name="x"/>
    </composite:interface>
  <composite:implementation>
    <h:outputText value="Hello, #{cc.attrs.x}!"/>
    </composite:implementation>
  </h:body>
</html>
```

Not surprisingly, for such a trivial component, the code is also trivial. But it tells you a lot about developing components with the composite library.

First of all, inside h:body, you find two elements, a composite:interface and a composite:implementation. Inside the former, you define the attribute named x, and inside the latter, you define the logic of the component.

To access the attribute from within the implementation, you use the expression #{cc.attrs.x}.

Listing 8-29 shows you how to use the new component, and Figure 8-10 shows how the page appears in a browser.

Listing 8-29. comp.xhtml

```xml
<?xml version="1.0" encoding="UTF-8"?>
<!DOCTYPE html PUBLIC "-//W3C//DTD XHTML 1.0 Transitional//EN"
    "http://www.w3.org/TR/xhtml1/DTD/xhtml1-transitional.dtd"
    >
<html xmlns="http://www.w3.org/1999/xhtml"
    xmlns:h="http://java.sun.com/jsf/html"
    xmlns:gz="http://java.sun.com/jsf/composite/gz"
    >
<h:head><title>Example of a composite component</title></h:head>
<h:body>
  <gz:hello x="wherever you are"/>
  </h:body>
</html>
```

Figure 8-10. *composite*

Have you noticed anything unusual in comp.xhtml? Instead of separately declaring the namespaces of the JSF composite library and of your custom components, you declare a single namespace composite/gz. For this to work, you need to create in the root of your application a folder named resources; create a folder (in the example, named gz) inside resources; and place your custom components there. The name of the component (e.g., hello) is obtained from the name of the component file (e.g., hello.xhtml) by removing its extension.

It is an established practice to use the same string for the prefix and for naming the folder inside resources, and I recommend that you follow it, but the two strings can be different.

Note that if you place elements in an interface body, you need to define a corresponding implementation. But you can have code in implementation with an empty interface, like in

```
<composite:interface/>
<composite:implementation>
  <h:outputText value="Hello, World!"/>
  </composite:implementation>
```

It simply means that your new component will not have any attribute to set.

To include in a composite component an input component, do exactly what you did for an output component in hello.xhtml. In fact, if you replace in hello.xhtml the line

```
<h:outputText value="Hello, #{cc.attrs.x}!"/>
```

with

```
<h:inputText value="Hello, #{cc.attrs.x}!"/>
```

you will see the page shown in Figure 8-11, but be aware that this is not a working page. It's just to show you how to use composite:attribute.

Figure 8-11. *composite with input element*

You can also use composite:attribute to set the action attribute of
h:commandButton and h:commandLink. For example, if you want to build a composite
component called, say, flip around the h:commandButton you used in templa a couple
of pages back, the body of flip.xhtml would look something like this:

```
<composite:interface>
  <composite:attribute name="act" targets="myB" method-signature="java.
lang.String action()"/>
  </composite:interface>
<composite:implementation>
  <h:commandButton id="myB" action="#{cc.attrs.act}" value="Page
#{actionBean.n}"
      actionListener="#{actionBean.swapPages}"
      />
  </composite:implementation>
```

Then, you would use the new composite component like this:

```
<gz:flip act="#{actionBean.goThere}"/>
```

As it was in the previous examples, you use the expression #{cc.attrs.act} to
access from the implementation the value of the act attribute declared in interface. In
addition, unlike what happened in the previous examples, you also need a reference in
the opposite direction, from interface to implementation. This is because JSF must be
able to wire the method set in gz:flip to the h:commandButton component for which
the method is meant. In fact, if there were more components in implementation, you
could wire the same method to several of them by writing their identifiers in the targets
attribute separated by spaces (this is why the name of the attribute is targets, plural,
instead of target).

The value of method-signature specifies that the value of act must evaluate to a
method and defines its signature. This means that <gz:flip act="go2"/> wouldn't
work. You would have to replace

```
method-signature="java.lang.String action()"
```

with

```
type="java.lang.String"
```

The two attributes are mutually exclusive, and if you leave out both of them, JSF assumes

```
type="java.lang.Object"
```

Now that you know how to make visible the action attribute of h:commandButton, you will perhaps be asking yourself how you expose its actionListener attribute as well. Here it is:

```
<composite:interface>
  <composite:attribute name="act" targets="myB" method-signature="java.
lang.String action()"/>
  <composite:actionSource name="myB"/>
  </composite:interface>
<composite:implementation>
  <h:commandButton id="myB" action="#{cc.attrs.act}" value="Page #{actionBean.n}"/>
  </composite:implementation>
```

Then, you would use the new composite component like this:

```
<gz:flip act="#{actionBean.goThere}">
  <f:actionListener for="myB" binding="#{actionBean.swapPages}"/>
  </gz:flip>
```

The element composite:actionSource exposes the h:commandButton component, and f:actionListener wires to it the appropriate action listener. Notice that the attribute actionListener has disappeared from h:commandButton.

A few words about composite:facet and composite:renderFacet. Close to the beginning of the section about the core library, I mentioned that facets are a means to let components do something special with a block of code. Now, suppose that you want to include a special word in several places within the composite component you are developing and that the page that uses the component should be able to define that word. You could do it like this:

```
<composite:interface>
  <composite:facet name="aWord"/>
  </composite:interface>
<composite:implementation>
```

320

```
<!-- ...some code... -->
<composite:renderFacet name="aWord"/>    <!-- say it here -->
<!-- ...some code... -->
<composite:renderFacet name="aWord"/>    <!-- and here -->
<!-- ...some code... -->
<composite:renderFacet name="aWord"/>    <!-- and again here -->
</composite:implementation>
```

And this is how you would use the component:

```
<gz:myFacetedComponent>
  <f:facet name="aWord"><h:outputText value="#@%!"/></f:facet>
</gz:myFacetedComponent>
```

JSF will take the body of the `facet` element defined in the using page and insert it where you invoke `composite:renderFacet`. If you like to insert those components *as a facet*, you need to use `composite:insertFacet` instead.

Normally, JSF ignores what is inside the body of your custom component, like in

```
<gz:myComponent>
  <h:outputText value="#@%! "/>
  <h:inputText value="#{aBean.whatever}"/>
</gz:myComponent>
```

If you want to include it in your composite component, you can do it with

```
<composite:insertChildren/>
```

Summary

In this chapter, we have covered a lot of ground. I gave you a first taste of JSF with simple applications. Then, after describing the JSF life cycle, I went on to talk about all four JSF tag libraries `html`, `core`, `facelet`, and `composite`. I listed their tags and showed you with simple examples how to use the most common or significant tags.

In the next chapter, we'll go back to `eshop` to see how we can convert it to a JSF application.

CHAPTER 9

JSF and Eshop

In Chapter 5, I introduced the eshop project, followed in Chapter 7 by eshopx, functionally identical to eshop except that I replaced the JSP pages containing scripting elements with JSP documents in XML format.

In this chapter, I am going to describe eshopf, a version of eshopx based on JSF. You will find both the WAR file and the expanded project in the software package for this chapter.

eshopf

Figure 9-1 shows the welcome page of eshopf. Although it is identical to that of eshop and eshopx, I include it here so that you can refer to it without having to flip forth and back across several chapters. Instead of commenting the listings of the whole application, I will concentrate on some interesting fragments as they relate to JSF.

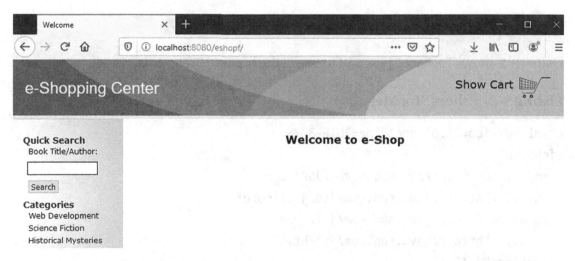

Figure 9-1. *eshopf's home page*

© Luciano Manelli and Giulio Zambon 2020
L. Manelli and G. Zambon, *Beginning Jakarta EE Web Development*,
https://doi.org/10.1007/978-1-4842-5866-8_9

As a basis for developing eshopf, I used eshopx. If you look at the welcome pages of eshopx and eshopf, both named index.jspx, you will see at once that, in order to use JSF, I added the two namespace declarations for the core and html JSF tag libraries and the element f:view to enclose all JSF actions.

But there is another update that is less obvious. Check out Listing 9-1, which shows the body of the f:view element.

Listing 9-1. eshopf: Body of f:view in index.jspx

```
<h:form>
  <jsp:include page="TopMenu.jspx" flush="true"/>
  <jsp:include page="LeftMenu.jspx" flush="true"/>
  </h:form>
<div class="content">
  <h1>Welcome to e-Shop</h1>
  </div>
```

In index.jspx of eshopx, the two jsp:includes were not wrapped inside a form. The reason for this change is due to the fact that, inside the jsp:included documents, as you will see in the following section, two HTML *anchor* elements are to be converted to h:commandLink components, which need to be inside h:form. It seemed reasonable to use a single form.

The Top Menu

Listing 9-2 shows TopMenu.jspx and its use of the h:panelGroup component.

Listing 9-2. eshopf: TopMenu.jspx

```
<?xml version="1.0" encoding="UTF-8"?>
<jsp:root
  xmlns:jsp="http://java.sun.com/JSP/Page"
  xmlns:c="http://java.sun.com/jsp/jstl/core"
  xmlns:f="http://java.sun.com/jsf/core"
  xmlns:h="http://java.sun.com/jsf/html"
  version="2.1"
  >
```

```
<jsp:directive.page
  language="java"
  contentType="application/xhtml+xml;charset=UTF-8"
  />
<f:subview id="viewcart">
  <h:panelGroup styleClass="header">
    <h:outputText styleClass="logo" value="e-Shopping Center"/>
    <h:commandLink action="showCart" immediate="true" styleClass="cart
    link2">
      <h:outputText value="Show Cart "/>
      <h:graphicImage url="/images/cart.gif"/>
    </h:commandLink>
  </h:panelGroup>
</f:subview>
</jsp:root>
```

The purpose of TopMenu.jspx is to provide a standardized access to the shopping cart.

Notice that I used f:subview to enclose all actions. Also notice that f:subview exists precisely to contain actions when they are included via jsp:include or any custom actions like c:include. Its purpose is equivalent to that of a pair of braces in Java: it limits the scope of its content. For example, the component IDs defined in one subview can be identical to those defined in other subviews of the same page.

With TopMenu.jspx, you don't necessarily need to wrap everything inside a subview, because the content of that document doesn't conflict with what is inside LeftMenu. jspx or with index.jspx. Nevertheless, it's good practice to avoid possible side effects of included modules. Subviews are required to have an ID, which is why I defined id="viewcart", even though we don't actually have any use for it.

The attribute styleClass is the JSF equivalent of the HTML attribute class. Refer to the file /css/eshopf.jspx to see the style definition for each class.

The function of h:panelGroup is grouping together UI components. In this case, it makes possible to apply the style class header to all elements it contains.

The JSF equivalent of the HTML element img is h:graphicImage.

Notice that the immediate attribute of h:commandLink is set to true. You will recall from the previous chapter that by doing so, you force the execution of the action listener already in the Apply Request Values phase. This guarantees that, regardless of what page the user is viewing, perhaps with a partially and inconsistently filled in form, control goes directly to the page of the shopping cart. The `action` attribute of `h:commandLink` sets the outcome to be `showCart`.

The Left Menu (Part 1)

Listing 9-3 shows the top-level structure of `LeftMenu.jspx`, with the `h:panelGrid` component.

Listing 9-3. eshopf: LeftMenu.jspx—Structure

```xml
<?xml version="1.0" encoding="UTF-8"?>
<jsp:root
  xmlns:jsp="http://java.sun.com/JSP/Page"
  xmlns:c="http://java.sun.com/jsp/jstl/core"
  xmlns:f="http://java.sun.com/jsf/core"
  xmlns:h="http://java.sun.com/jsf/html"
  version="2.1"
  >
<jsp:directive.page
  language="java"
  contentType="application/xhtml+xml;charset=UTF-8"
  />
<f:subview id="leftMenu">
  <h:panelGrid styleClass="menu">
    Here goes the Search Box - See Listing 9-4
    Here goes the Category Selection Box - See Listing 9-6
    </h:panelGrid>
  </f:subview>
</jsp:root>
```

As I showed in the previous chapter (see Listing 8-11), the `h:panelGrid` component is rendered with an HTML `table`; each component it contains is rendered as an HTML `td` element; and the optional attribute `columns` determines the length of the rows.

In `LeftMenu.jspx`, you could have written `columns="1"`, but I omitted it because 1 is the default. Here you need `h:panelGrid` instead of `h:panelGroup`, because otherwise the search and category selection boxes would have not been rendered one below the other.

The rows are filled in from left to right with the components in the order in which they appeared inside h:panelGrid, from top to bottom. The search box shown in Listing 9-4 consists of some descriptive text, an input text field, and a button to submit the search.

Listing 9-4. eshopf: LeftMenu.jspx—Search Box

```
<h:panelGroup styleClass="box">
  <h:outputText styleClass="box_title" value="Quick Search"/>
  <h:outputText styleClass="box_p" value="Book Title/Author:"/>
  <h:inputText size="15"
      styleClass="box_searchTxt"
      binding="#{shopManager.searchTxt}"
      />
  <h:commandButton
      type="submit" value="Search"
      styleClass="box_searchBtn"
      action="#{shopManager.searchBooks}"
      immediate="true"
      />
</h:panelGroup>
```

Notice that the action attribute of h:commandButton is set to a method of a managed bean instead of to a string literal. You encountered this mechanism in the section of the last chapter about Action Controllers and Action Listeners.

The attribute binding="#{shopManager.searchTxt}" shows how you can wire the input field to a data object on the server. You can establish a similar link with the value attribute, as I explained in the previous chapter (e.g., see Listing 8-1).

The difference is that with binding, you establish a two-way link, which lets your backing bean modify the value of the field, while with value, the backing bean cannot modify the data entered by the user. The shopManager bean doesn't need to modify the search string entered in LeftMenu.jspx, but you still use binding for reasons that will become clear in a moment.

As with the shopping cart in TopMenu.jspx, the attribute immediate="true" tells JSF that the action should be executed during Apply Request Values, rather than during Invoke Application, which is the default for all actions. In this way, you can be sure that the user is always able to resume shopping from any page, even if it contains invalid input fields (e.g., from the checkout page with empty fields).

327

This immediate execution of the search action is why you need to use the binding attribute in the h:inputText component. With the value attribute, you could access the search string with the method getValue, but only during Invoke Application, after Process Validation and Update Model Value have done their job. This would have been too late, because, as I've just explained, the search action takes place during Apply Request Values. By using the binding attribute, you make available to the shop manager *the whole h:inputText component*. As a result, you can invoke the method getSubmittedValue (see line 120 of Listing 9-5) already during Apply Request Value, when the search action is executed.

Before completing the study of LeftMenu.jspx, we should look at the ShopManager Java bean, which I have already mentioned a couple of times.

The Shop Manager

The shop manager is a managed bean defined in the session scope.

In the previous section, I said that the following two attributes realize the linking of user inputs and server entities:

```
binding="#{shopManager.searchTxt}"
action="#{shopManager.searchBooks}"
```

To understand exactly how this works, let's go through the relevant parts of ShopManager.java, as shown in Listing 9-5.

Listing 9-5. eshopf Fragment: Searching for Books in ShopManager.java

```
014: private List<Book>     books;
...
023: private HtmlInputText searchTxt = new HtmlInputText();
...
103: public HtmlInputText getSearchTxt() {
104:    return searchTxt;
105:    }
...
118: public String searchBooks() {
119:    categoryName=null;
120:    String searchKeyword = (String)searchTxt.getSubmittedValue();
```

```
121:    books = dataManager.getSearchResults(searchKeyword);
122:    return "listBooks";
123:    }
...
147: public void setSearchTxt(HtmlInputText val) {
148:    searchTxt = val;
149:    }
```

The binding attribute listed means that during Update Model Values, the JSF servlet saves the search string typed by the user in the attribute searchTxt, which is of type javax.faces.component.html.HtmlInputText. It does so by using the method setSearchTxt. Later in the life cycle, during Render Response, it uses the getSearchText method to get the value needed to prefill the input text field in HTML. The HtmlInputTxt class has a series of properties and methods that enable you, among other things, to make it a required input and to validate the value typed in by the user.

The action attribute of the Search button causes the JSF servlet to execute the method searchBooks during Invoke Application. As you can see in Listing 9-5, the method simply obtains the value of the search string, executes the dataManager method to obtain the list of books from the database, saves the list in the object books, and returns the string "listBooks".

If you now look at the following fragment of faces-config.xml, you'll see that by returning "listBooks", the searchBooks method forces JSF to switch from the current page to ListBooks.jspx:

```
<from-outcome>listBooks</from-outcome>
<to-view-id>/jsp/ListBooks.jspx</to-view-id>
<redirect/>
```

The presence (or absence) of the redirect element determines how this switch is done. If redirect is present, as in the example, JSF will send a redirect response to the client that will cause the browser to request the new page. Without the redirect element, during Render Response, JSF will directly use the content of the books object to render in HTML the list of books found in the database. But in that case, the list will effectively be a new rendering of the page that the user launched the search from. As a result, the URL shown in the browser will remain unchanged (e.g., http://localhost:8080/eshopf/).

The Left Menu (Part 2)

Now that you know how eshopf binds user inputs and actions to data objects and methods, we can complete the study of LeftMenu.jspx. Listing 9-6 shows the part where you select books by category.

Listing 9-6. eshopf: LeftMenu.jspx—Category Selection Box

```
01: <h:panelGroup styleClass="box" id="categBox">
02:    <h:outputText styleClass="box_title" value="Categories"/>
03:    <h:dataTable value="#{shopManager.categories}" var="category">
04:      <h:column>
05:        <h:commandLink
06:            action="#{shopManager.selectCategory}"
07:            value="#{category.name}"
08:            immediate="true"
09:            />
10:      </h:column>
11:    </h:dataTable>
12:  </h:panelGroup>
```

JSF renders the h:dataTable component (line 03) with an HTML table element, in which every column is identified by an h:column component (line 04). In addition to the table functionality as you know it from HTML, JSF also provides an iteration mechanism similar to that of c:forEach and linked to the data model. The mechanism is based on two attributes: value, which contains an EL expression that returns a list of items, and var, which contains the name of a variable to which the items of the list are assigned one by one in sequence.

In this case, the EL expression #{shopManager.categories} executes the following method of shopManager:

```
068 public ListDataModel<Category> getCategories() {
069   categoriesDataModel.setWrappedData(dataManager.getCategories());
070   return categoriesDataModel;
071   }
```

with `categoriesDataModel` defined as follows:

```
017 private ListDataModel<Category> categoriesDataModel = new
ListDataModel<Category>();
```

The result is that the `List` of categories obtained from the database via the `dataManager.getCategories` method is assigned to the `value` attribute of `h:dataTable`.

JSF implements an index that goes through all the items of the list, and the attribute `var="category"` defines the name of the variable that gives access to the current item. In practical terms, this means that when the JSF servlet renders the `h:dataTable` component during the Render Response phase, it renders the `h:commandLink` of lines 05–09 for each category found in the database.

The Checkout Page

The `Checkout.jspx` module of the `eshopf` application asks the user to provide the payment data (name, address, and credit-card information). Listing 9-7 shows the code associated with one of the input items.

Listing 9-7. eshopf: Checkout.jspx—Address Entry

```
<h:panelGrid columns="3" rendered="#{!shopManager.shoppingCartEmpty}"
    style="width:auto">
  ...
  <h:outputText value="Delivery Address"/>
  <h:inputText id="address" required="true"
      value="#{shopManager.customer.deliveryAddress}"
      requiredMessage="Value is required!"
      />
  <h:message for="address" styleClass="error"/>
  ...
</h:panelGrid>
```

The value of the `h:inputText` component is associated with the `deliveryAddress` attribute of the object `customer`, which is an instantiation of the class `eshop.beans.Customer`. Because the attribute `required` of `h:inputText` is set to true, if the user omits to fill in the field, the value of the attribute `requiredMessage` is displayed. If you define the the JSF element `h:message`, its location within the page and its style determine where the error message is displayed and how, as shown in Figure 9-2.

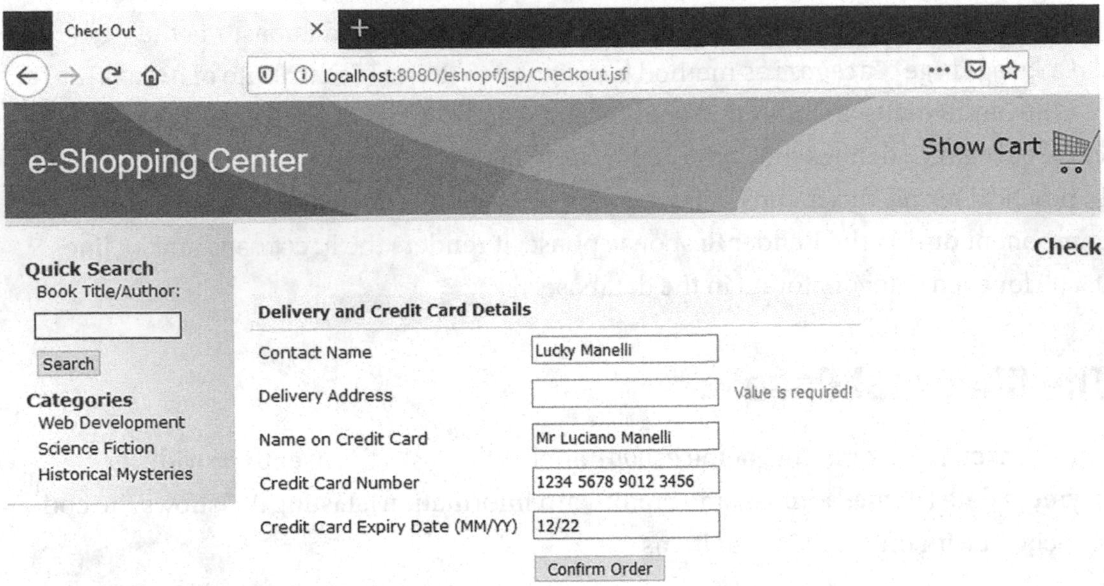

Figure 9-2. *Incomplete input on Checkout.jspx*

web.xml

Listing 9-8 shows the file `WEB-INF\web.xml` for the application `eshopf`.

Listing 9-8. eshopf: web.xml

```
<?xml version="1.0" encoding="UTF-8"?>
<web-app version="2.5" xmlns="http://java.sun.com/xml/ns/javaee"
  xmlns:xsi="http://www.w3.org/2001/XMLSchema-instance"
  xsi:schemaLocation="http://java.sun.com/xml/ns/javaee ~CCC
http://java.sun.com/xml/ns/javaee/web-app_2_5.xsd">
  <display-name>eshop</display-name>
  <context-param>
    <param-name>javax.faces.DEFAULT_SUFFIX</param-name>
    <param-value>.jspx</param-value>
    </context-param>
```

```
<servlet>
  <servlet-name>Faces Servlet</servlet-name>
  <servlet-class>javax.faces.webapp.FacesServlet</servlet-class>
  <load-on-startup>1</load-on-startup>
  </servlet>
<servlet-mapping>
  <servlet-name>Faces Servlet</servlet-name>
  <url-pattern>*.jsf</url-pattern>
  </servlet-mapping>
<login-config>
  <auth-method>BASIC</auth-method>
  </login-config>
<resource-ref>
  <res-ref-name>jdbc/mysql</res-ref-name>
  <res-type>javax.sql.DataSource</res-type>
  <res-auth>Container</res-auth>
  </resource-ref>
</web-app>
```

Most of the tags should be familiar to you from previous examples.

The context-parameter element sets the file extension to be jspx, which is the extension of JSP documents, as those of eshopf. If you had left out this element, the extension would have been jsp, which is the extension of JSP pages.

The servlet element points to the class of the standard JSF servlet. By setting the element servlet-mapping to *.jsf, you specify that the JSP documents are to be accessed with that extension instead of their real extension, which is jspx. For example, when you select a book category in eshopf, the URL displayed in the browser is

```
http://localhost:8080/eshopf/jsp/ListBooks.jsf
```

while the JSP document is actually called ListBooks.jspx. This is called *extension mapping*.

The last element, resource-ref, states that the resource named jdbc/mysql is of type DataSource and that Tomcat does its own authentication. Tomcat provides a Java Naming and Directory Interface (JNDI) InitialContext for each application. This means that once you've registered a resource in web.xml, you can provide in a separate context file all the information necessary to link it to your server environment. For eshopf, the information is shown in Listing 9-9.

Listing 9-9. context.xml

```
<?xml version="1.0" encoding="UTF-8"?>  <!-- MySQL database context -->
<!DOCTYPE Context [<!ELEMENT Context ANY> <!ATTLIST Context debug CDATA
#IMPLIED
  reloadable CDATA #IMPLIED crossContext CDATA #IMPLIED>]>
<Context debug="5" reloadable="true" crossContext="true">
  <Resource
      name="jdbc/mysql"
      auth="Container"
      type="javax.sql.DataSource"
      username="root"
      password="root"
      driverClassName="com.mysql.cj.jdbc.Driver"
      url="jdbc:mysql://localhost:3306/shop"
      maxActive="8"
      maxIdle="4"
      />
  <Valve
      className="org.apache.catalina.valves.AccessLogValve"
      directory="logs"
      prefix="eshopf-access."
      suffix=".log"
      pattern="common"
      resolveHosts="false"
      />
</Context>
```

As you can see, the resource attributes url, username, and password specify the MySQL database used in all versions of E-shop application and how to access it. The context file must be named context.xml and placed in the META-INF folder of your application directory.

In eshop and eshopx, you defined the database parameters in web.xml with init-param elements and retrieved them in the eshop.ShopServlet.init method to make them available to the data manager (see Listings 5-1, 5-2, and 5-3).

In eshopf, as you have just seen, you define the same parameters (it actually is the same database) in context.xml and make them accessible to the application by defining a resource-ref element in web.xml.

Accordingly, you have to update the data manager's method getConnection. In practical terms, after removing all checks from the actual code for clarity, the line

```
conn = DriverManager.getConnection(getDbURL(), getDbUserName(),
getDbPassword());
```

of eshop and eshopx is replaced in eshopf by the following four lines:

```
Context ctx = new InitialContext();
Context envContext  = (Context)ctx.lookup("java:/comp/env");
DataSource ds = (DataSource)envContext.lookup("jdbc/mysql");
conn = ds.getConnection();
```

The mechanism used in eshop and eshopx could not be used in eshopf because ShopServlet has been replaced by the JSF servlet. The mechanism relying on context.xml is in fact more flexible and elegant than the original one, but I think it was good for you to see both mechanisms.

Using and Creating Converters

As I said when describing the JSF life cycle, the JSF servlet executes the decode method of each component during Apply Request Values. The method saves the parameter values locally, but it first needs to convert the input strings to the corresponding types defined in the components, except when the components expect values of type String. JSF provides standard converters for the java.lang types Boolean, Byte, Character, Double, Enum, Float, Integer, Long, and Short and for the java.math types BigDecimal and BigInteger.

The standard converters perform a series of checks that you can use to validate, at least in part, the user's input. To do so, you have to enable the reporting of converter messages.

For example, in the `eshopf` application, the user can update the number of copies of a book that is already in the shopping cart. Clearly, it doesn't make any sense to type a fractional number or a string that is not numeric. Therefore, you can write the input component in the `ShoppingCart.jspx` document as follows:

```
<h:inputText id="quantity" value="#{item.quantity}" size="2"
    required="true"
    requiredMessage="What? Nothing?"
    converterMessage="An integer, please!"
    />
```

Then, you only need to add this line to display the error messages of the standard Integer converter:

```
<h:message for="quantity" styleClass="error"/>
```

This is not yet a perfect solution, because the application still accepts negative integers. That is, you can type in `-1`, and the application will happily display negative prices! To see how to solve this problem, you'll have to wait for the section about validators.

Sometimes the standard converters are not sufficient. For example, you might like to save in a database a credit-card number without any dashes or spaces. To make a custom converter, you need to create an implementation of the `javax.faces.Converter` interface that overrides its methods `getAsObject` and `getAsString`. You must implement both directions of the converter. During Apply Request Values, JSF uses the `getAsObject` method to convert the input string to the data model object. During Render Response, JSF uses the `getAsString` method to do the conversion in the opposite direction, so that a string can be included in the HTML response. Once you complete the converter, you have to register it with the application.

To invoke the converter, you need to nest it as a property of `f:converter` or assign it to the `converter` attribute of the input component. Let's go through the three steps (i.e., develop, register, and invoke) one at a time. The converter will just clean up a credit-card number of any non-numeric character. Notice that it is the task of a validator to check that the credit-card number is valid. This normally takes place during Process Validation, while the conversions, as I just said, take place during phases Apply Request Values and Render Response.

Writing the Converter in Java

Listing 9-10 shows the full code of the converter used in eshopf to convert the credit-card number when checking out.

Listing 9-10. CCNumberConverter.java

```
package eshop.converters;
import javax.faces.convert.Converter;
import javax.faces.context.FacesContext;
import javax.faces.component.UIComponent;
import javax.faces.convert.ConverterException;
public class CCNumberConverter implements Converter {
  //
  // getAsObject extracts from the input string all numeric characters
  public Object getAsObject(FacesContext ctx, UIComponent cmp,
      String val) {
    String convVal = null;
    if ( val != null ) {
      char[] chars = val.trim().toCharArray();
      convVal = "";
      for (int k = 0; k < chars.length; k++) {
        if (chars[k] >= '0' && chars[k] <= '9') {
          convVal += chars[k];
          }
        }
/*
      System.out.println("CCNumberConverter.getAsObject: '"
          + val + "' -> '" + convVal + "'");
*/
      }
    return convVal;
    }
  //
  // getAsString inserts into the object string spaces to make it readable
  // default: nnnn nnnn nnnn nnnn, Amex: nnnn nnnnnn nnnn
```

337

```java
  public String getAsString(FacesContext ctx, UIComponent cmp, Object val)
     throws ConverterException {
    String convVal = null;
    if (val != null) {
      int[] spaces = {3, 7, 11, 99};
      int[] amex = {3, 9, 99};
      String sVal = null;
      try {
        sVal = (String)val; // The val object should be a String!
        }
      catch (ClassCastException e) {
        throw new ConverterException("CCNumberConverter: Conversion Error");
        }
      int kSpace = 0;
      char[] chars = sVal.toCharArray();
      if (chars.length == 15) spaces = amex;
      convVal = "";                              .
      for (int k = 0; k < chars.length; k++) {
        convVal += chars[k];
        if (spaces[kSpace] == k) {
          convVal += ' ';
          kSpace++;
          }
        }
/*
      System.out.println("CCNumberConverter.getAsString: '"
          + sVal + "' -> '" + convVal + "'");
*/
      }
    return convVal;
    }
  }
```

The getAsObject method simply removes from the input string all the characters that are not decimal digits. The getAsString method inserts spaces to make the credit-card numbers more readable.

For example, if you during checkout type something such as 12-34. 56Abc78;90123--456, it will be reformatted to 1234 5678 9012 3456 as soon as you press the Check Out button. To verify that the object is correct, you can use the two println statements that you see commented out in the code. Here are a few examples taken from stdout_*yyyymmdd*.log in Tomcat's logs folder:

```
CCNumberConverter.getAsObject: 'abc1234 5678 1111x2222' ->
'1234567811112222'
CCNumberConverter.getAsString: '1234567811112222' -> '1234 5678 1111 2222'
CCNumberConverter.getAsObject: '  1  23456789  012345' -> '123456789012345'
CCNumberConverter.getAsString: '123456789012345' -> '1234 567890 12345'
```

As you can see, the output of getAsObject, which is also the input of getAsString, is always stripped of nondigit characters, while the output of getAsString is always formatted with spaces. Once more, the checking of correctness is a task for the validator, not for the converter.

Registering the Converter with the Application

You can register the converter with the application by adding the following lines to the faces-config.xml file:

```xml
<converter>
  <converter-id>CCNumberConverter</converter-id>
  <converter-class>eshop.converters.CCNumberConverter</converter-class>
</converter>
```

You can choose any name you like inside the converter-id element, while the class in the converter-class element must match that of the converter that I described in the previous section.

Using the Converter

Here's how to write the input element for the credit-card number in the Checkout.jspx module:

```
<h:inputText id="ccnumber" required="true"
    value="#{shopManager.customer.ccNumber}"
    requiredMessage="Value is required!"
    converter="CCNumberConverter"
    />
```

As you can see, you only need to include the converter attribute and assign to it the converter-id you've registered in faces-config.xml. Alternatively, you could have nested an f:converter element inside the h:input component:

```
<f:converter converterId="CCNumberConverter"/>
```

The result would have been the same. This is a permissive converter, because it accepts almost everything without complaining. You could ask yourself whether a 30-character-long string that happens to include 16 digits is a valid credit-card number. I'll leave that up to you.

Using and Creating Validators

How do you ensure that the user of the eshopf application doesn't succeed in buying a negative number of books? Actually, the application should also reject any attempt of buying zero books. And what about checking the validity of a credit-card number? These are tasks for validators.

JSF features four types of validation mechanisms:

- Built-in validation components

- Application-level validation

- Custom validation components

- Validation methods in backing beans

Let's go through them one by one.

Built-In Validators

JSF provides the following validation components:

- `f:validateBean`: It delegates validation of the bean's local value to the Bean Validation API.

- `f:validateDoubleRange`: It validates that a numeric input is within a given range. It is applicable to values that you can convert to a `double`.

- `f:validateLength`: It validates that the length of the input string is within a given range.

- `f:validateLongRange`: It validates that a numeric input is within a given range. It is applicable to values that you can convert to a `long`.

- `f:validateRegex`: It checks whether the String value of the component matches a given regular expression.

- `f:validateRequired`: It checks whether a value is present. It is equivalent to setting the `required` attribute to `true`.

To use these validation components, you simply nest them inside the `h:input` component you need to validate. For example, to check that only positive quantities can be entered in the `eshopf` shopping cart, you modify the `h:inputText` component in `ShoppingCart.jspx` as follows:

```
<h:inputText id="quantity" value="#{item.quantity}" size="2"
   required="true"
   requiredMessage="What? Nothing?"
   converterMessage="An integer, please!"
   validatorMessage="At least one copy!"
   >
 <f:validateLongRange minimum="1"/>
 </h:inputText>
```

All three validators also accept the `maximum` attribute to set the upper limit of the range. For example, you can force the user to enter the correct number of credit-card digits by modifying the corresponding `h:inputText` in `Checkout.jspx`:

```
<h:inputText id="ccnumber" required="true"
    value="#{shopManager.customer.ccNumber}"
    converter="CCNumberConverter"
    requiredMessage="Value is required!"
    validatorMessage="Only 15 or 16 digits accepted!"
    >
  <f:validateLength minimum="15" maximum="16"/>
  </h:inputText>
```

As the validation takes place after the conversion, the limits of 15 (for American Express) and 16 (for all other credit cards) are applied to the user's input after removing all nondigit characters.

Application-Level Validation

Application-level validation consists of performing checks inside the backing beans. This makes sense if you need to validate the business logic of your application, as opposed to validating formal correctness of individual fields. For example, before accepting an order, you might like to check that your bank has not blacklisted the credit-card number. Let's see how it works.

In eshopf, when the user clicks the Check Out button after entering his or her name and credit-card data, the checkOut method of shopManager is executed, as shown in the following line taken from Checkout.jspx:

```
<h:commandButton value="Check Out" action="#{shopManager.checkOut}"/>
```

The method is as follows:

```
public String checkOut() {
  orderId = dataManager.insertOrder(customer, shoppingCart);
  if (orderId != 0) {
    customer = null;
    shoppingCart.clear();
    }
  return "orderConfirmation";
  }
```

The dataManager.insertOrder method saves the order information in the database. The checkOut method returns an outcome that tells JSF what page should be displayed next.

If you want to do some application-level validation, you could insert its logic at the beginning of the checkOut method and make the database update and the method outcome dependent on the validation result. In case of validation failure, you could also send a message to the user, as shown in the following few lines:

```
FacesContext ctxt = FacesContext.getCurrentInstance();
FacesMessage mess = new FacesMessage();
mess.setSeverity(FacesMessage.SEVERITY_ERROR);
mess.setSummary("This is the summary text");
mess.setDetail("This is the detail text");
ctxt.addMessage(null, mess);
```

The message created in this way is a global message, not bound to any particular component, and you can display it with the following JSF component:

```
<h:messages globalOnly="true" styleClass="error"/>
```

If you want to create a message for a particular component, you need to replace the null argument of ctxt.addMessage with the clientId of the component. The clientId is a string containing all the IDs necessary to identify a particular component. For example, if you have <h:inputText id="it"...> inside <h:form id="fm"...>, the clientId of the input component is fm:it. I recommend that you don't use this option, because it forces you to hard-code the clientId in your Java method.

Custom Validators

In the section "Using and Creating Converters" of this chapter, I explained how to implement a custom converter. To implement a custom validator, you follow an almost identical process:

- Create an implementation of the interface javax.faces. validator.Validator that overrides the validate method.

- Register the validator in faces-config.xml.

- Within your JSF application, refer to the validator in an attribute or a component.

Suppose you want to ensure that the credit-card expiry date provided by the user during checkout is in the form MM/YY and that the card has not expired. Listing 9-11 shows the validator code.

Listing 9-11. CCExpiryValidator.java

```java
package eshop.validators;
import javax.faces.validator.Validator;
import javax.faces.context.FacesContext;
import javax.faces.component.UIComponent;
import javax.faces.application.FacesMessage;
import javax.faces.validator.ValidatorException;
import java.util.GregorianCalendar;
import java.util.Calendar;

public class CCExpiryValidator implements Validator {
  public CCExpiryValidator() {
    }
  public void validate(FacesContext cntx, UIComponent cmp, Object val) {
    String messS = null;
    String[] fields = ((String)val).split("/", 3);
    if (fields.length != 2) {
      messS = "Expected MM/YY!";
      }
    else {
      int month = 0;
      int year = 0;
      try {
        month = Integer.parseInt(fields[0]);
        year = Integer.parseInt(fields[1]);
        }
      catch (NumberFormatException e) {
        }
      if (month <= 0  ||  month > 12) {
        messS = "Month " + fields[0] + " not valid!";
        }
```

```
    else if (year < 0  ||  year > 99) {
      messS = "Year " + fields[1] + " not valid!";
      }
    else {
      GregorianCalendar cal = new GregorianCalendar();
      int thisMonth = cal.get(Calendar.MONTH) + 1;
      int thisYear = cal.get(Calendar.YEAR) - 2000;
      if (year < thisYear  ||  year == thisYear && month < thisMonth) {
        messS = "Credit card expired!";
        }
      }
    }
  if (messS !- null) {
    FacesMessage mess = new FacesMessage(FacesMessage.SEVERITY_ERROR,
    messS, messS);
    throw new ValidatorException(mess);
    }
  }

}
```

To register the validator with the application, you only need to add the following lines to `faces-config.xml`, for example, immediately below the registration of the converter:

```
<validator>
  <validator-id>CCExpiryValidator</validator-id>
  <validator-class>eshop.validators.CCExpiryValidator</validator-class>
  </validator>
```

Then, to validate the credit-card expiry date, you modify the `h:inputText` component used in `Checkout.jspx` as follows:

```
<h:inputText id="ccexpiry" required="true"
    value="#{shopManager.customer.ccExpiryDate}"
    requiredMessage="Value is required!"
    >
  <f:validator validatorId="CCExpiryValidator"/>
  </h:inputText>
```

You'll be rewarded with error messages like those shown in Figure 9-3 (which I obtained by taking several screenshots and then putting them together with a graphics program).

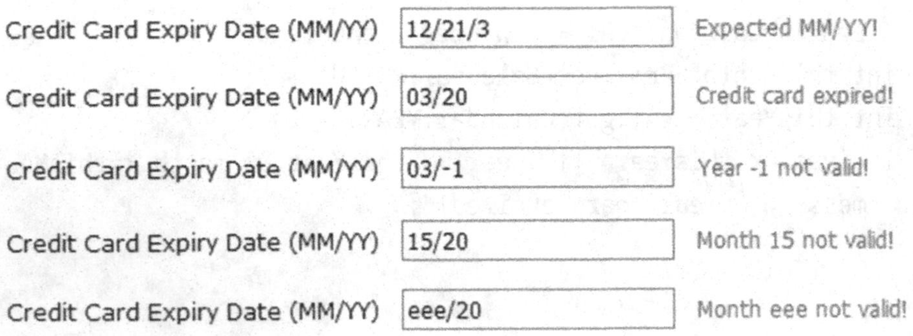

Credit Card Expiry Date (MM/YY)	12/21/3	Expected MM/YY!
Credit Card Expiry Date (MM/YY)	03/20	Credit card expired!
Credit Card Expiry Date (MM/YY)	03/-1	Year -1 not valid!
Credit Card Expiry Date (MM/YY)	15/20	Month 15 not valid!
Credit Card Expiry Date (MM/YY)	eee/20	Month eee not valid!

Figure 9-3. Expiry-date validation in Checkout.jspx

Validation Methods in Backing Beans

Instead of creating a new class as described in the previous section, you can add a method to a backing bean. In this case, you could do the following steps:

- Copy the validate method from CCExpiryValidator.java to ShopManager.java, inside the class ShopManager, and rename it validateCCExpiry.

- Copy the imports of FacesContext, UIComponent, FacesMessage, GregorianCalendar, and Calendar from CCExpiryValidator.java to the beginning of shopManager.java.

- Replace in validateCCExpiry the line that throws the ValidatorException with ctxt.addMessage(cmp.getClientId(ctxt), mess);.

That's it! To use this validator instead of the previous one, modify the h:inputText in Checkout.jspx as follows:

```
<h:inputText id="ccexpiry" required="true"
    value="#{shopManager.customer.ccExpiryDate}"
    validator="#{shopManager.validateCCExpiry}"
    requiredMessage="Value is required!"
    />
```

The `validator` element in `faces-config.xml`, the element `f:validator` in `Checkout.jspx`, and the module `CCExpiryValidator.java` are then no longer needed.

Tip   To modify projects, always use Eclipse: duplicate the project by selecting its icon in Eclipse's Project Explorer bar, and then copy and paste it. Eclipse will ask you to provide a new name for the duplicate project. In this way, it will be easier to go back to the original should you want to.

Creating Custom Components

The functionality of a component is centered on converting a user's inputs (i.e., the HTTP request parameters) to component values (via the `decode` method during Apply Request Values) and converting component values back to HTML (via the `encode` method during Render Response).

In the previous chapter, you saw how to create custom components with the facelets and composite JSF tag libraries. In this chapter, I want to give you an example of how to create a new JSF component without those tags. This will give you a better understanding of how JSF works. I am always a great defender of doing things "by hand" at least once!

When you design a JSF component, you can choose to move encoding and decoding to a separate renderer class. The advantage of this approach is that you can develop more than one renderer for the same component, each with a different representation in HTML. You will then have the same behavior associated with different ways of reading data from the request and writing it to the response.

In general, considering that JSF is open source, you might consider modifying an existing component instead of developing a new one; or, thanks to the separation of components and renderers, perhaps you can modify an existing renderer.

The root class of all JSF components is the abstract `javax.faces.component.UIComponent`, and the root class of all renderers is `javax.faces.render.Renderer`. To develop a component, though, you're *always* better off extending an existing component or, at the very least, the `UIComponentBase` class, which provides default implementations of all abstract methods of `UIComponent`. In this way, you only develop code for the methods you need to override. The same goes with the renderer.

To complete the picture of how to develop your custom component, you also need to create a custom tag that's useable with JSP. The root class of all tag classes is `javax.faces.webapp.UIComponentELTag`.

In summary, to develop a custom component, you need to follow these steps:

1. Create a component class that subclasses `UIComponent` by extending an existing component.

2. Register the component in `faces-config.xml`.

3. Create a renderer class that subclasses `Renderer` and overrides the methods for encoding and decoding.

4. Register the renderer in `faces-config.xml`.

5. Create a custom tag that subclasses `UIComponentELTag`.

6. Create a TLD for the custom tag.

One last word about components and renderers: unless you really think that you'll reuse the same component for different applications, it will be much easier to keep the renderer inside the component. I'll first show you what to do when they're separate, and then I'll tell you how to keep them together.

I'll show you how to develop a component that combines the functionality of all three standard components needed for accepting a user's input: a label explaining what is expected, the text field to accept the input, and a message to report input errors. In other words, I'll show you how to replace the following JSF code:

```
<h:outputText value="Contact Name"/>
  <h:inputText id="name" required="true"
      value="#{shopManager.customer.contactName}"
      requiredMessage="Value is required!"
      />
  <h:message for="name" styleClass="error"/>
```

with this custom component:

```
<eshop:inputEntry label="Contact Name" required="true"
    value="#{shopManager.contactName}"
    errorStyleClass="error" requiredMessage="Value is required!"
    />
```

I'll also show you how this new eshop:inputEntry component prints an asterisk beside the label if you set required to true.

Component

The component is actually the easiest part. Let's go through the methods one by one (see Listing 9-12).

Listing 9-12. InputEntryComponent.java

```
01: package eshop.components;
02: import javax.faces.component.UIInput;
03: import javax.faces.context.FacesContext;
04:
05: public class InputEntryComponent extends UIInput {
06:     private String label;
07:     public InputEntryComponent(){
08:         this.setRendererType("eshop.inputEntry");
09:     }
10:     public String getLabel() {
11:         return label;
12:     }
13:     public void setLabel(String label) {
14:         this.label = label;
15:     }
16:
17:     // Overridden methods
18:     public String getFamily() {
19:         return "eshop.inputEntry";
20:     }
21:     public void restoreState(FacesContext ctxt, Object state) {
22:         Object val[] = (Object[])state;
23:         super.restoreState(ctxt, val[0]);
24:         label = (String)val[1];
25:     }
```

```
26:    public Object saveState(FacesContext ctxt) {
27:       Object val[] = new Object[2];
28:       val[0] = super.saveState(ctxt);
29:       val[1] = label;
30:       return ((Object)val);
31:       }
32:    }
```

InputEntryComponent is the component initialization. Its only task is to register with the component the string that identifies the renderer. The only property of the component defined in InputEntryComponent.java is label. This is because you're extending UIInput, which takes care of defining everything that has to do with the input field.

The getter and setter methods of the label property are getLabel and setLabel. Nothing special there.

You use the getFamily method to find all the renderers associated with this component. We're going to create only one renderer, but it's still appropriate to define a family rather than inherit the family of UIInput, because you couldn't use UIInput's renderers with InputEntryComponent. By overriding the default getFamily, you ensure that only your renderer is visible.

The state of the component consists of the state of UIInput plus the label property. Therefore, you define its state as an array of two objects. The saveState method forms the array and returns it, so that JSF can save it. The restoreState method receives the state, unpacks it, and stores it locally. Notice how the operations that have to do with UIInput are always delegated to it.

Now that you have the component, you have to register it. You do this by inserting the following lines into faces-config.xml:

```
<component>
  <component-type>eshop.inputEntry</component-type>
  <component-class>eshop.components.InputEntryComponent</component-class>
</component>
```

Renderer

The renderer is a bit trickier than the component. To implement it, you define a class that extends javax.faces.render.Renderer. Start by looking at the three methods that you need to override (see Listing 9-13).

Listing 9-13. InputEntryRenderer.java—Overridden Methods

```
59: public void decode(FacesContext ctxt, UIComponent cmp) {
60:    InputEntryComponent ieCmp = (InputEntryComponent)cmp;
61:    Map<String, String> requestMap =
62:        ctxt.getExternalContext().getRequestParameterMap();
63:    String clientId = cmp.getClientId(ctxt);
64:    String val = (String)requestMap.get(clientId);
65:    ((UIInput)ieCmp).setSubmittedValue(val);
66:    }
67:
68: public void encodeBegin(FacesContext ctxt, UIComponent cmp)
69:        throws IOException {
70:    InputEntryComponent ieCmp = (InputEntryComponent)cmp;
71:    ResponseWriter respWr = ctxt.getResponseWriter();
72:    encodeLabel(respWr, ieCmp);
73:    encodeInput(respWr, ieCmp);
74:    encodeMessage(ctxt, respWr, ieCmp);
75:    respWr.flush();
76:    }
77:
78: public Object getConvertedValue(FacesContext ctxt, UIComponent cmp,
79:    Object subVal) throws ConverterException {
80:    Object convVal = null;
81:    ValueExpression valExpr = cmp.getValueExpression("value");
82:    if (valExpr != null) {
83:      Class valType = valExpr.getType(ctxt.getELContext());
84:      if (valType != null) {
85:        convVal = subVal;
86:        if (!valType.equals(Object.class) && !valType.equals(String.
           class)) {
87:          Converter converter = ((UIInput)cmp).getConverter();
88:          converter =  ctxt.getApplication().createConverter(valType);
89:          if (converter != null ) {
90:            convVal = converter.getAsObject(ctxt, cmp, (String)subVal);
91:            }
```

```
92:           }
93:         }
94:       }
95:   return convVal;
96:   }
```

As I said before, the only property that you add to UIInput is label, which the user cannot modify. Therefore, not surprisingly, as you don't need to do anything concerning the label, you only need to decode the input field. In line 60, you typecast the component object to InputEntryComponent, so that you can work with it more comfortably. In lines 61–62, you get the map of the input parameters, and in line 63, you get from the FacesContext the clientId of the component, so that in line 64, you can finally get the input string as typed by the user. After that, you only need to save the input string as a submitted value. Remember that this method is executed during Apply Request Values.

The encoding process requires more work than the decoding process, because you have to send to the HTTP response all three components that were combined to form InputEntryComponent. This takes place during Render Response. In line 71 of the encodeBegin method, you get the response writer from the FacesContext. After executing the functions that write the three subcomponents, you flush the output, and you're done.

Listing 9-14 shows the method to encode the label. It opens the HTML label element with the startElement method, writes the label with a plain write method, writes an asterisk—but only if the component is required—and closes the label element with the endElement method. The result is something like <label>Contact Name*</label>.

Listing 9-14. InputEntryRenderer.java—encodeLabel

```
31: private void encodeLabel(ResponseWriter respWr, InputEntryComponent cmp)
32:     throws IOException {
33:   respWr.startElement("label", cmp);
34:   respWr.write(cmp.getLabel());
35:   if (cmp.isRequired()) {
36:     respWr.write("*");
37:   }
38:   respWr.endElement("label");
39:   }
```

Listing 9-15 shows the method to encode the input field. It opens the HTML `input` element, adds the attributes with the `writeAttribute` method, and closes the element. The three parameters of `writeAttribute` are the name and value of the HTML attribute and the name of the component property. The result is something like the following element:

```
<input type="text" id="form:nameEntry" name="form:nameEntry" value=""/>
```

Listing 9-15. InputEntryRenderer.java—encodeInput

```
18: private void encodeInput(ResponseWriter respWr, InputEntryComponent cmp)
19:     throws IOException {
20:   FacesContext ctxt = FacesContext.getCurrentInstance();
21:   respWr.startElement("input", cmp);
22:   respWr.writeAttribute("type", "text", "type");
23:   respWr.writeAttribute("id", cmp.getClientId(ctxt), "id");
24:   respWr.writeAttribute("name", cmp.getClientId(ctxt), "name");
25:   if(cmp.getValue() != null) {
26:     respWr.writeAttribute("value", cmp.getValue().toString(), "value");
27:   }
28:   respWr.endElement("input");
29: }
```

Listing 9-16 shows the method to encode the error message. It gets the list of all messages queued for the component but only displays the first one. If you want to display them all, you just need to replace the `if` keyword with a `while`. To display the message, the method opens the HTML `span` element, adds the `class` attribute to show the message with the correct style, displays the message itself, and closes the element. The result is something like the following element:

```
<span class="error">Value is required!</span>
```

Listing 9-16. InputEntryRenderer.java—encodeMessage

```
41: private void encodeMessage(FacesContext ctxt, ResponseWriter respWr,
42:     InputEntryComponent cmp) throws IOException {
43:    Iterator it = ctxt.getMessages(cmp.getClientId(ctxt));
44:    // Notice: an if instead of a while
45:    if (it.hasNext()){
46:      FacesMessage mess = (FacesMessage)it.next();
47:      if (!cmp.isValid()) {
48:        String errorStyleClass =
49:            (String)cmp.getAttributes().get("errorStyleClass");
50:        respWr.startElement("span", cmp);
51:        respWr.writeAttribute("class", errorStyleClass, "class");
52:        respWr.write(mess.getDetail());
53:        respWr.endElement("span");
54:      }
55:    }
56:  }
```

To register the renderer, insert the following lines into `faces-config.xml`:

```
<render-kit>
  <renderer>
    <component-family>eshop.inputEntry</component-family>
    <renderer-type>eshop.inputEntry</renderer-type>
    <renderer-class>eshop.renderers.InputEntryRenderer</renderer-class>
  </renderer>
</render-kit>
```

Tag

The custom component is done, but to use it with JSP, you need to define a corresponding custom tag I already explained how to define. Listing 9-17 shows the Java class that implements the tag handler.

Listing 9-17. InputEntryTag.java

```java
package eshop.tags;
import javax.el.ValueExpression;
import javax.faces.component.UIComponent;
import javax.faces.webapp.UIComponentELTag;

public class InputEntryTag extends UIComponentELTag {
  private ValueExpression  errorStyleClass;
  private ValueExpression  label;
  private ValueExpression  required;
  private ValueExpression  requiredMessage;
  private ValueExpression  value;

  // Setters
  public void setErrorStyleClass(ValueExpression errorStyleClass) {
    this.errorStyleClass = errorStyleClass;
    }
  public void setLabel(ValueExpression label) {
    this.label = label;
    }
  public void setRequired(ValueExpression required) {
    this.required = required;
    }
  public void setRequiredMessage(ValueExpression requiredMessage) {
    this.requiredMessage = requiredMessage;
    }
  public void setValue(ValueExpression value) {
    this.value = value;
    }

  // Overridden methods
  public String getComponentType() {
    return "eshop.inputEntry";
    }
  public String getRendererType() {
    return "eshop.inputEntry";
    }
```

```
protected void setProperties(UIComponent cmp) {
  super.setProperties(cmp);
  if (errorStyleClass != null) {
    cmp.setValueExpression("errorStyleClass", errorStyleClass);
    }
  if (label != null) {
    cmp.setValueExpression("label", label);
    }
  if (required != null) {
    cmp.setValueExpression("required", required);
    }
  if (requiredMessage != null) {
    cmp.setValueExpression("requiredMessage", requiredMessage);
    }
  if (value != null) {
    cmp.setValueExpression("value", value);
    }
  }
public void release() {
  super.release();
  errorStyleClass = null;
  label = null;
  requiredMessage = null;
  value = null;
  required = null;
  }
}
```

As you can see, you define a property for each attribute supported by the tag, but not for the id attribute. The reason is that UIComponentELTag already defines it. Notice that you only have setter methods, without the corresponding getters. This is because you never need the get methods. The setProperties method copies the attribute values from the tag to the component, and the release method cleans up what is no longer needed.

Before you can use the custom tag in JSP, you still need to create a TLD to be placed in WEB-INF\tlds\. See Listing 9-18.

Listing 9-18. eshop.tld

```
01: <?xml version="1.0" encoding="UTF-8"?>
02: <taglib xmlns="http://java.sun.com/xml/ns/javaee"
03:     xmlns:xsi="http://www.w3.org/2001/XMLSchema-instance"
04:     xsi:schemaLocation="http://java.sun.com/xml/ns/javaee ➥
http://java.sun.com/xml/ns/j2ee/web-jsptaglibrary_2_1.xsd"
05:     version="2.1">
06:   <description>Eshopf Custom Tags</description>
07:   <tlib-version>1.0</tlib-version>
08:   <short-name>eshop</short-name>
09:   <tag>
10:     <display-name>inputEntry</display-name>
11:     <name>inputEntry</name>
12:     <tag-class>eshop.tags.InputEntryTag</tag-class>
13:     <body-content>empty</body-content>
14:     <attribute>
15:       <name>id</name>
16:       <required>false</required>
17:       <rtexprvalue>true</rtexprvalue>
18:     </attribute>
19:     <attribute>
20:       <name>value</name>
21:       <required>false</required>
22:       <deferred-value><type>java.lang.Object</type></deferred-value>
23:     </attribute>
24:     <attribute>
25:       <name>required</name>
26:       <required>false</required>
27:       <deferred-value><type>boolean</type></deferred-value>
28:     </attribute>
29:     <attribute>
30:       <name>label</name>
31:       <required>false</required>
32:       <deferred-value><type>java.lang.String</type></deferred-value>
33:     </attribute>
```

357

```
34:      <attribute>
35:        <name>errorStyleClass</name>
36:        <required>false</required>
37:        <deferred-value><type>java.lang.String</type></deferred-value>
38:      </attribute>
39:      <attribute>
40:        <name>requiredMessage</name>
41:        <required>false</required>
42:        <deferred-value><type>java.lang.String</type></deferred-value>
43:      </attribute>
44:    </tag>
45:  </taglib>
```

In lines 09, 12, and 13, you define the eshop:inputEntry tag and associate it with the tag handler. The eshop.tags.InputEntryTag string means that you have to place InputEntryTag.class in the folder WEB-INF\classes\eshop\tags\. In the rest of the TLD, you define all attributes and set them to accept the JSF expressions as values, with the exception of id.

With this, you're ready to use the new JSF UI component h:inputEntry. You only need to add the eshop namespace declaration to the jsp:root element at the beginning of the JSP document:

```
xmlns:eshop="urn:jsptld:/WEB-INF/tlds/eshop.tld"
```

The result will look like the field shown in Figure 9-4. The version of eshopf you find in the software package for this chapter already has everything in it. To see the field, you only need to remove the comments around the relevant lines of code in Checkout.jspx.

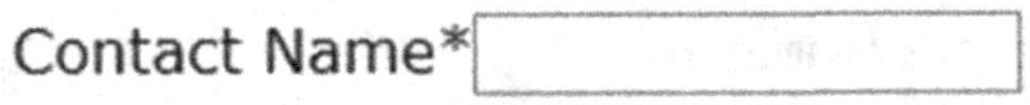

Contact Name*[   ]

Figure 9-4. *Checkout.jspx—eshop:inputEntry*

Inline Renderer

It's possible to include the rendering functionality inside the component class, so that the component effectively renders itself. As I mentioned before, unless you plan to use more than one renderer with the same component, you might choose not to bother with a separate renderer.

358

To make eshop:inputEntry self-rendering, you need to do these:

1. Move the methods of InputEntryRenderer.java to
    InputEntryComponent.java. You'll need to make some cosmetic
    changes that I'll explain in a moment. After you have done the
    move, you can delete the renderer file.

2. Add the encodeEnd method to InputEntryComponent.java (more
    about this in a moment).

3. Return null in the getRendererType method of InputEntryTag.
    java.

4. Remove the registration of the renderer from faces-config.xml.

The UIInput class, which you extend to make the component, supports the
three methods decode, encodeBegin, and getConvertedValue that you used in the
separate renderer, but without the UIComponent parameter. It makes sense because the
component object is directly accessible with the keyword this.

When you remove the cmp parameter from the three methods, you should also
remove the line

```
InputEntryComponent ieCmp = (InputEntryComponent)cmp;
```

from decode and encodeBegin, because it has become useless. Then, make a global
replace of ieCmp with this and replace the four occurrences of cmp in decode and
getConvertedValue with this.

You need the encodeEnd method to override the method in UIComponentBase, which
throws a NullPointerException. In fact, you don't need to do anything in encodeEnd;
you can just write an empty method:

```
public void encodeEnd(FacesContext context) throws IOException { }
```

Note that you only need this method when a component renders itself, not when it
uses a separate renderer class.

In InputEntryTag.java, the getRendererType method returns "eshop.inputEntry".
If the method is to use its internal rendering methods, getRendererType has to return
null. Finally, remove the seven lines of the render-kit element from faces-config.xml.

faces-config.xml

I've already explained all the elements of this file when I talked about the Shop Manager (`<managed-bean>` and `<navigation-rule>`) and when registering a converter (`<converter>`), a validator (`<validator>`), a component (`<component>`), and a renderer (`<render-kit>`). In this section, I only want to summarize with Table 9-1 the navigation rules of eshopf.

Table 9-1. *Eshopf Navigation Rules*

from-outcome	to-view-id	redirect
checkOut	/jsp/Checkout.jspx	Yes
listBooks	/jsp/ListBooks.jspx	Yes
orderConfirmation	/jsp/OrderConfirmation.jspx	No
showBook	/jsp/BookDetails.jspx	Yes
showCart	/jsp/ShoppingCart.jspx	Yes

Summary

In this chapter, I described how to use JSF to reimplement the user interface of eshopx, to create the application eshopf.

I showed how to work with the standard JSF components and then explained how to create your own converters, validators, and components. On the way, I also briefly described how to tie together the application with web.xml, faces config.xml, and context.xml.

Based on the content of this chapter and the previous one, you should now be able to write your own application.

CHAPTER 10

Conclusion

In several chapters of this book, I've used examples taken from three different versions of an online bookshop application: eshop (see Chapter 5), eshopx (introduced in Chapter 7), and eshopf (the subject of Chapter 9). In this chapter, I'll complete the description of those applications so that you can use them as models for your own.

All three versions have the same functionality and generate almost identical HTML pages. Their differences are in their implementation. The main difference between the first two versions, eshop and eshopx, is that the JSP code in eshop is in standard JSP syntax, while the code in eshopx is in XML syntax. The third version of the application, eshopf, is quite different from the first two, because I implemented it with JSF. This required me to replace the original servlet with the JSF servlet.

The eshop Application

In Chapter 4 and Chapter 5, where I introduced eshop, I described the objects this application deals with (product categories, books, shopping cart, and orders) and the operations the user can perform on those objects. In Chapter 4, I described the SQL scripts shop_create.sql (Listing 4-5) and shop_populate.sql (Listing 4-7), which create the shop database containing categories, books, and orders. I also showed you the code of Category.java (Listing 4-10). In Chapter 5, I described the MVC architecture of eshop. In particular, I listed the methods of the DataManager class (Table 5-1), described the initialization of the servlet (Listing 5-1 and Table 5-2), summarized how the servlet handles incoming requests, and listed the JSP pages (Table 5-3). I also took you through a typical user session.

Then, I devoted the whole "DB Access in eshop" section to describing how the data manager updates the database via the *peer* methods (Figure 5-6 and Listings 5-5 to 5-8).

In this chapter, I'll start by listing all the subfolders and files in the eshop application folder (see Listing 10-1, where the folder names are in bold).

© Luciano Manelli and Giulio Zambon 2020
L. Manelli and G. Zambon, *Beginning Jakarta EE Web Development*,
https://doi.org/10.1007/978-1-4842-5866-8_10

Listing 10-1. The eshop Files

```
css
    eshop.css
images
    1.jpg, 2.jpg, 3.jpg, 4.jpg, 5.jpg, 6.jpg
    bg_header.gif
    bg_menu.gif
    cart.gif
jsp
    BookDetails.jsp
    Checkout.jsp
    LeftMenu.jsp
    OrderConfirmation.jsp
    SearchOutcome.jsp
    SelectCatalog.jsp
    ShoppingCart.jsp
    TopMenu.jsp
META-INF
    MANIFEST.MF
WEB-INF
    web.xml
    classes
        eshop
            ShopServlet.class
            ShopServlet.java
            beans
                Book.class, Book.java
                CartItem.class, CartItem.java
                Category.class, Category.java
                Customer.class, Customer.java
            model
                BookPeer.class, BookPeer.java
                CategoryPeer.class, CategoryPeer.java
                DataManager.class, DataManager.java
                OrderDetailsPeer.class, OrderDetailsPeer.java
                OrderPeer.class, OrderPeer.java
                shop.sql
```

To complete the description of the ShopServlet class, I need to show you how it selects the appropriate JSP page on the basis of the request, thereby fulfilling its role as a controller. Listing 10-2 shows the code of the doPost method (as I mentioned already in Chapter 5, doGet simply executes doPost).

Listing 10-2. ShopServlet.java—doPost Method

```java
protected void doPost(HttpServletRequest request,
    HttpServletResponse response) throws ServletException, IOException {
  String base = "/jsp/";
  String url = base + "index.jsp";
  String action = request.getParameter("action");
  if (action != null) {
      switch (action) {
      case "search":
        url = base + "SearchOutcome.jsp";
        break;
      case "selectCatalog":
        url = base + "SelectCatalog.jsp";
        break;
      case "bookDetails":
        url = base + "BookDetails.jsp";
        break;
      case "checkOut":
        url = base + "Checkout.jsp";
        break;
      case "orderConfirmation":
        url = base + "OrderConfirmation.jsp";
        break;
      default:
        if (action.matches("(showCart|(add|update|delete)Item)"))
          url = base + "ShoppingCart.jsp";
        break;
      }
  }
```

```
RequestDispatcher requestDispatcher =
  getServletContext().getRequestDispatcher(url);
requestDispatcher.forward(request, response);
}
```

As you can see, doPost obtains the request parameter named action and then uses it to form the correct URL of the JSP page. It then uses the request dispatcher obtained from the servlet context to forward control to the page. If no action parameter exists or if it doesn't match any of the expected strings, the servlet will execute the default page (/jsp/index.jsp).

To cover the eshop functionality in detail, I'll show you what happens in a typical user session and I'll look at the behavior of the application on the server. The architecture of eshop is consistent with the general MVC architecture shown in Figure 3-2.

What Happens When the Application Starts

The user starts the application by typing http://localhost:8080/eshop/shop/ in his or her browser. The doGet method of ShopServlet is executed, and that simply executes doPost. The doPost method, as I just explained, doesn't find a request parameter named action, so it forwards the request to index.jsp.

The index.jsp page, like all other pages of eshop, displays a header with a link to the shopping cart and a menu on the left-hand side with search and selection controls (see Figure 10-1). It does so by including two separate modules, as follows:

```
<jsp:include page="TopMenu.jsp" flush="true"/><jsp:include
page="LeftMenu.jsp" flush="true"/>
```

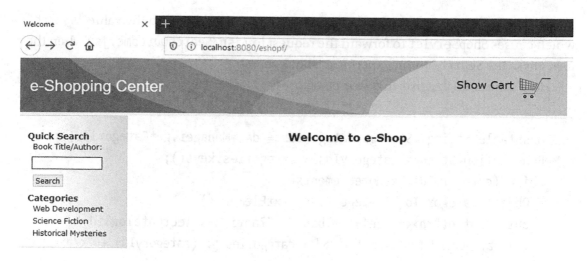

Figure 10-1. *E-shop's home page*

The central area of the page only displays the text Welcome to e-Shop.

The TopMenu.jsp module is trivial. Essentially, it consists of the following elements:

```
<a class="link2" href="<%=base%>?action=showCart">Show Cart
  <img src="<%=imageURL%>/cart.gif" border="0"/></a>
```

where the two variables are obtained from the application scope

```
String base = (String)application.getAttribute("base");
String imageURL = (String)application.getAttribute("imageURL");
```

The action parameter set to showCart causes ShopServlet to forward the request to /jsp/ShoppingCart.jsp.

The LeftMenu.jsp module has to do more. It displays a search field and a list of selectable book categories. The code to accept a search request is as follows:

```
<p>Book Title/Author:</p>
  <form style="border: 0px solid; padding: 0; margin: 0;">
    <input type="hidden" name="action" value="search"/>
    <input id="text" type="text" name="keyword" size="15"/>
    <input id="submit" type="submit" value="Search"/>
  </form>
```

Notice the presence of the hidden parameter named `action` with the value `"search"`, which causes `ShopServlet` to forward the request to `/jsp/SearchOutcome.jsp` when the user clicks the `Search` button to perform a book search.

Here's the code that lists the book categories:

```
<%
    Hashtable<String, String> categories = dataManager.getCategories();
    Enumeration<String> categoryIds = categories.keys();
    while (categoryIds.hasMoreElements()) {
      Object categoryId = categoryIds.nextElement();
      out.println("<p><a href=" + base + "?action=selectCatalog&id="
        + categoryId.toString() + ">" + categories.get(categoryId) + "</a></p>"
        );
    }
  %>
```

The `DataManager` method `getCategories` only executes another method of the data model

```
  public Hashtable<String, String> getCategories() {
    return CategoryPeer.getAllCategories(this);
    }
```

that interrogates the database to obtain identifiers and names of the available categories (see Listing 10-3).

Listing 10-3. CategoryPeer.java—getAllCategories Method

```
public static Hashtable<String, String>
    getAllCategories(DataManager dataManager) {
  Hashtable<String, String> categories = new Hashtable<String, String>();
  Connection connection = dataManager.getConnection();
  if (connection != null) {
    try {
      Statement s = connection.createStatement();
      String sql = "select category_id, category_name from categories";
      try {
        ResultSet rs = s.executeQuery(sql);
```

```
  try {
    while (rs.next()) {
      categories.put(rs.getString(1), rs.getString(2));
      }
    }
  finally { rs.close(); }
  }
  finally {s.close(); }
  }
catch (SQLException e) {
  System.out.println("Could not get categories: " + e.getMessage());
  }
finally {
  dataManager.putConnection(connection);
  }
}
return categories;
}
```

I've highlighted the lines that do all the work: first, the database query is performed, and then the result is saved in a hashtable in which the key is the category ID and the value is the category name.

LeftMenu.jsp uses the content of the hashtable to generate one link for each category with the statement

```
out.println("<p><a href=" + base + "?action=selectCatalog&id="
  + categoryId.toString() + ">" + categories.get(categoryId) + "</a></p>"
  );
```

as shown in the following example for action novels:

```
<p><a href=/eshop/shop?action=selectCatalog&id=3>Action Novels</a></p>
```

Notice that the action parameter is set to selectCatalog. This is done for all categories and causes ShopServlet to forward the request to /jsp/SelectCatalog.jsp when the user clicks a category name.

As you can see from the code of CategoryPeer.java, I took great care to ensure that the database connection is closed before the method returns.

Handling Requests for Book Selection and Book Search

As you saw in the previous section, when the user selects a book category or performs a search, the pages displayed are `SelectCatalog.jsp` and `SearchOutcome.jsp`, respectively. Both pages display a list of books and are similar to each other. Actually, they are so alike that I merged them into a single page in the JSF version of the application, `eshopf`, as you'll see later in this chapter. Figure 10-2 shows the list you will see when you search for the letter F (or f, as the searches are case-insensitive), while Figure 10-3 shows the list of books in the category `Science Fiction`.

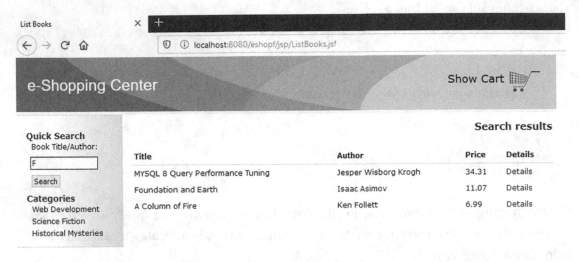

Figure 10-2. *Titles and author names containing an F*

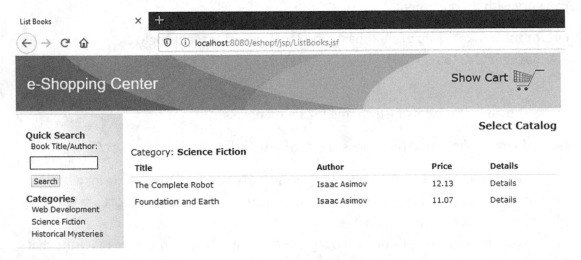

Figure 10-3. *Science Fiction category*

In `SelectCatalog.jsp`, the requested category is specified by the `id` parameter. To obtain the category name, you execute the `DataManager` method `getCategoryName`

```
public String getCategoryName(String categoryID) {
  Category category = CategoryPeer.getCategoryById(this, categoryID);
  return (category == null) ? null : category.getName();
  }
```

and this loads the category record from the database via the corresponding peer method.

In `SearchOutcome.jsp`, the search string is in the `keyword` parameter.

To obtain the list of books, `SelectCatalog.jsp` executes the following statement in a scriptlet:

```
ArrayList books = dataManager.getBooksInCategory(categoryId);
```

while `SearchOutcome.jsp` executes the statement

```
ArrayList books = dataManager.getSearchResults(keyword);
```

For each book in the list, both pages generate a link such as the following one:

```
<a class="link1" href="/eshop/shop?action=bookDetails&bookId=3">Details</a>
```

With the `action` parameter set to `bookDetails`, `ShopServlet` forwards the request to `BookDetails.jsp`.

Displaying the Book Details

By now, the mechanism should be pretty clear: each JSP page passes its key request parameter to a `DataManager` method that encapsulates the business logic. This is how the *view* and the *model* of the MVC architecture are kept separate, making it possible for the web-page designers and the software developers to work independently. One creates visually appealing and clear pages, and the other handles the databases. The signatures of the data model methods are the only interface needed between page designers and software developers.

`BookDetails.jsp` passes the `bookId` request parameter to the `DataManager` method `getBookDetails`:

```
public Book getBookDetails(String bookID) {
  return BookPeer.getBookById(this, bookID);
  }
```

and the `BookPeer` method `getBookById` gets the corresponding book record from the database.

To buy the book (see Figure 10-4), the user then clicks a link that looks like this in HTML:

```
<a class="link1" ="/eshop/shop?action=addItem&bookId=4">Add To Cart</a>
```

With the `action` parameter set to `addItem`, `ShopServlet` forwards the request to `ShoppingCart.jsp`.

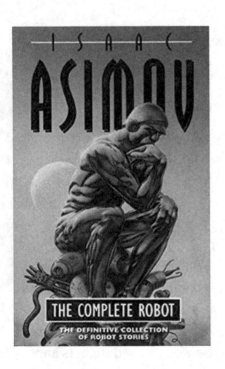

The Complete Robot
Isaac Asimov
Price: 12.13

Add to Cart

Figure 10-4. *Buying a book*

Managing the Shopping Cart

The application displays the shopping cart (see Figure 10-5) not only when the user clicks the Add to Cart link while viewing the book details but also when the user clicks the shopping cart link in the header of any page. The difference is that in the first case, the action parameter passed to ShoppingCart.jsp has the value addItem, while in the second case the value is showCart.

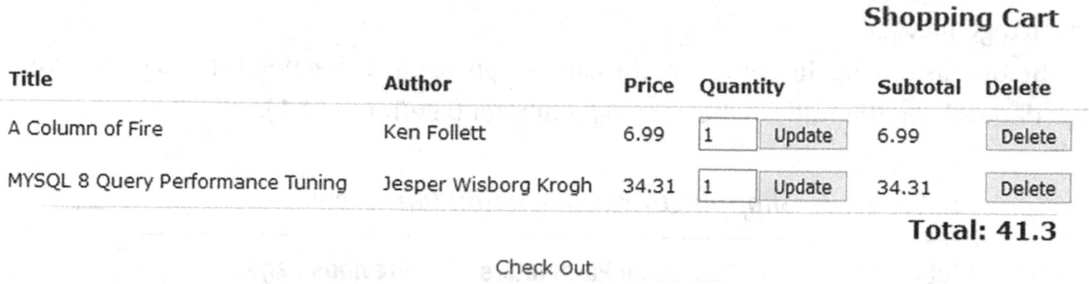

Shopping Cart

Title	Author	Price	Quantity		Subtotal	Delete
A Column of Fire	Ken Follett	6.99	1	Update	6.99	Delete
MYSQL 8 Query Performance Tuning	Jesper Wisborg Krogh	34.31	1	Update	34.31	Delete

Total: 41.3

Check Out

Figure 10-5. *The shopping cart*

The shopping cart itself is an object of type Hashtable<String, String> stored as a session attribute. Note that the scope of the attribute must be session, because the shopping cart must be available across multiple HTTP requests. The hashtable key is the book ID, while the value is an object of type CartItem. The CartItem class has no methods except the getters and setters for the author, title, price, bookID, and quantity properties.

It's appropriate to save the book price in the shopping cart, because the user should pay the price shown in the book details when he or she clicks Add to Cart, even if the book price stored in the database is then changed before the order is completed.

For each shopping cart item, ShoppingCart.jsp displays the quantity of books in an input field and adds the Update and Delete buttons enclosed in separate forms. This makes it possible for the user to modify the number of copies ordered or to remove an item altogether. Here's an example of an update form:

```
<form>
    <input type="hidden" name="action" value="updateItem"/>
    <input type="hidden" name="bookId" value="4"/>
    <input type="text" size="2" name="quantity" value="1"/>
    <input type="submit" value="Update"/>
</form>
```

and here's an example of a delete form:

```
<form>
  <input type="hidden" name="action" value="deleteItem"/>
  <input type="hidden" name="bookId" value="4"/>
  <input type="submit" value="Delete"/>
</form>
```

When the user clicks one of the buttons, ShopServlet forwards the request back to ShoppingCart.jsp.

Before displaying the content of the cart, ShoppingCart.jsp needs to do some work that depends on the value of the action parameter (see Table 10-1).

Table 10-1. *ShoppingCart.jsp—Action Parameter*

Action Value	Additional Parameters	Previous Page
showCart	None	Any
addItem	bookId	BookDetails.jsp
updateItem	bookId, quantity	ShoppingCart.jsp
deleteItem	bookId	ShoppingCart.jsp

To handle addItem, ShoppingCart.jsp obtains the book details from the data manager via the getBookDetails method and creates a new CartItem object, which it then adds to the cart. To handle updateItem, ShoppingCart.jsp uses the setQuantity method to update the quantity in the cart item identified by bookId. To handle deleteItem, ShoppingCart.jsp simply removes the cart item identified by bookId from the cart.

After listing the cart content, ShoppingCart.jsp displays this link:

```
<a class="link1" href="<%=base%>?action=checkOut">Check Out</a>
```

With the action parameter set to checkOut, ShopServlet forwards the request to Checkout.jsp.

Accepting an Order

Checkout.jsp asks the user to provide his or her personal and financial data (see Figure 10-6).

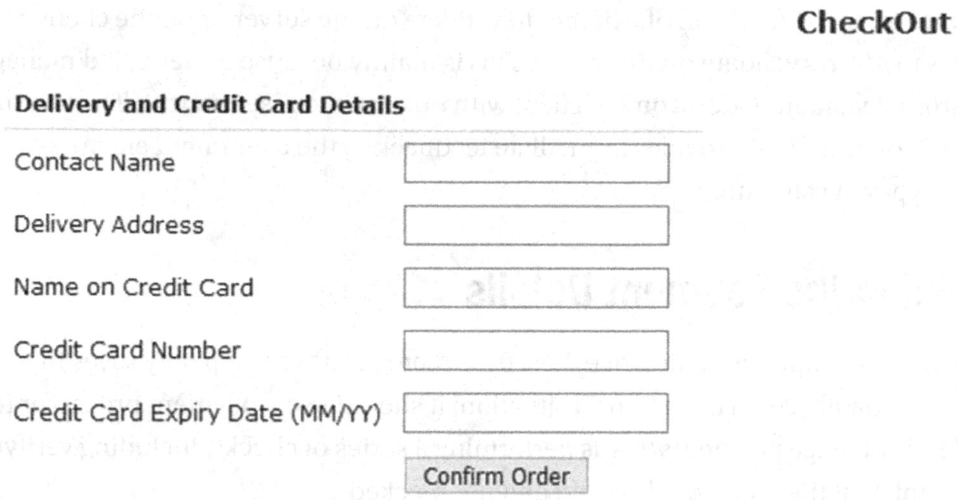

CheckOut

Delivery and Credit Card Details

Contact Name

Delivery Address

Name on Credit Card

Credit Card Number

Credit Card Expiry Date (MM/YY)

Confirm Order

Figure 10-6. *Checking out*

When the user clicks the Confirm Order button, the hidden action parameter is set to orderConfirmation, which causes ShopServlet to forward the request to OrderConfirmation.jsp. In real life, you should implement validation on as many fields as possible.

To perform validation of the user's inputs, you have to decide what fields to validate, whether the validation should take place on the client or on the server (or on both), whether to check the fields one by one or all together, and what technique to use.

There are some fields that you cannot really validate (e.g., the contact name). Others might not be critical enough to warrant the effort you would need to spend in order to implement validation. For example, to check the delivery address provided via a simple form like that of Figure 10-6, you could parse the field; extract the country, if present, the ZIP/post code; and check whether they are consistent. To minimize the risk of input errors, it would make more sense to break down the address into several fields and give a multiple choice of countries and, depending on the chosen country, on ZIP codes. This would involve quite a bit of work, and the lists would have to be kept up to date, for example, by downloading them from an online service. All in all, you might decide to forego such complex checks. That said, it is not uncommon for websites to check that the *format* of the ZIP code is consistent with the country.

In general, how far you go with validation is something you need to decide on a case-by-case basis.

Concerning the question of whether to validate on the server or on the client, my advice is to *always* validate on the server. This is mainly because a user could manage to work around validation done on the client with unknown consequences. The fact that validation on the client provides immediate feedback to the user might encourage you to do both types of validation.

Providing the Payment Details

In this skeleton implementation of eshop, OrderConfirmation.jsp only saves the order in the database. In a real-world situation, it should use a payment processor to completely manage payments/cards performing a series of checks, including verifying with a bank that the credit card is valid and not blocked.

All the work to store the order in the database is done in the DataManager method insertOrder, which I've already discussed in Chapter 5.

The eshopx Application

After completing eshop, I showed you how to create the eshopx application by replacing the JSP pages with JSP documents (i.e., modules in XML syntax). This required us to move scriptlet code to JSP custom tags.

Listing 10-4 shows the annotated list of files and folders that constitute eshopx.

Listing 10-4. The Eshopx Files

css
      eshop.jspx (replaces eshop.css)
images (content unchanged)
jsp (all pages rewritten as XML documents)
      BookDetails.jspx
      Checkout.jspx

```
    LeftMenu.jspx
    OrderConfirmation.jspx
    SearchOutcome.jspx
    SelectCatalog.jspx
    ShoppingCart.jspx
    TopMenu.jspx
META-INF  (content unchanged)
WEB-INF
    web.xml  (minor update)
    classes
        eshop  (ShopServlet unchanged)
            beans  (content unchanged)
            model  (content unchanged)
            tags  (new folder)
                AddBookTag.class, AddBookTag.java
                BookDetailsTag.class, BookDetailsTag.java
                BooksInCartTag.class, BooksInCartTag.java
                BooksInCategoryTag.class, BooksInCategoryTag.java
                CategoryNameTag.class, CategoryNameTag.java
                DeleteBookTag.class, DeleteBookTag.java
                InsertOrderTag.class, InsertOrderTag.java
                RoundToCentTag.class, RoundToCentTag.java
                SearchResultsTag.class, SearchResultsTag.java
                UpdateBookTag.class, UpdateBookTag.java
    tlds (new folder)
        eshop.tld
```

As you can see, I only changed the *view* part of the application (i.e., the JSP modules), while I didn't need to touch the *controller* and the *model* (i.e., the servlet, the beans, the peer classes, and the data manager). This confirms the advantage of implementing an MVC architecture.

As I already mentioned, the views of eshop and eshopx differ in the implementation but are functionally identical.

Style Sheet

I replaced the shop.css file used in eshop with shop.jspx. Listing 10-5 shows the differences between the two files.

Listing 10-5. shop.jspx

```
<?xml version="1.0" encoding="UTF-8"?>
<jsp:root
  xmlns:jsp="http://java.sun.com/JSP/Page"
  xmlns:c="http://java.sun.com/jsp/jstl/core"
  version="2.1"
  >
<jsp:directive.page
  language="java"
  contentType="text/css; charset=UTF-8"
  pageEncoding="UTF-8"
  />
<c:url var="imgUrl" value="/images"/>
<jsp:text>
  ----------  shop.css lines 1 - 42  ----------
  background: url(${imgUrl}/bg_header.gif) no-repeat top left;
  ----------  shop.css lines 44 - 82  ----------
  background: url(${imgUrl}/bg_menu.gif) repeat-y top left;
  ----------  shop.css lines 84 - 105  ----------
  background: url(${imgUrl}/menubar.gif) repeat-x bottom left;
  ----------  shop.css lines 107 - 206 (the last one)  ----------
</jsp:text>
</jsp:root>
```

As you can see, I only wrapped shop.css inside a jsp:text element and changed three lines. If you look at the original lines, it should become clear why I did it:

```
background: url(/eshop/images/bg_header.gif) no-repeat top left;
background: url(/eshop/images/bg_menu.gif) repeat-y top left;
background: url(/eshop/images/menubar.gif) repeat-x bottom left;
```

The string "/eshop/images" of shop.css has become "${imgUrl}" in shop.jspx, and if you look at the beginning of shop.jspx, you'll notice that the variable imgUrl is set as follows:

```
<c:url var="imgUrl" value="/images"/>
```

The advantage of doing it with the EL expression is that c:url takes care of adding the application folder (i.e., /eshop) before the relative URL /images. This makes it possible to deploy the application in any folder. You should try to avoid hard-coding paths.

Obviously, you need to change the way in which the style sheet is loaded in the JSP modules. In eshop, with shop.css, you needed to include the following line in the <head> element:

```
<link rel="stylesheet" href="/eshop/css/eshop.css" type="text/css"/>
```

In eshopx, with shop.jspx, you need to write the line

```
<c:url var="cssUrl" value="/css/eshop.jspx"/>
```

and then include the following line in the <head>:

```
<link rel="stylesheet" href="${cssUrl}" type="text/css"/>
```

By doing so, you remove the hard-coded /eshop path from all JSP modules, which is a good thing to do.

web.xml

When moving from eshop to eshopx, I needed to modify in web.xml the definitions of two parameters: base and imageURL. The definition of base changed from /eshop/shop to /shop, because in eshop, I used base as follows:

```
<a class="link1" href="<%=base%>?action=checkOut">Check Out</a>
```

while in eshopx, I first define the page attribute myURL as

```
<c:url value="${base}" var="myURL">
  <c:param name="action" value="checkOut"/>
  </c:url>
```

and then use the attribute to make the link, as follows:

```
<a class="link1" href="${myURL}">Check Out</a>
```

As I said when talking about the style sheet, `c:url` accepts in the `value` attribute URLs relative to the application folder and then completes them to make them relative to the server root. Within `eshop`, you had to include the application folder in `base`, because you didn't form the URL with `c:url`.

The definition of `imageURL` changed from `/eshop/images/` to `/images/` because I used `imageURL` in `eshop` as follows:

```
<img src="<%=imageURL%>cart.gif" border="0"/>
```

while in `eshopx`, I first define the page attribute `imgURL`:

```
<c:url value="${imageURL}" var="imgURL"/>
```

and then use the attribute in the `img` element:

```
<img src="${imgURL}cart.gif" border="0"/>
```

Thanks to these two changes, I could remove all hard-coded references to the application directory in `eshopx`.

But these small changes in the handling of the images cause a problem in the welcome page of the application.

Perhaps you will recall that in Chapter 6, when talking about `c:url`, I mentioned that Tomcat attaches a `jsessionid` string to a URL before sending it to the client in the response.

Tomcat does it when it opens a new session, to handle clients that don't accept cookies. When Tomcat receives subsequent requests from the same client and they contain the session cookie, it stops appending the session ID string to the URLs, because it knows that it is unnecessary.

Now, the welcome page (`index.jspx`) includes `TopMenu.jspx`, which contains the two lines

```
<c:url value="${imageURL}" var="imgURL"/>
...
<img src="${imgURL}cart.gif" border="0"/>
```

to display the image of the shopping cart.

JSP Documents

To explain how I converted the JSP pages of eshop (with extension jsp) to the corresponding JSP documents of eshopx (with extension jspx), I'll go through one example in detail.

Listing 10-6 shows OrderConfirmation.jsp. I choose it because it is one of the simplest modules.

Listing 10-6. OrderConfirmation.jsp

```
01: <%@page language="java" contentType="text/html"%>
02: <%@page import="java.util.Hashtable"%>
03: <%@page import="eshop.beans.CartItem"%>
04: <jsp:useBean id="dataManager" scope-"application"
05:    class="eshop.model.DataManager"/>
06: <html>
07: <head>
08:    <meta http-equiv="Content-Type" content="text/html; charset=UTF-8"/>
09:    <title>Order</title>
10:    <link rel="stylesheet" href="/eshop/css/eshop.css" type="text/css"/>
11:    </head>
12: <body>
13: <jsp:include page="TopMenu.jsp" flush="true"/>
14: <jsp:include page="LeftMenu.jsp" flush="true"/>
15: <div class="content">
16:    <h2>Order</h2>
17:    <jsp:useBean id="customer" class="eshop.beans.Customer"/>
18:    <jsp:setProperty property="*" name="customer"/>
19: <%
20:      @SuppressWarnings("unchecked")
21:      Hashtable<String, CartItem> cart =
22:          (Hashtable<String, CartItem>)session.getAttribute("shoppingCart");
23:      long orderId = dataManager.insertOrder(customer, cart);
24:      if (orderId > OL) {
25:        session.invalidate();
26:    %>
```

```
27:          <p class="info">
28:             Thank you for your purchase.<br/>
29:             Your Order Number is: <%=orderId%>
30:          </p>
31: <%
32:       }
33:    else {
34:       %><p class="error">Unexpected error processing the order!</p><%
35:       }
36:    %>
37:    </div>
38: </body>
39: </html>
```

When converting to the XML syntax, you first need to replace the first 11 lines of the JSP page with those shown in Listing 10-7.

Listing 10-7. Top Portion of OrderConfirmation.jspx

```
01: <?xml version="1.0" encoding="UTF-8"?>
02: <jsp:root
03:    xmlns:jsp="http://java.sun.com/JSP/Page"
04:    xmlns:c="http://java.sun.com/jsp/jstl/core"
05:    xmlns:eshop="urn:jsptld:/WEB-INF/tlds/eshop.tld"
06:    version="2.1"
07:    >
08: <jsp:directive.page
09:    language="java"
10:    contentType="application/xhtml+xml;charset=UTF-8"
11:    />
12: <jsp:output omit-xml-declaration="false"/>
13: <jsp:output
14:    doctype-root-element="html"
15:    doctype-public="-//W3C//DTD XHTML 1.0 Strict//EN"
16:    doctype-system="http://www.w3.org/TR/xhtml1/DTD/xhtml1-strict.dtd"
17:    />
18: <c:url var="cssUrl" value="/css/eshop.jspx"/>
```

```
19: <html xmlns="http://www.w3.org/1999/xhtml">
20: <head>
21:   <title>Order</title>
22:   <link rel="stylesheet" href="${cssUrl}" type="text/css"/>
23:   </head>
```

In XML format, you no longer need to declare the Java classes, but you need to declare the namespaces of JSP, the JSTL core, and the custom library. The `page` directive becomes a `jsp:directive.page` element. Also, notice that the style sheet is loaded as I explained in a previous section.

Lines 12–18 of `OrderConfirmation.jsp` remain practically the same, the only difference being that now the two modules have the extension `jspx`. The last three lines (37–39) also remain the same. You only have to append the end tag of `jsp:root`.

The major changes take place in lines 19–36. They are replaced by the code shown in Listing 10-8.

Listing 10-8. Central Portion of OrderConfirmation.jspx

```
31: <eshop:insertOrder var="orderID" customer="${customer}"/>
32: <c:choose>
33:   <c:when test="${orderID > 0}">
34:     <p class="info">
35:       Thank you for your purchase.<br/>
36:       Your Order Number is: <c:out value="${orderID}"/>
37:     </p>
38:   </c:when>
39:   <c:otherwise>
40:     <p class="error">Unexpected error processing the order!</p>
41:   </c:otherwise>
42: </c:choose>
```

Line 31 of `OrderConfirmation.jspx` is the XML equivalent of lines 20–25 plus line 32 of `OrderConfirmation.jsp`. Notice that in eshop, the order ID is returned by the `insertOrder` method and stored in the scripting variable `orderID`, while in eshopx, the order ID is stored into the EL variable `orderID` directly by the custom tag `eshop:insertOrder`.

The if/else of lines 24 and 33 in the JSP code is replaced in the JSPX code by the elements c:choose/c:when/c:otherwise of lines 32–33 and 39. As I said on other occasions, you cannot use c:if because a c:else doesn't exist.

To complete the picture, let's look at Listing 10-9, which shows the doEndTag method of InsertOrderTag.java.

Listing 10-9. InsertOrderTag.java—doEndTag Method

```
public int doEndTag() {
    ServletContext context = pageContext.getServletContext();
    DataManager dataManager =(DataManager)context.getAttribute("dataManager");
    HttpSession session = pageContext.getSession();
    @SuppressWarnings("unchecked")
    Hashtable<String, CartItem> cart =
        (Hashtable<String, CartItem>)session.getAttribute("shoppingCart");
    long orderID = dataManager.insertOrder(customer, cart);
    if (orderID > 0L) session.invalidate();
    pageContext.setAttribute(var, new Long(orderID).toString());
    return EVAL_PAGE;
}
```

Not surprisingly, here you find (highlighted in bold) the code originally in lines 20–25 of OrderConfirmation.jsp that executes the dataManager method insertOrder and terminates the user session if the insertion succeeds. On the basis of this example, you should now be able to figure out how to convert the other modules. In the next section, you'll find additional information concerning the eshop custom-tag library.

Custom Tags and TLD

EL expressions can include bean properties. This means that they can invoke "getter" methods. What they cannot do is invoke methods that require input parameters. You can work around that difficulty by setting an attribute with c:set and picking it up in a bean method.

For example, in SelectCatalog.jspx, the request parameter id specifies a book category, and you need to know the category name. This operation requires a database search, which you can implement with the following custom tag:

```
<eshop:categoryName var="cat" catID="${param.id}"/>
```

It accepts the ID as an input and sets the variable cat to the category name. The doEndTag method of CategoryNameTag.java is simple:

```
public int doEndTag() {
  ServletContext context = pageContext.getServletContext();
  DataManager dataManager =(DataManager)context.
  getAttribute("dataManager");
  pageContext.setAttribute(var, dataManager.getCategoryName(catID));
  return EVAL_PAGE;
  }
```

The getCategoryName method of the data manager (invoked exclusively by the doEntTag method of CategoryNameTag.java) is even simpler:

```
public String getCategoryName(String categoryID) {
  Category category = CategoryPeer.getCategoryById(this, categoryID);
  return (category == null) ? null : category.getName();
  }
```

Instead of defining the custom tag, you could add the categoryID property to the data manager

```
private String categoryID = "0";
public void setCategoryID(String categoryID) {
  this.categoryID = categoryID;
  }
```

and remove its input parameter from the getCategoryName method.

Then, in SelectCatalog.jspx, you could replace the eshop:categoryName element with jsp:setProperty to set the categoryID in the data manager and c:setVar to invoke the getCategoryName method:

```
<jsp:setProperty name="dataManager" property="categoryID"
    value="${param.id}"/>
<c:set var="cat" value="${dataManager.categoryName}"/>
```

The result would be the same. I didn't do it in that way because it makes the code less "transparent," but it is ultimately a matter of taste. I just want to make the point that you can replace the input parameters of bean methods by setting bean properties with jsp:setProperty. Then, you only need to name the getter methods appropriately (e.g., getWhatever), and you'll be able to execute them with an expression such as ${myBean. whatever}.

In any case, I introduced a total of ten tags, as listed in Table 10-2.

Table 10-2. *eshop Custom-Tag Library*

Name	Attributes	Where Used
bookDetails	var, bookID	BookDetails.jspx
insertOrder	var, customer	OrderConfirmation.jspx
searchResults	var, keyword	SearchOutcome.jspx
categoryName	var, catID	SelectCatalog.jspx
booksInCategory	var, catID	SelectCatalog.jspx
addBook	bookID	ShoppingCart.jspx
updateBook	bookID, quantity	ShoppingCart.jspx
deleteBook	bookID	ShoppingCart.jspx
booksInCart	items	ShoppingCart.jspx
roundToCent	var, value	ShoppingCart.jspx

Listing 10-10 shows an example of a TLD tag element.

Listing 10-10. A TLD Tag Element

```
<tag>
  <description>Insert an order into storage</description>
  <display-name>insertOrder</display-name>
  <name>insertOrder</name>
  <tag-class>eshop.tags.InsertOrderTag</tag-class>
  <body-content>empty</body-content>
  <attribute>
    <name>var</name>
    <type>java.lang.String</type>
    <rtexprvalue>true</rtexprvalue>
    </attribute>
```

```
<attribute>
  <name>customer</name>
  <type>eshop.beans.Customer</type>
  <rtexprvalue>true</rtexprvalue>
  </attribute>
</tag>
```

The eshopf Application

Although I used eshopx as a basis for the JSF version of the application, its architecture is quite different from that of the first two versions. This is partly due to the fact that I had to replace ShopServlet with the standard FacesServlet class. In the process, I also removed the custom tags I had introduced in eshopx. In this section, I'll refer to the eshopf application as described in Chapter 9 after the addition of a custom converter, a custom validator, and a custom component with a separate renderer.

Listing 10-11 shows the annotated list of files and folders that constitute eshopf. The folders marked "= eshopx" have the same content as the corresponding folders of eshopx (not of the original eshop); the modules marked "rewritten" are completely different from the previous versions; and those marked "~ eshop" are those obtained by updating the corresponding modules in eshop.

Listing 10-11. The Eshopf Files

css
```
    eshopf.jspx  (updated version of eshop.jspx)
```
images (content = eshopx)
jsp
```
    BookDetails.jspx  (~ eshop)
    Checkout.jspx  (~ eshop)
    LeftMenu.jspx  (~ eshop)
    ListBooks.jspx  (update of SelectCatalog.jspx + SearchOutcome.jspx)
    OrderConfirmation.jspx  (~ eshop)
    ShoppingCart.jspx  (~ eshop)
    TopMenu.jspx  (~ eshop)
```

META-INF
    MANIFEST.MF   (= eshopx)
    context.xml   (new file)

WEB-INF
    faces-config.xml   (new file)
    web.xml   (rewritten)
    classes
        eshop   (ShopServlet removed)
            beans
                Book.class, Book.java   (= eshopx)
                CartItem.class, CartItem.java   (~ eshop)
                Category.class, Category.java   (= eshopx)
                Customer.class, Customer.java   (= eshopx)
                ShopManager.class, ShopManager.java   (new file)
            components   (new folder)
                InputEntryComponent.class, InputEntryComponent.java
            converters   (new folder)
                CCNumberConverter.class, CCNumberConverter.java
            model
                BookPeer.class, BookPeer.java   (= eshopx)
                CategoryPeer.class, CategoryPeer.java   (~ eshop)
                DataManager.class, DataManager.java   (~ eshop)
                OrderDetailsPeer.class, OrderDetailsPeer.java   (= eshopx)
                OrderPeer.class, OrderPeer.java   (= eshopx)
                shop.sql   (= eshopx)
            renderers   (new folder)
                InputEntryRenderer.class, InputEntryRenderer.java
            tags   (removed all the custom tags of eshopx)
                InputEntryTag.class, InputEntryTag.java   (new file)
            validators   (new folder)
                 CCExpiryValidator.class, CCExpiryValidator.java
  tlds
      eshop.tld   (rewritten)

In fact, I described almost everything in Chapter 9. In this chapter, I'll systematically go through the changes I made to eshopx to transform it into eshopf.

web.xml and context.xml

In eshopx, I defined ShopServlet.java to implement the controller part of the MVC architecture. In eshopf, this function is performed by the standard FacesServlet. As a result, I had to rewrite most of web.xml. In particular, I replaced the servlet element used in the web.xml version of eshopx

```
<display-name>ShopServlet</display-name>
<servlet-name>ShopServlet</servlet-name>
<servlet-class>eshop.ShopServlet</servlet-class>
```

with this:

```
<servlet-name>Faces Servlet</servlet-name>
<servlet-class>javax.faces.webapp.FacesServlet</servlet-class>
<load-on-startup>1</load-on-startup>
```

I also changed the body of servlet-mapping from this:

```
<servlet-name>ShopServlet</servlet-name>
<url-pattern>/shop/*</url-pattern>
```

to this:

```
<servlet-name>Faces Servlet</servlet-name>
<url-pattern>*.jsf</url-pattern>
```

In eshopx, to access the database containing books, book categories, and orders, I defined the initialization parameters jdbcDriver, dbURL, dbUserName, and dbPassword. They were used in ShopServlet to set up an object of type DataManager, which implemented the model part of the MVC architecture and interfaced to the database. The replacement of ShopServlet with FacesServlet forced me to implement a different mechanism in eshopf for passing the database parameters to the data manager.

I defined the database as a resource external to the application by creating the context.xml file in the META-INF folder with the following content:

```
<Context debug="5" reloadable="true" crossContext="true">
  <Resource
      name="jdbc/mysql"
      auth="Container"
```

```
        type="javax.sql.DataSource"
        username="root"
        password="root"
        driverClassName="com.mysql.cj.jdbc.Driver"
        url="jdbc:mysql://localhost:3306/shop"
        maxActive="8"
        maxIdle="4"
        />
    <Valve
        className="org.apache.catalina.valves.AccessLogValve"
        directory="logs"
        prefix="eshopf-access."
        suffix=".log"
        pattern="common"
        resolveHosts="false"
        />
    </Context>
```

I then registered the resource in the web.xml file as follows:

```
<resource-ref>
  <res-ref-name>jdbc/mysql</res-ref-name>
  <res-type>javax.sql.DataSource</res-type>
  <res-auth>Container</res-auth>
  </resource-ref>
```

Note that with this mechanism, you effectively pool the connections to the database, thereby achieving a more efficient use of resources. I leave up to you to retrofit eshopx with this mechanism. To complete the conversion from eshopx to eshopf, I also removed the definition of the initialization parameters base and imageURL from web.xml, because they were no longer needed, and I added the element to direct Tomcat to perform the basic authentication needed to access the database resource. Listing 9-8 shows the full web.xml file of eshopf.

Style Sheet

CSS lets you define new styles by adding attributes to already defined styles. This "cascading" mechanism is a form of inheritance, and therefore it requires an underlying hierarchical structure. CSS uses the structure provided by HTML documents instead of creating its own. This is fine as long as you write the HTML code yourself or generate it with JSP. When you use JSF, though, the control you have on the generated HTML is reduced. As a result, you have to pay greater attention when designing the style sheets.

When converting eshopx to eshopf, I encountered this issue in several places and had to modify the style-sheet file accordingly.

For example, in eshopx\css\eshop.jspx, I first defined .box (lines 130–133)

```
.box {
  padding: 0px 0px 10px 0px;
  margin: 0px;
  }
```

and then extended it to define .box p (lines 134–139)

```
.box p {
  font-size: 12px;
  padding: .2em 1em .2em 1em;
  margin: 0px;
  border: 0px;
  }
```

LeftMenu.jspx uses the two styles as follows:

```
<div class="box">
  ...
  <p>Book Title/Author:</p>
  ...
  </div>
```

In eshopf, I replaced the HTML p element with a h:outputText component, which generates an HTML span element, not a p. Therefore, I defined in eshopf\css\eshopf. jspx also the new style .box_p as follows (lines 153–159):

```
.box_p {
  font-size: 12px;
  padding: .2em 1em .2em 1em;
  margin: 0px;
  border: 0px;
  display: block;
  }
```

By writing in eshopf\jsp\LeftMenu.jspx the code

```
<h:panelGroup styleClass="box">
  ...
  <h:outputText styleClass="box_p" value="Book Title/Author:"/>
  ...
  </h:panelGroup>
```

I could generate the following HTML output:

```
<span class="box">
  ...
  <span class="box_p">Book Title/Author:</span>
  </span>
```

and this resulted in the correct formatting of the search box.

This issue concerning style sheets can be a disadvantage of using JSF, but it becomes less and less important as you become familiar with the HTML code that JSF generates. Furthermore, you'll normally start developing directly with JSF. When converting eshopx into eshopf, I was dealing with an existing user interface that I wanted to alter as little as possible.

JSP Documents

I had to modify all JSP documents. This shouldn't be a surprise, considering that the JSP documents generate the HTML pages that the user sees in his or her web browser. In Chapter 9, I described all the JSF components you need for eshopf. Therefore, it wouldn't make much sense to do it again here. In this section, I'll only tell you how JSF allows you to merge two separate JSP documents of eshopx (SelectCatalog.jspx and SearchOutcome.jspx) into a single document of eshopf (ListBooks.jspx).

The two modules were already very similar in eshopx. Without considering page titles, text headers, and error messages, the differences boiled down to less than a handful of lines. In SearchOutcome.jspx, I was using the custom tag eshop:searchResults, while in SelectCatalog.jspx, I was first obtaining the category name with eshop:categoryName and then the list of books with eshop:booksInCategory.

After converting the two modules to use JSF, the list of books in both cases was obtained from a property of shopManager: when the user performed a search via the search field of LeftMenu.jspx, the method that filled in the list of books in shopManager was searchBooks, and when the user selected a category, the method was selectCategory.

The only difference left between the two modules was in a couple of messages. To make the merging possible, I added the categoryName property to shopManager and reset it to null within the searchBooks method. In this way, I could use the name of the category as a flag, because it would be null after a search and non-null after a category selection.

Java Modules

One major change I made was to replace the custom tags defined in eshopx with the eshop.beans.ShopManager class. I did this to take advantage of JSF.

For example, to update the number of copies of a book in eshopx, you use the custom tag UpdateBook. Listing 10-12 shows the code to implement the tag.

Listing 10-12. Eshopx—UpdateBookTag.java

```java
package eshop.tags;

import java.util.Hashtable;
import javax.servlet.jsp.tagext.TagSupport;
import javax.servlet.http.HttpSession;
import eshop.beans.CartItem;

public class UpdateBookTag extends TagSupport {
  static final long serialVersionUID = 1L;
  private String bookID;
  private String quantity;
```

```
public void setBookID(String bookID) {
  this.bookID = bookID;
  }

public void setQuantity(String quantity) {
  this.quantity = quantity;
  }

public int doEndTag() {
  HttpSession session = pageContext.getSession();
  @SuppressWarnings("unchecked")
  Hashtable<String, CartItem> shoppingCart =
      (Hashtable<String, CartItem>)session.getAttribute("shoppingCart");
  CartItem item = (CartItem)shoppingCart.get(bookID);
  if (item != null) {
    item.setQuantity(quantity);
    }
  return EVAL_PAGE;
  }
}
```

In eshopf, the following JSF component of ShoppingCart.jspx takes care of updating the number of copies:

```
<h:inputText id="quantity" value="#{item.quantity}" size="2"
    required="true"
    requiredMessage="What? Nothing?"
    converterMessage="An integer, please!"
    validatorMessage="At least one copy!"
    >
  <f:validateLongRange minimum="1"/>
  </h:inputText>
```

As a result, when you trigger an update by pressing the corresponding button

```
<h:commandButton action="#{shopManager.updateItem}" value="Update"/>
```

there's nothing left for the updateItem method of the shop manager to do:

```
public String updateItem() {
  return null;
}
```

Another example is the RoundToCent tag, which rounds amounts in dollars to two decimal places in eshopx. This is necessary because sometimes the result of multiplying the price of a book by the ordered quantity results in a sequence of '9's after the decimal point. Here is an example of its usage taken from ShoppingCart.jspx:

```
<eshop:roundToCent var="itemPrice" value="${item.quantity * item.price}"/>
```

In eshopf, I introduced the subtotal attribute to the CartItem bean and added the functionality to recalculate it and round it to two decimals after every shopping cart update. This is the only update I made to the four eshop.beans modules.

Of the eshop.model modules, I only needed to modify CategoryPeer.java and DataManager.java. In CategoryPeer.java, I changed the getAllCategories method to return a list of categories instead of an object of type java.util.Hashtable. I then changed the getCategories methods in DataManager.java and ShopManager.java accordingly. This allowed me to display the list of categories in LeftMenu.jspx with the following JSF element without having to do any type conversion:

```
<h:dataTable value="#{shopManager.categories}" var="category">
```

In DataManager, besides the change to the getCategories method that I've already discussed and the removal of the getCatIDs method that was no longer needed, I only updated the algorithm used in the getConnection method to open a database connection. This was necessary because I had replaced the database initialization parameters of eshopx with a JNDI resource.

In eshopx, DataManager opened a database connection by invoking the static getConnection method of the java.sql.DriverManager class:

```
conn = DriverManager.getConnection(getDbURL(), getDbUserName(),
getDbPassword());
```

The dbURL, dbUserName, and dbPassword attributes were set by ShopServlet using the servlet initialization parameters. In eshopf, the code to obtain a database connection is as follows:

```
Context ctx = new InitialContext();
if (ctx != null){
  Context envContext  = (Context)ctx.lookup("java:/comp/env");
  if (envContext != null) {
    DataSource ds = (DataSource)envContext.lookup("jdbc/mysql");
    if (ds != null) {
      conn = ds.getConnection();
    }
  }
}
```

Finally, I added Java modules to implement a custom JSF component, a converter, a renderer, and a validator. Please refer to the corresponding sections of Chapter 9 for their description.

Tomcat

Now, I want to spend some words about Tomcat I've been using in all the chapters to show you examples of servlets, JSP pages, and documents.

Tomcat, an open source Servlet/JSP server/container from Apache Software Foundation, is essentially three things:

- A web server

- An application that executes Java servlets

- An application that converts JSP pages and documents into Java servlets

Tomcat is a project of the Apache Software Foundation. Therefore, the authoritative source for obtaining further information on Tomcat is `http://tomcat.apache.org/`, which provides extensive documentation (`https://tomcat.apache.org/tomcat-9.0-doc/index.html`). At the moment of writing this chapter, the latest release of Tomcat is 9.0.34, which runs on Java 8 (or later), and implements the Servlet 4.0 and JSP 2.3 specifications (`https://tomcat.apache.org/whichversion.html`).

Tomcat consists of a series of functional components that can be combined according to well-defined rules. The structure of each server is defined in the file server.xml, which is located in the conf subdirectory of Tomcat's folder. An interesting element of Tomcat's components called containers is Context that represents a single web application. Tomcat automatically instantiates and configures a standard context upon loading your application. As part of the configuration, Tomcat also processes the properties defined in the \WEB-INF\web.xml file of your application folder and makes them available to the application.

Directory Structure

If you've installed Tomcat as I explained in Chapter 1, Tomcat will be in the directory named apache-tomcat-9.0.34.

The Tomcat folder contains the following subdirectories: bin, conf, lib, logs, temp, webapps, and work, as shown in Figure 10-7. Two of them are pretty obvious: bin is where the Tomcat executable resides, and temp is a working directory for temporary files.

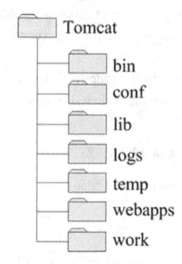

Figure 10-7. *Tomcat's top directories*

conf

The conf directory contains the configuration files that apply to all applications. Besides server.xml, you'll also see context.xml, tomcat-users.xml, and web.xml, which define defaults for all the applications of the server. In Chapter 9, I showed you how to use a context.xml file containing a Context element to make the information concerning a MySQL database accessible to eshopf (see Listing 9-9). On that occasion, context.xml was in the META-INF application subfolder. The same file placed in the conf folder would make the same database data accessible to all applications.

lib

All the JAR files are kept in the lib directory described in the previous chapters. Your Tomcat release might have slightly different JARs.

logs

Tomcat keeps its log files in the logs directory. On any given day of operation, you'll see the following files: catalina.*yyyy-mm-dd*.log, commons-daemon.*yyyy-mm-dd*.log, host-manager.*yyyy-mm-dd*.log, localhost.*yyyy-mm-dd*.log, localhost_access_log.*yyyy-mm-dd*.txt, manager.*yyyy-mm-dd*.log, tomcat9-stderr.*yyyy-mm-dd*, and tomcat9-stdout.*yyyy-mm-dd*.log.

If you want to write something to the stdout log from JSP, you can simply write to System.out. For example, the following code writes a line containing "bla bla bla" in the file stdout_*yyyy-mm-dd*.log:

```
<% System.out.println("bla bla bla"); %>
```

The output of System.err also goes to stdout.

webapps

The webapps directory is the application base directory of localhost. The content of any subdirectory of webapps is accessible by browsers. For example, if you create the folder aaa inside webapps and copy into it the file bbb.jsp, you'll be able to execute it by typing this in your browser:

```
http://localhost:8080/aaa/bbb.jsp
```

You can also drop into `webapps` a WAR file at any time and Tomcat will automatically expand it.

work

Tomcat keeps the translation of JSP into Java in the `work` directory: that is, Tomcat will translate a `page.jsp` into `page_jsp.java` and compile it into `page_jsp.class`. The two files will be in `work\Catalina\localhost\_\org\apache\jsp\`, where `Catalina` is the engine name, `localhost` is the hostname, and the underscore indicates that it is the default application of the host.

Application Deployment

The simplest way to deploy an application with Tomcat is to create an application folder and place it inside the application base directory of the host (`webapps` by default).

For example, if you go to the Source Code/Download area of the Apress website (`www.apress.com`) and download the software package containing the examples I developed for this manual, you'll find that the folder with the examples for Chapter 5 contains a folder named `eshop folder` that contains a folder named `eshop`. Copy the folder `eshop` to the directory `webapps` and you'll be able to launch the application with the following URL:

```
http://localhost:8080/eshop/shop
```

Another way of deploying an application is to create a WAR file (as I described in Chapter 3) and place it in the application base directory of the host. Tomcat will then expand it into the application folder. For example, copy the `eshop.war` file you find in the same `folder` I mentioned earlier to the directory `webapps` and wait a few seconds while Tomcat expands it.

You might decide to define hosts that don't support automatic deployment. This would improve security, but it would also force you to restart Tomcat in order to deploy or redeploy applications. To resolve this issue, Tomcat's developers have created a manager application that lets you deploy your applications without having to restart Tomcat.

To be able to use the manager application, edit the `tomcat-users.xml` file in `conf` folder and insert the following elements before the final tag </tomcat-users>:

```
<role rolename="manager-gui"/>
<user username="tomcat" password="root" roles="manager-gui"/>
```

The file contains the credentials to let you use manager webapp. I created a user tomcat with role manager-gui. You can see the role for the manager application at the local URL http://localhost:8080/docs/manager-howto.html.

Now, if you click *manager app* button or type the URL `http://localhost/manager/html` in a browser, you will be requested to enter user ID and password of an admin/manager user. After logging in, you'll see a page with the list of the deployed applications and additional information. Figure 10-8 shows the top of the page, including the first application, which is the root application of `localhost`.

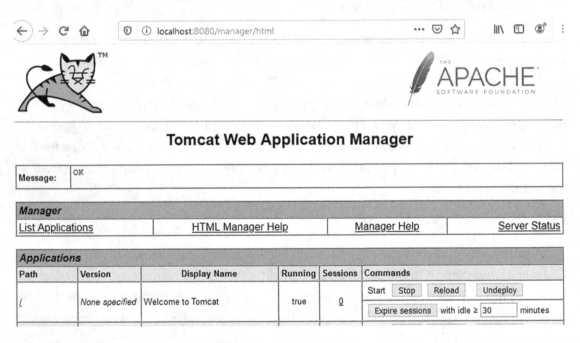

Figure 10-8. *Top of Tomcat's Web Application Manager page*

Notice that you can undeploy (i.e., remove) the application, reload it, and stop it. You can also change the session idle timeout, which is currently set to the default value of 30 minutes.

If you scroll down, you will find a part of the page that lets you deploy new applications as shown in Figure 10-9.

Deploy	
Deploy directory or WAR file located on server	
Context Path:	[ ]
Version (for parallel deployment):	[ ]
XML Configuration file path:	[ ]
WAR or Directory path:	[ ]
	Deploy
WAR file to deploy	
Select WAR file to upload	Sfoglia... Nessun file selezionato.
	Deploy

Figure 10-9. *Deploy of Tomcat's Web Application Manager page*

If you want to know more about your server, you only need to click the Server Status tab you see in Figure 10-8. If you do so, you will see that the tab changes to Complete Server Status. Click it again and you will get detailed information on all the applications.

What About TomEE?

We have analyzed many applications in the book based on Tomcat. It is a very light server and its administration is easy, but in some cases, we needed external libraries. Now, is it possible to use another typology of server including all this jar? The better answer could be a server of the same "family"; in fact, Apache Tomcat has many implementations of a full Java EE server. You will find a server called TomEE that is the Java Enterprise Edition of Apache Tomcat: it combines several Java projects including, in the simpler edition, the Apache MyFaces Java ServerFaces (JSF) and delivering—besides Servlets and JSP—also JSF, JTA, and JPA as you can see at http://tomee.apache.org/comparison.html. The choice depends on you: if you need only a servlet container (maintaining less complexity and resource use adding some libraries) or you think that it is better to use an application server. In the book I chose Tomcat, but I also tried to use TomEE. You can go to TomEE-plus home page at https://tomee.apache.org/ and follow the same steps of Chapter 1:

1. Go to the URL `https://tomee.apache.org/download-ng.html` and download TomEE Plus 8.0.1 by clicking the zip link.

2. Start the download from the mirror site of the file apache-tomee-plus-8.0.1.zip (60.3MB).

3. Unzip the downloaded file: at this point, you should have the folder apache-tomee-plus-8.0.1.

Now the server is ready to start up. Go to \apache-tomee-plus-8.0.1\bin and double-click startup.bat file. Now try it! Use eshopf project, delete libraries from lib folder, and copy the project in webapps. At last, go to the URL `http://localhost:8080/eshopf/`. You will see the working application!

Summary

In this chapter, I completed the description of the various versions of the online bookshop example and explained what I had to do in order to convert standard JSP syntax to XML syntax and then to use JSF. At last, I provided a very brief introduction to Tomcat.

This chapter completes the main body of the book. After the first introductory chapter, I took you through six chapters about JSP, application architectures, JSP actions, XML, and databases, followed by two chapters about JSF.

I hope that you'll find this book useful. Perhaps in a few areas I could have gone a bit deeper or provided additional examples, but a lot of ground had to be covered in a limited space.

I wish you all the best. Happy programming!

Index

A

Action elements, 55
Application object, 66, 68
aStringBean.getStr() method, 276
Atomicity, consistency, isolation, and
        durability (ACID), 112

B

Binding attribute, 329
bufferSize field, 71

C

Cascading Style Sheets (CSS), 15, 107, 215
Checkout.jspx module, 331, 340
Command-line interface (CLI), 33, 112
context-parameter element, 333
Create, read, update, and delete (CRUD), 112

D

Data Access Object (DAO), 156
Database management system (DBMS)
    CLI, 112
    CRUD, 112
    GUIs, 112
Databases
    Category.java, 137
    client, 136
    columns, 111

    field, 111
    foreign key, 111
    rows, 111
    schema, 111
    SQL statements, 136, 138
    transaction, 112
    UPDATE statement, 137
    web application, 136
Data Control Language (DCL), 138
Data Definition Language (DDL), 113, 138
dataManager.getCategories method, 331
Data Manipulation
    Language (DML), 113, 138
Declaration scripting element, 57
decode method, 284, 286, 335
Directive elements
    JSP container, 55
    page, 82, 83, 85
    Tomcat data, 82
doEndTag method, 182
doGet method, 364
doPost method, 363

E

E-bookshop
    Book.java, 105
    business logic and presentation, 91
    Checkout.jsp, 106
    eclipse, 94
    home page, 95, 96

401

© Luciano Manelli and Giulio Zambon 2020
L. Manelli and G. Zambon, *Beginning Jakarta EE Web Development*,
https://doi.org/10.1007/978-1-4842-5866-8